Mel Bay Presents . . . The Guitar Masters Series

COMPLETE JOE PASS

Solo Transcriptions by Roland Leone

2 3 4 5 6 7 8 9 0

Visit us on the Web at www.melbay.com — E-mail us at email@melbay.com

Contents

Joe Pass Introduction

It is with great pleasure that Mel Bay Publications, Inc. releases *Complete Joe Pass* as an integral part of the Guitar Masters Series. Both music critics and performers have hailed Joe Pass as one of the finest jazz musicians to have ever lived. This book is a collage of many of Joe's thoughts about the guitar as an accompanying and solo instrument. Also, many of Joe's transcribed solos, as well as transcriptions of the famous Joe Pass and Herb Ellis duos, are presented in this text. We hope the music and life of Joe Pass will continue to inspire and guide musicians through this work.

Corey Christiansen

Senior Music Editor

MAJOR KEY SIGNATURES

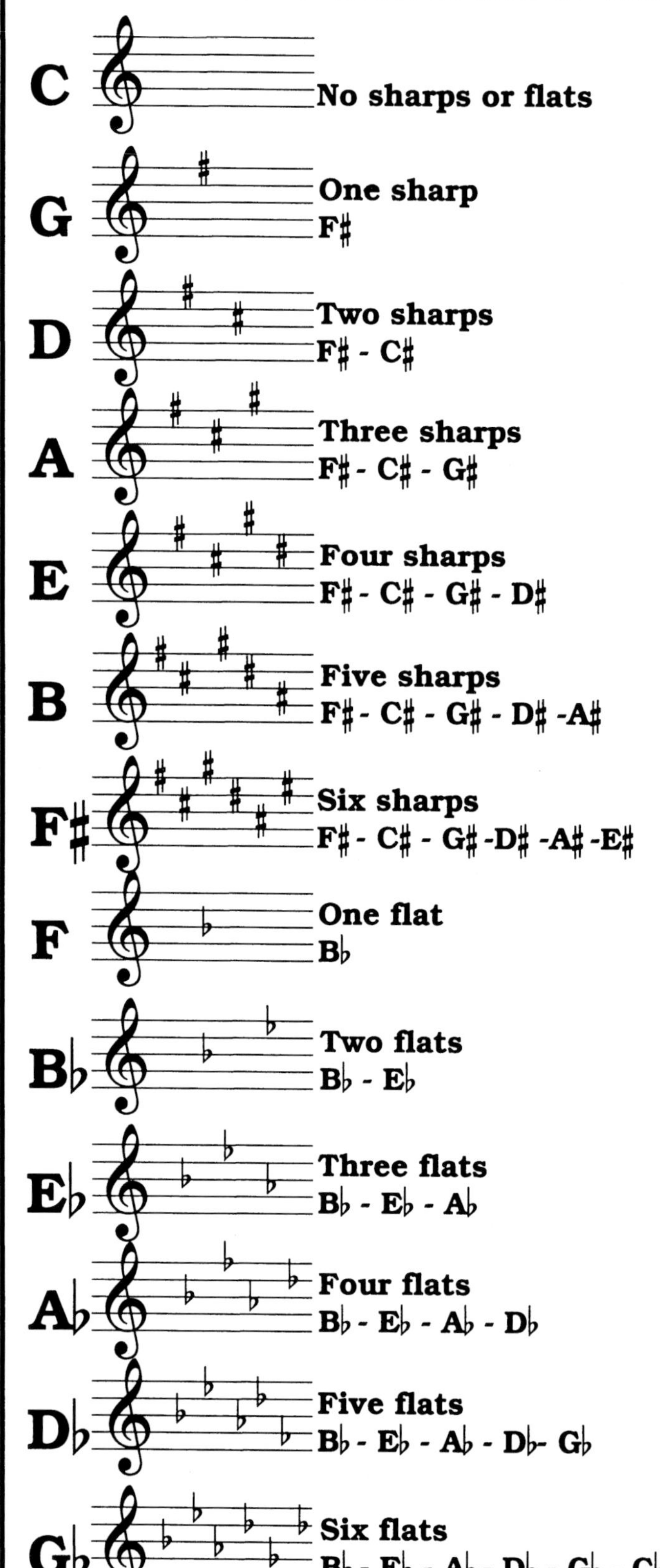

THE CYCLE OF KEYS

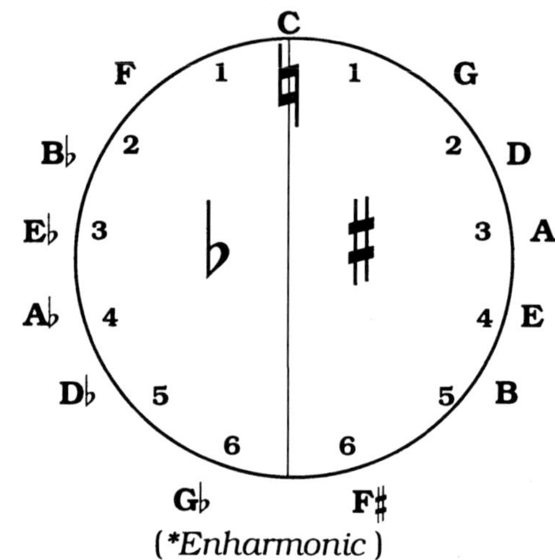

G♭ F♯
(*Enharmonic)

Going around the circle clockwise will take us through the **Dominant keys.**

Going around the circle counterclockwise will take us through the **Sub-Dominant keys.**

* *Enharmonic:* Written differently as to notation but sounding the same.

The Major and Relative Minor Keys

MAJOR KEYS	RELATIVE MINOR KEYS
C	Am
G	Em
D	Bm
A	F♯m
E	C♯m
B	G♯m
F♯	D♯m
F	Dm
B♭	Gm
E♭	Cm
A♭	Fm
D♭	B♭m
G♭	E♭m

PART ONE

HARMONY

MUSIC COMPONENTS

For the next several pages, you will find the essential elements required to make music: chords and scales. Many guitar books spell out literally thousands of chords. However, most masters of the guitar concentrate on selected chords that *sound* good to them. *Sound* is what Joe Pass emphasizes again and again.

Within the variations of chords are *chord inversions and chord substitutions. Scale families* follow.

While there are many approaches to learning how to play the guitar, the information contained within this book is the:

Joe Pass Approach

Definitions:

- **Chords**..three or more notes played together at the same time.
- **Chord Inversions**...first, second and third inversions are determined by the note in the bass*.
- **Chord Substitutes**...alternative chords to play that *sound* good, creating flavor and texture to songs.
- **Scale Families...**arrangement of chromatic notes (one note following the next note in a series of whole and half steps) as governed by the key signature (how many flats or sharps at the beginning of the exercise or song). These families include:

Major
Minor
Dominant
Diminished
Whole-tone (augmented)
Half-diminished
Blues

* Root in the Bass = Root position
3rd in the Bass = 1st inversion
5th in the Bass = 2nd inversion
7th in the Bass = 3rd inversion

HOW TO PLAY AND MOVE BARRE CHORD FORMS

You will be learning how to play and move chords that flow and make harmonic sense. Joe Pass uses the ***Barre Chord Forms***.

These are referred to as the ***C-A-G-E-D Forms***. All of these forms are moveable. As you move up the neck, barre the fret as illustrated on the **Chord Form** page (p.24).

All references to chords and scales in this section are in the key of "C."

RHYTHM

Joe Pass on *Rhythm*: The key to accompanying singers is to *listen to them!*

"Learn and use pull-offs, hammer-ons, slurs and slides because they make your lines sound more interesting. Learn to make smooth transitions from chords and scales.

"If you are playing for a singer who does not improvise, play simply. Stay with the same voicing and movements. Good singers don't need you to play exactly the same all the time.

" The alternate picking style does not get as good a jazz sound as does the down stroke. The back picking is not as strong; it does not have the punch on the 2nd and 4th beats."

Rhythm **is the principle of making musical sense through the combination of chords and scales together.**

Picking techniques are as varied as there are guitarists who play. Size and shape of guitar picks vary greatly, also. Joe often breaks an already small pick in half and uses the point of that small piece. He is not as concerned with the "brand" name of a pick as he is, as with everything else involved in his music, the *sound*. Does the pick give him the *sound* he is listening for?

When he is not using the pick, he uses his fingers to play. During solos, he often uses his fingers together as a plectrum; or strums, or alternately picks strings. When he is comping (accompanying), he uses the same techniques, depending upon the style of song and the effect he wants to create.

Using the fingernails in the style of the great classical guitarists that Joe admires so much, such as André Segovia, John Williams or Julian Breem, is an art unto itself and requires special study and a lifetime of practice in order to perfect. There are many books that speak to that particular art and can be found in the *Mel Bay Music Books* catalog.

The most used guitar techniques by the fretboard hand include the:

- Hammer-ons
- Pull-offs
- Slurs
- Glissandos

Intelligent improvising depends on a working understanding of the relationship between chords and melodic lines. The purpose of this section is to provide the necessary harmonic foundation for the solos in Part Two.

The chordal theory is presented in its briefest form, as it directly relates to the guitar. If some of the explanations differ from those in "formal" theory books, you're free to change the words to suit your own way of thinking. It is the idea that's important, not its explanation.

This material is designed more as a reference than a method. If these ideas are TOTALLY new to you, there may be other books you might investigate before finishing this one.

Chord Construction

The C Major/Minor Scale

MAJOR CHORDS: add chord NAME to basic triad

major	1	3	5 (basic triad)	C	C	E	G			
major 6th	1	3	5 and 6	C6	C	E	G	A		
major 7th	1	3	5 and ma7	Cma7	C	E	G	B		
added 9th	1	3	5 and 9	Cadd9	C	E	G	D		
major 9th	1	3	5 and ma7 and 9	Cma9	C	E	G	B	D	
6th/9th	1	3	5 and 6 and 9	C6/9	C	E	G	A	D	

SEVENTH CHORDS: add chord name to a 7th (or 9th) chord

7th	1	3	5	7	C7	C	E	G	B♭		
9th	1	3	5	7 and 9	C9	C	E	G	B♭	D	
11th*	1	3	5	7 (9)and11	C11	C	E	G	B♭	(D)	F
13th**	1	3	5	7 (9)and13	C13	C	E	G	B♭	(D)	A

* In most guitar inversions, the 3rd is omitted from 11th chords. The 9th is often omitted from both 11th and 13th chords.

** In theory, a 13th chord also contains the 11th, but that tone is normally omitted in guitar fingerings

MINOR CHORDS: add chord name to basic triad

minor	1	mi3	5 (basic triad)	Cm	C	E♭	G		
minor 6th	1	mi3	5 and 6	Cm6	C	E♭	G	A	
minor (ma7th)	1	mi3	5 and ma7	Cm+7	C	E♭	G	B	

MINOR SEVENTH CHORDS: add chord name to a m7th chord

minor 7th	1	mi3	5 7	Cm7	C	E♭	G	B♭	
minor 9th	1	mi3	5 7 and 9	Cm9	C	E♭	G	B♭	D
minor 11th	1	mi3	5 7 and 11	Cm11	C	E♭	G	B♭	F

DIMINISHED SEVENTH chords are built by flatting all but the root of a 7th chord.

C7	1	3	5	7	C	E	G	B♭
*C°	1	♭3	♭5	6 (♭7)	C	E♭	G♭	A (B♭♭)

*may be written: Cdim, Cdim7, C7dim, C°, C°7, C7°

The word "AUGMENTED" in a chord name normally applies to the sharped (augmented) 5th chord tone.**

C+, Caug	1	3	♯5		C	E	G♯	
C+7, C7+, C7aug	1	3	♯5	7	C	E	G♯	B♭

**EXCEPTION: the AUGMENTED ELEVENTH chord is a regular 11th chord, but the 11th is sharped.

C+11	1	3	(5)	7	(9)	♯11	C	E	(G)	B♭	(D)	F♯

ALTERED CHORDS (sharp or flat 5th or 9th): just do as instructed.

C7+5-9	1	3	♯5	7	♭9		C	E	G♯	B♭	D♭	
C13-5-9	1	3	♭5	7	♭9	13	C	E	G♭	B♭	D♭	A

"SHORTCUT" CHORD SYMBOLS

Cma7	C△7
Cma9	C9
Cm7	C-7
Cm7-5	Cø

Chord Embellishment

MAJOR CHORDS: add 6, ma7, 9 and (in blues) 7. To C major chord add the notes A, B, D or (blues) B♭. For C major, play:

SEVENTH CHORDS: add 9, 13 or use 11 in sets: 11 to 7, 11 to 9, 11 to 13. To C7 add the notes D, A, or F. For C7, play:

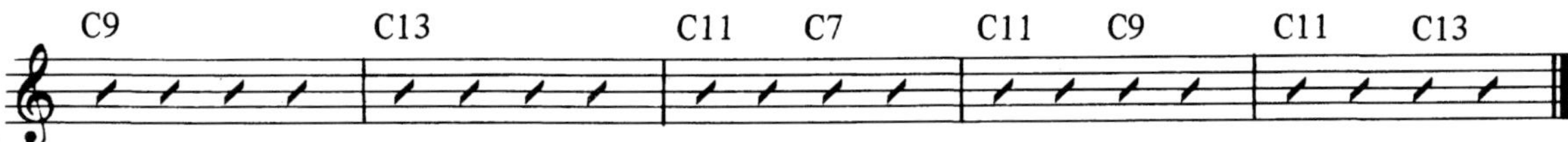

MINOR CHORDS: add 6, 7, ma7, 9 or 11. To Cm add the notes A, B♭, B, D or F. For Cm, play:

ALTERED CHORDS: the 5th may be sharped or flatted in any chord.
the 9th may be sharped or flatted in 7th chords.

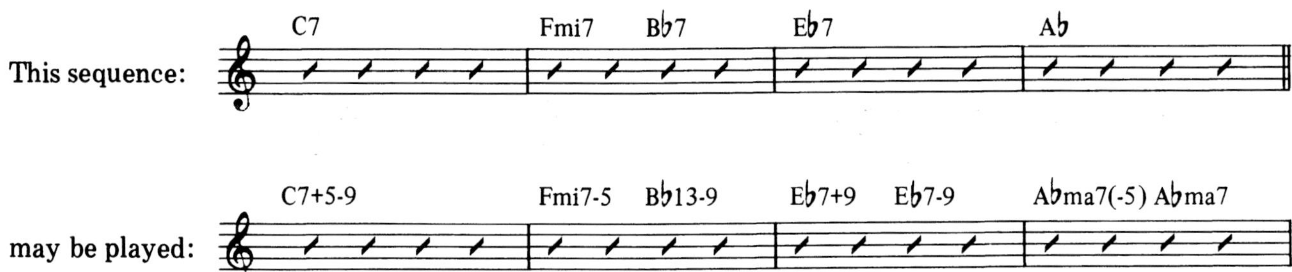

Reduce all chords to their basic form:

Cma7, C6, Cma9, C6/9	reduce to C MAJOR
C9, C11, C13-9, C9-5	reduce to C SEVENTH
Cm7, Cm9, Cm11, Cm7-5	reduce to C MINOR

Chord Substitution

MAJOR CHORDS: Substitute RELATIVE MINOR or SECONDARY RELATIVE MINOR chords. For C use Am or Em

Optional:

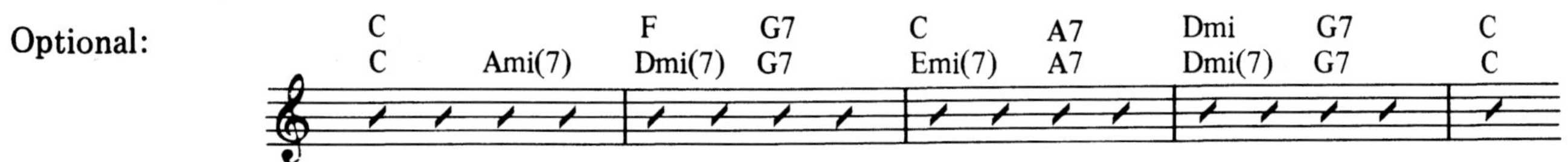

MINOR CHORDS: Substitute RELATIVE MAJOR. For Am use C

This:
becomes:

SEVENTH CHORDS: Substitute DOMINANT MINOR. For C7 use Gm

This rule may sometimes be reversed, as shown below:

ALL CHORDS: Substitute any chord which has as its root the FLAT FIFTH of the original chord. For C use G♭. The type of chord used (major, minor, seventh) depends upon the desired harmony. A few examples:

Gma7 Emi7 Ami11 D7

Gma7 B♭9 E♭ma7 A♭7-5

Bmi7 B♭7 Ami11 A♭7-5

G6/9 B♭13 E♭ma7 A♭ma7-5

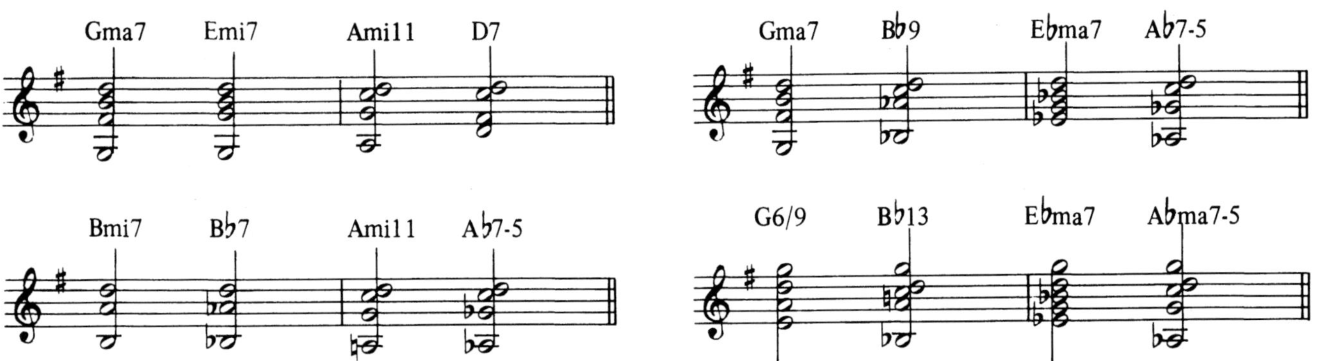

In places where the melody indicates no STRONG preference for chord type (as in the last two "turn-around" measures of a song where no melody exists), seventh chords may replace minors. Each of the following examples could be played in place of C Am Dm G7:

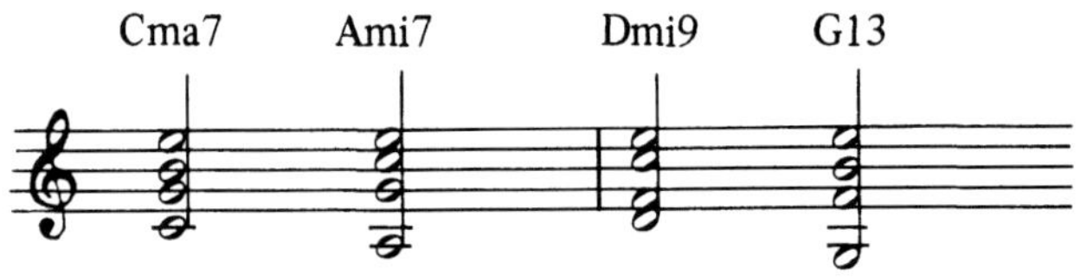

Cma7 Ami7 Dmi9 G13

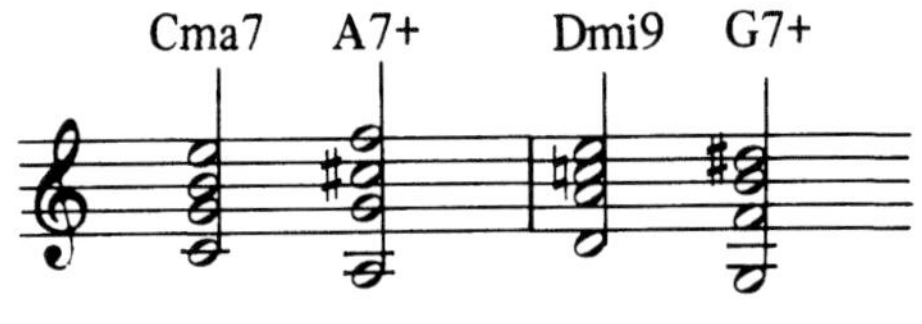

Cma7 A7+ Dmi9 G7+

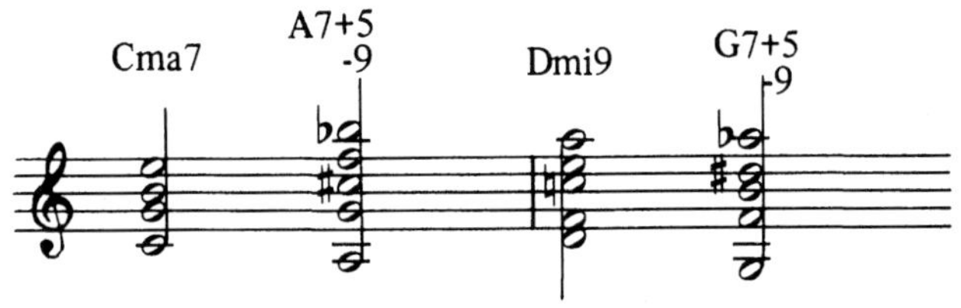

Cma7 A7+5 -9 Dmi9 G7+5 -9

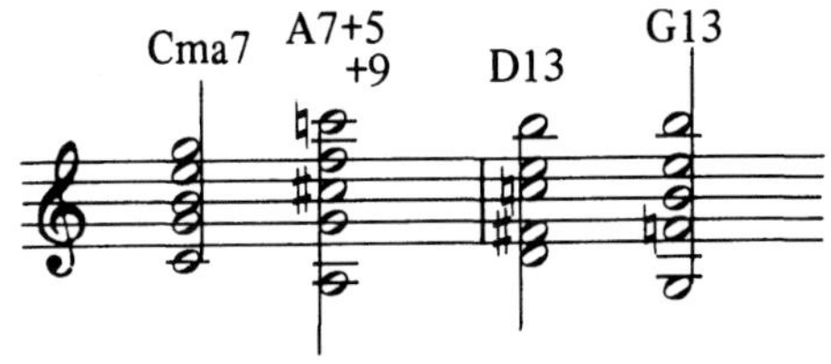

Cma7 A7+5 +9 D13 G13

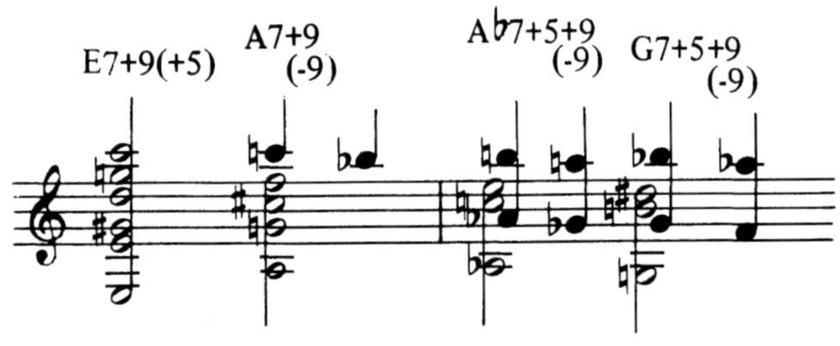

E7+9(+5) A7+9 (-9) A♭7+5+9 (-9) G7+5+9 (-9)

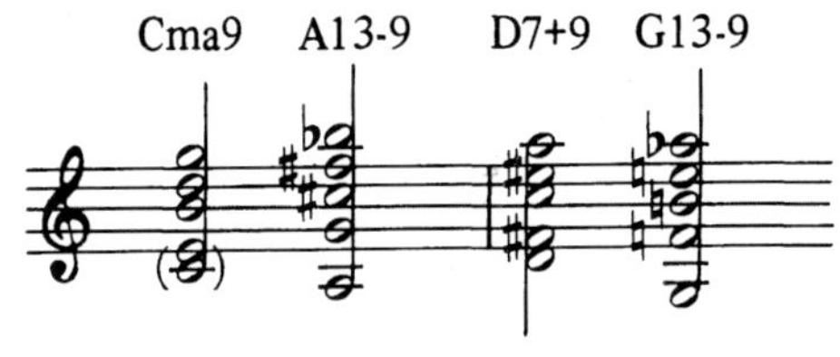

Cma9 A13-9 D7+9 G13-9

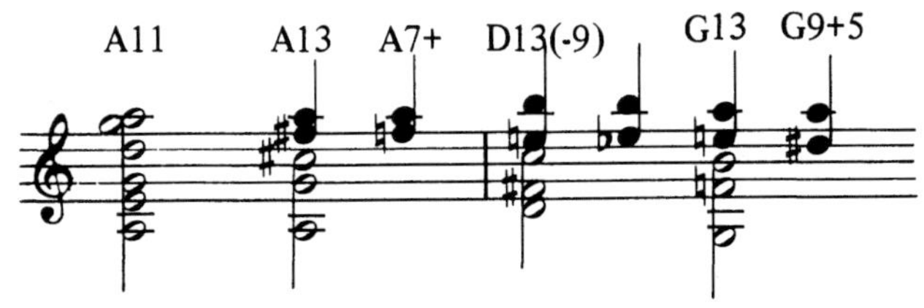

A11 A13 A7+ D13(-9) G13 G9+5

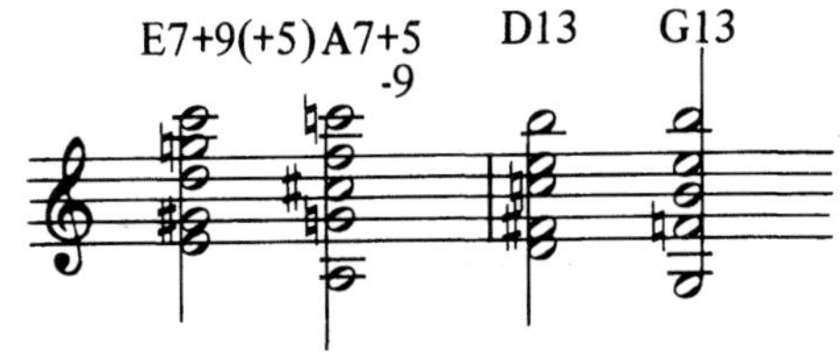

E7+9(+5) A7+5 -9 D13 G13

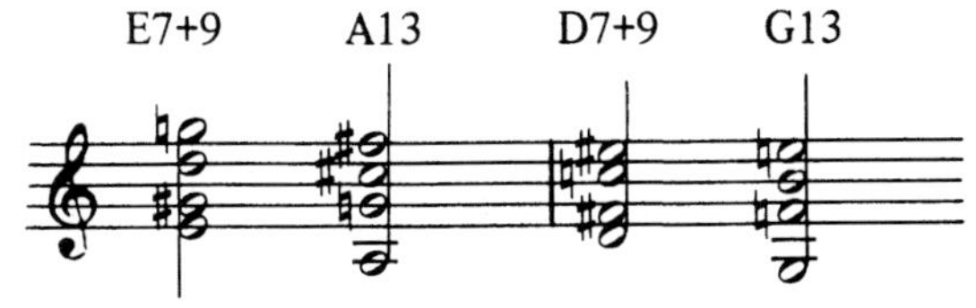

E7+9 A13 D7+9 G13

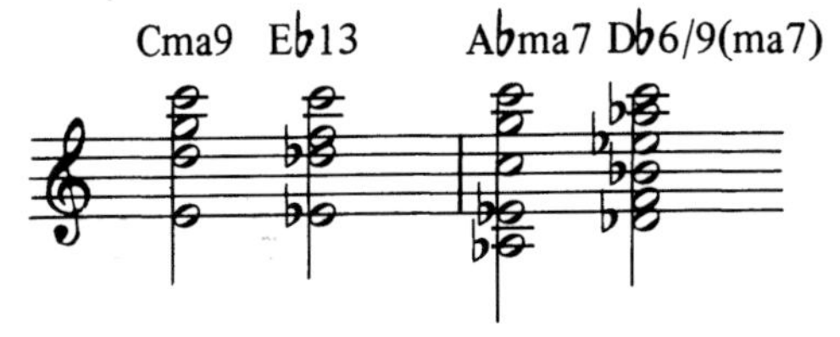

Cma9 E♭13 A♭ma7 D♭6/9(ma7)

Substitute Patterns

The following patterns substitute for C major. There are many possible variations, so experiment.

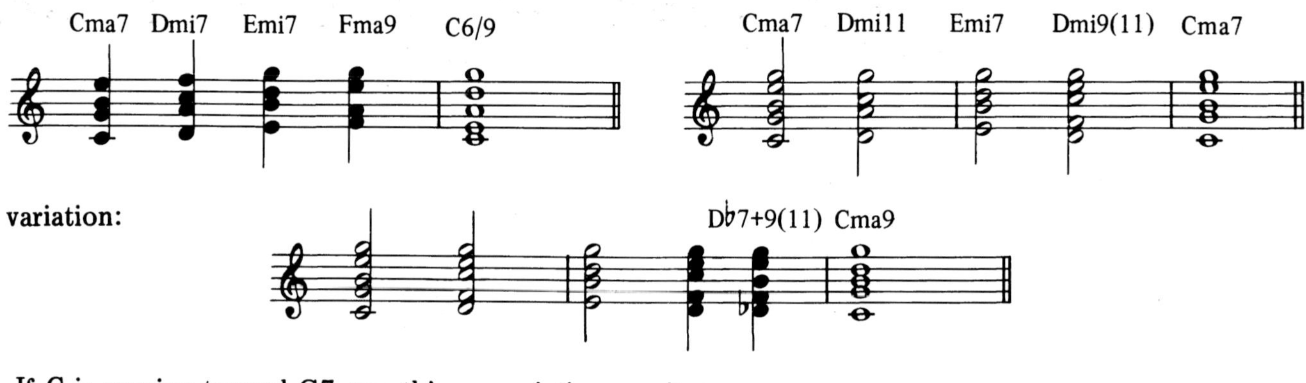

variation:

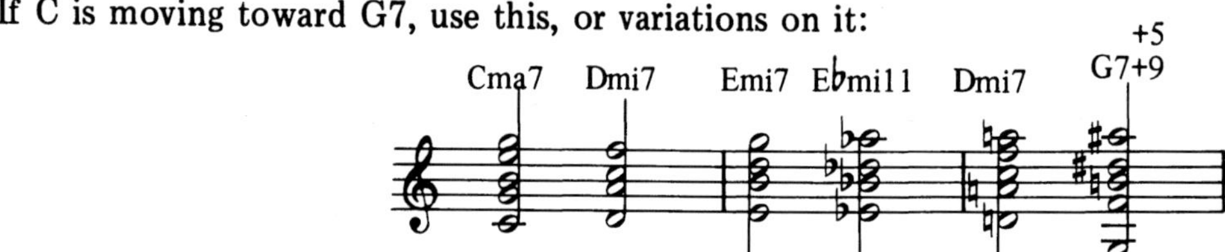

If C is moving toward G7, use this, or variations on it:

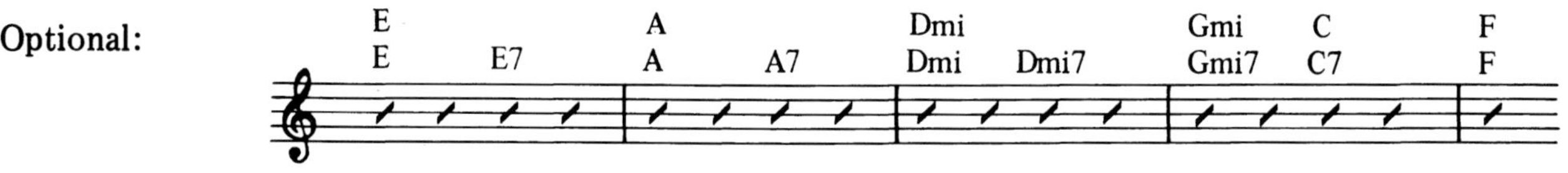

Chord Connection

SEVENTHS connect dominants, as shown below:

Optional:

AUGMENTED chords also connect dominants:

DIMINISHED chords connect subdominants. Use the diminished chord with the SAME NAME as (1) the chord being entered or (2) the chord being left:

DIMINISHED chords also connect chromatically:

CHORD SUBSTITUTIONS

Chord pattern substitutions for the I-VI-II-V progression are as follows:

I =	**VI** =	**II** =	**V** =
C Major 7	Am 7	Dm 7	G 7
or C Major 9	or Am 6	or Dm 6	
or C Major 11	or Am 9	or Dm 9	

- The chords have to have common tones (most often the Root).
- For any minor chord, you can substitute a dominant chord if you're not in a minor key.

Chord substitution patterns for the chord progression (I-VI-II-V) as demonstrated above in the key of C are:

I	VI	II	V
C Major 7	A m 7	D m 7	G 7
or E 7	A +	D m 7	G 7
or E 7	E♭ 7	D m 9	G 7
or B♭7	A 7	A♭ 7	G 7
or E m	A 7	D m	G 7
or E 7+ 9	A 13	D 7+ 9	G13
or B♭ 13	A 13	A♭ 13	G 13
or E 7+ 9	E♭ 7+ 9	D 7+ 9	G 7+ 9

- Or you can use any combination of these chords to form chord pattern = **Chord Pattern Substitutions**
- Voice your chords with common tones in them; especially on the top strings... this makes a moving line.

JOE PASS TIPS ON VOICE LEADING IN CHORDS:

1. Chord moves with a common tone on the top string.
2. Keep chords or notes in motion, connected with voice movement or musical line.
3. Put altered notes on the top strings (G, B, E).
4. Leave the Root in the bass or omit it altogether.
5. Joe often leaves out the 5th tone note.
6. Play a ♭9 chord with the Root on the bottom. That is, put the ♭9 note somewhere *inside* the chord.

Standard Pattern Chord Substitutions

In this section you will find basic chord patterns and substitute patterns utilizing the chords presented in the first two parts of this book. These chord symbols are written so that the order of appearance of notes coincides with the spelling of the chord symbol. For example, D7+9+5 means D7 with the raised 9th next, and the raised 5th on top.

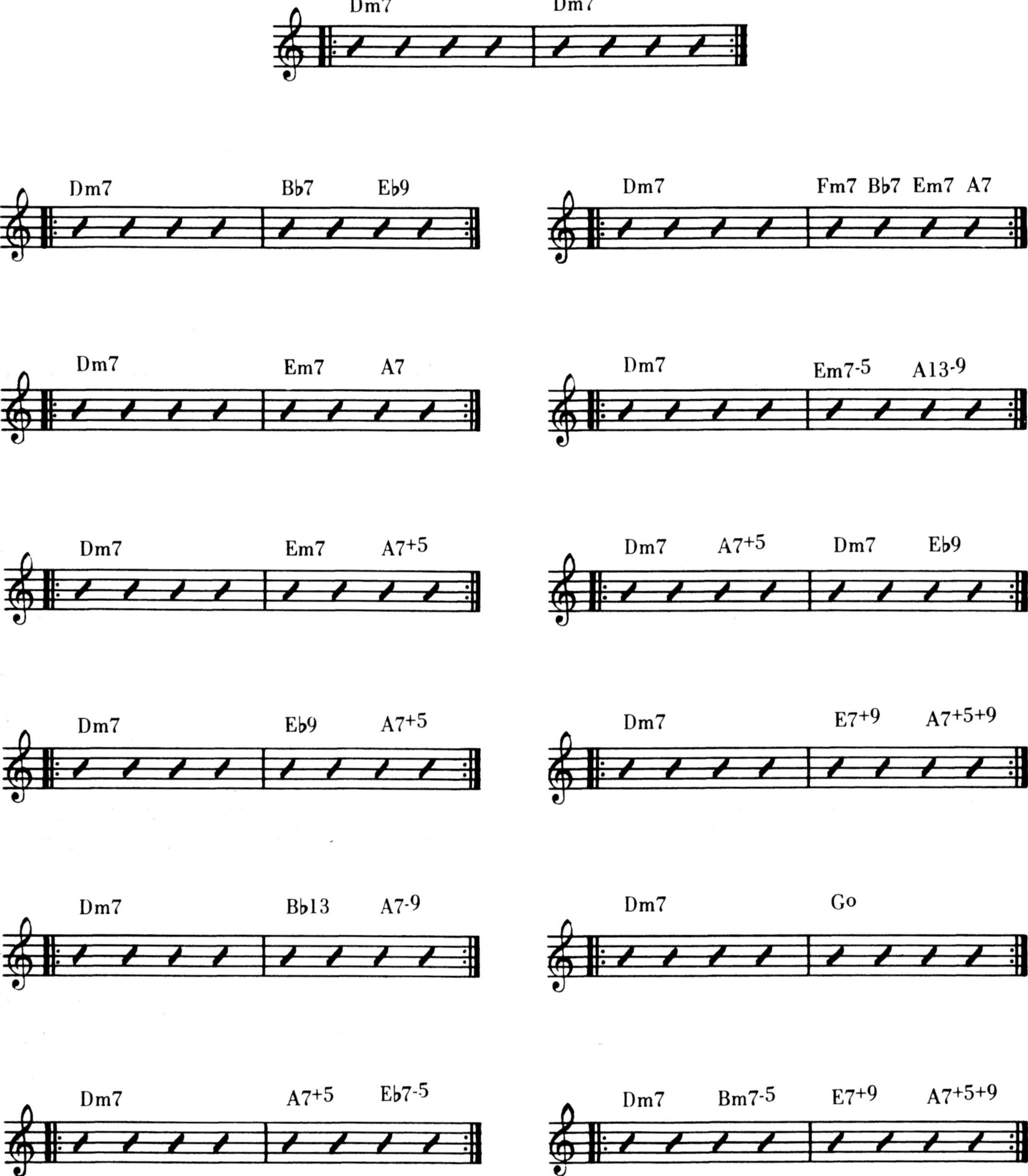

BASIC PATTERN:

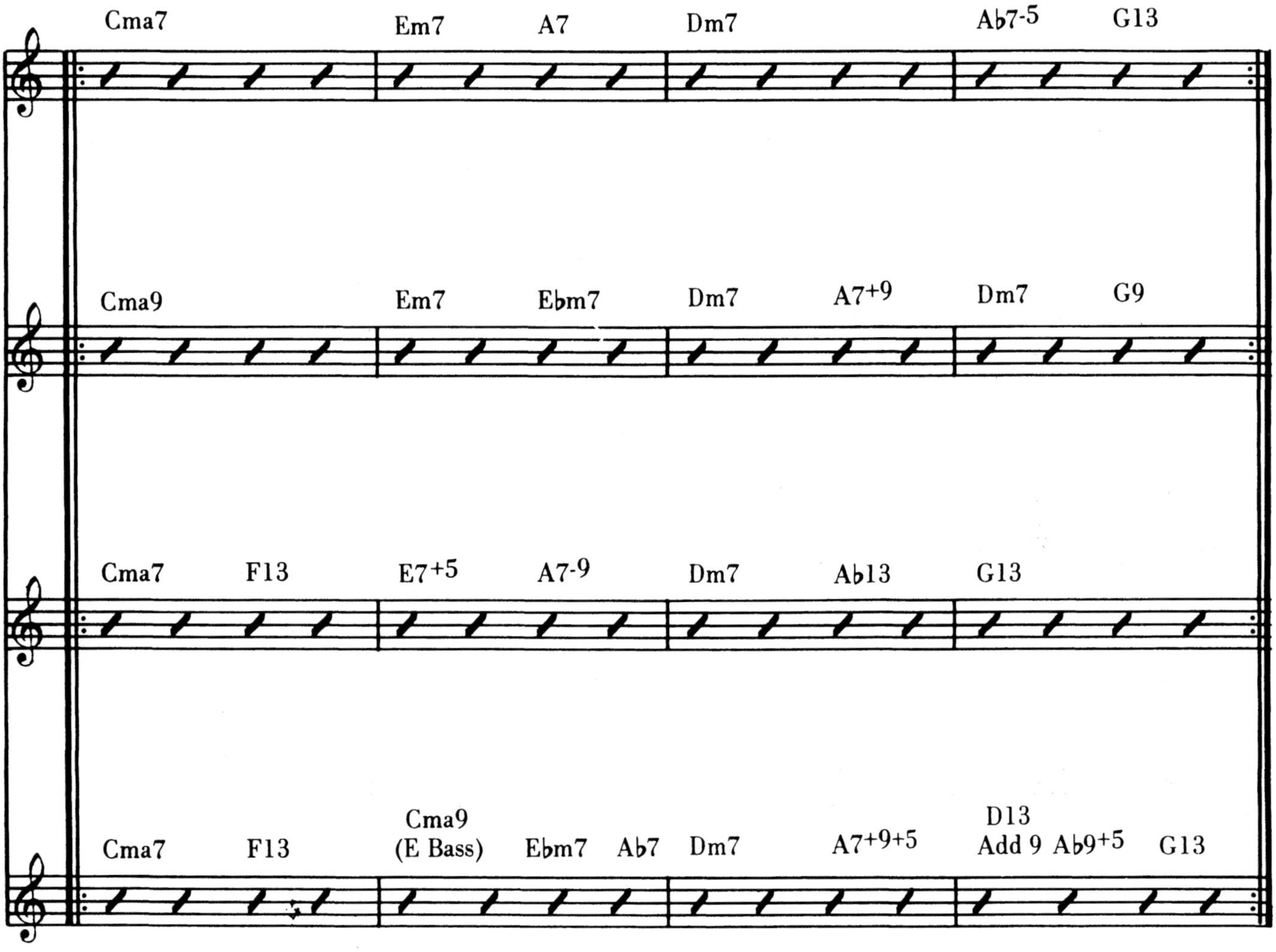

Cma7	Em7 A7	Dm7	A♭7^{-5} G13
Cma9	Em7 E♭m7	Dm7 A7^{+9}	Dm7 G9
Cma7 F13	E7^{+5} A7^{-9}	Dm7 A♭13	G13
Cma7 F13	Cma9 (E Bass) E♭m7 A♭7	Dm7 A7^{+9+5}	D13 Add 9 A♭9^{+5} G13

BASIC PATTERN:

Cma7 Dma7 Em7 Fma7 Em7 Dm7 Cma7

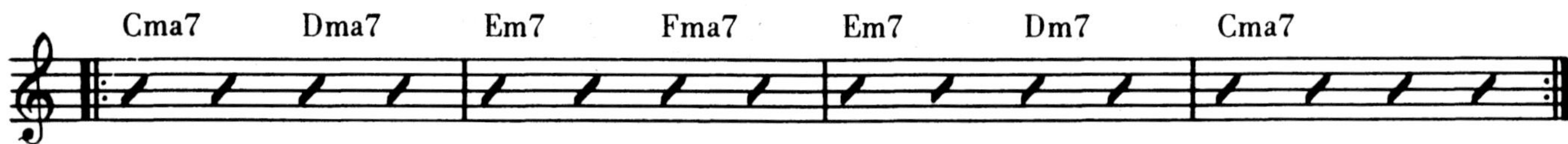

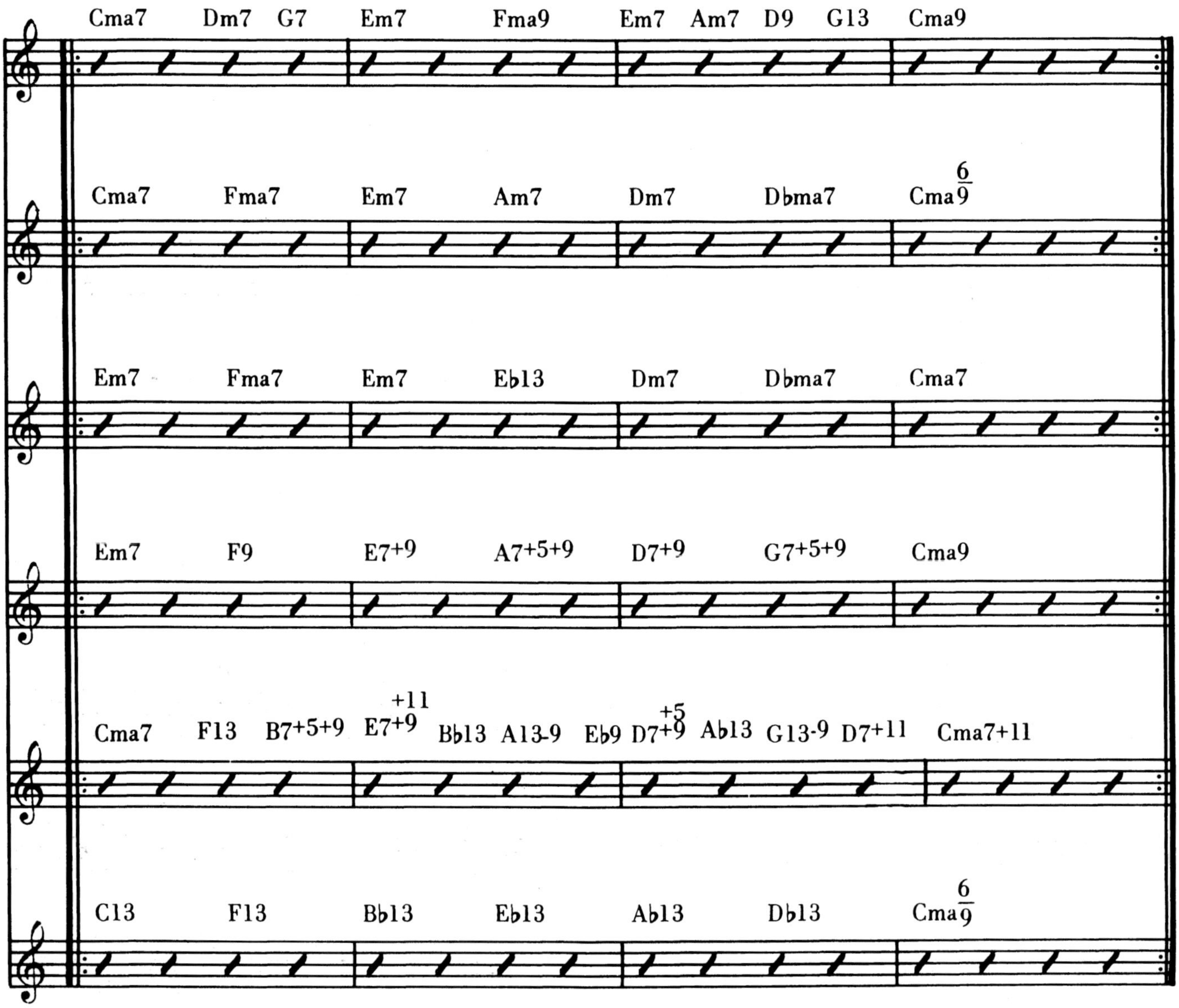
Cma7 Dm7 G7 Em7 Fma9 Em7 Am7 D9 G13 Cma9
Cma7 Fma7 Em7 Am7 Dm7 Dbma7 Cma 6/9
Em7 Fma7 Em7 Eb13 Dm7 Dbma7 Cma7
Em7 F9 E7+9 A7+5+9 D7+9 G7+5+9 Cma9
Cma7 F13 B7+5+9 E7+9+11 Bb13 A13-9 Eb9 D7+5+9 Ab13 G13-9 D7+11 Cma7+11
C13 F13 Bb13 Eb13 Ab13 Db13 Cma 6/9

BASIC PATTERN:

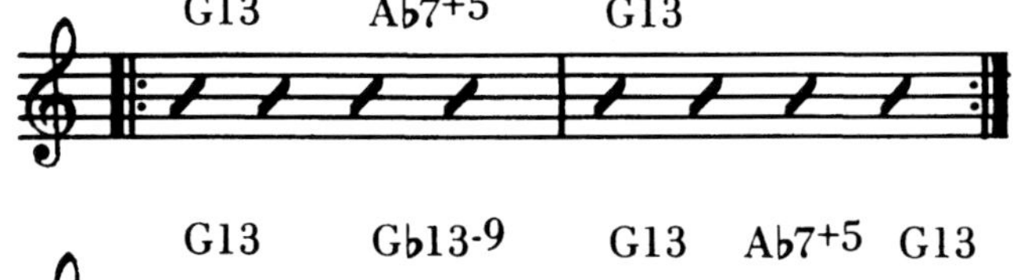

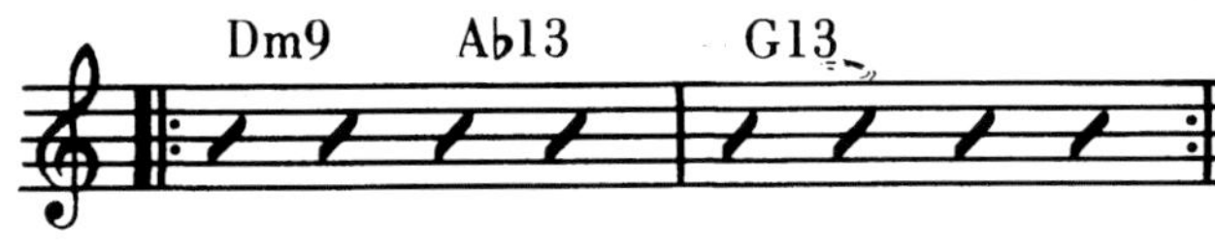

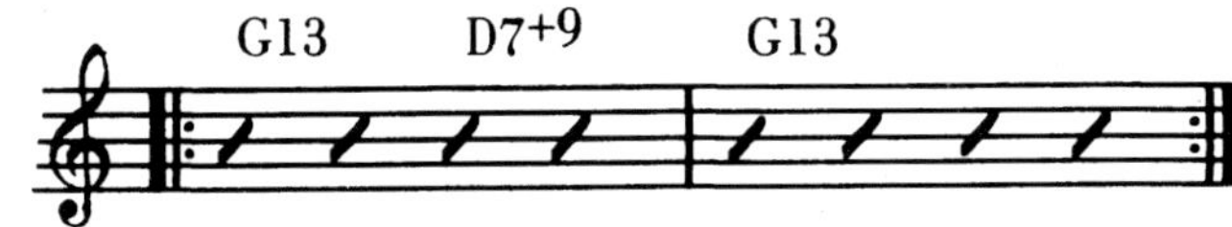

"STANDARD" CHANGES

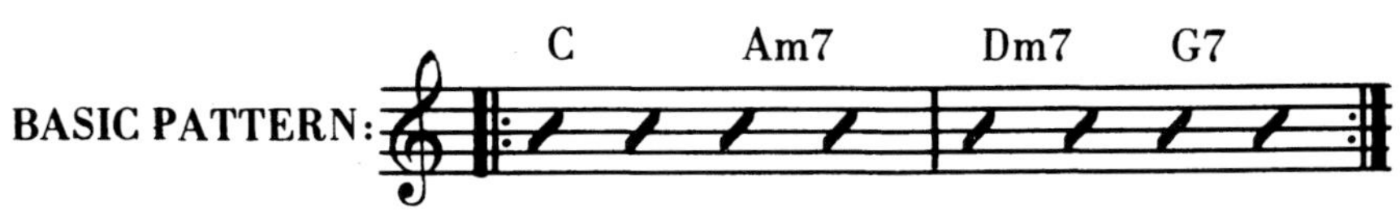

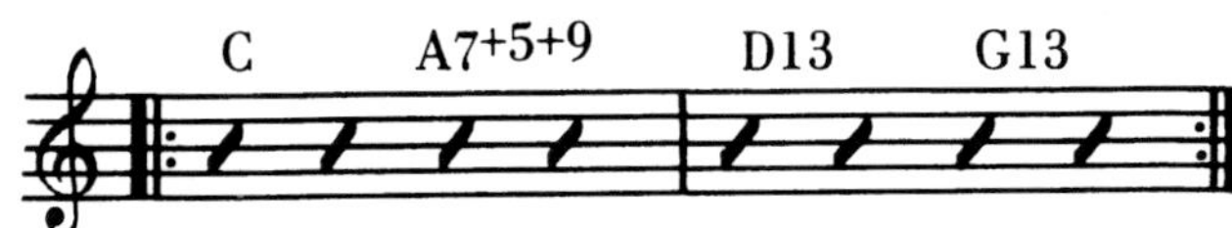

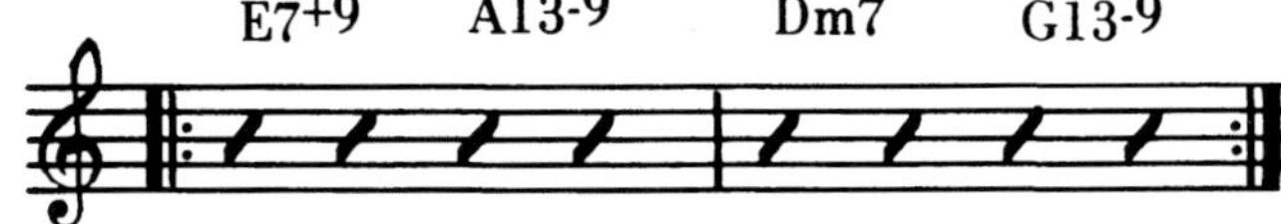

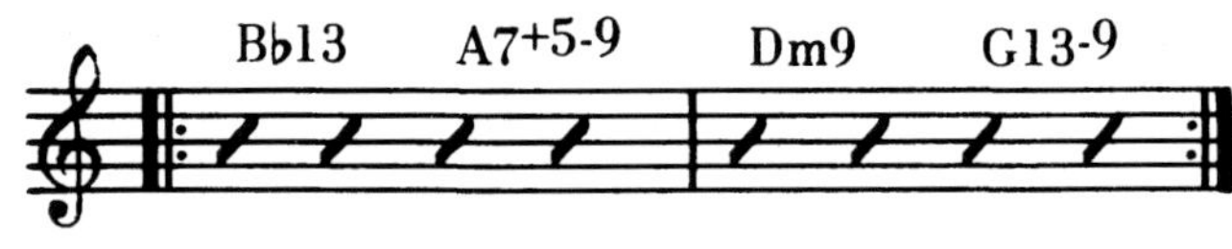

BASIC PATTERN:

BLUES

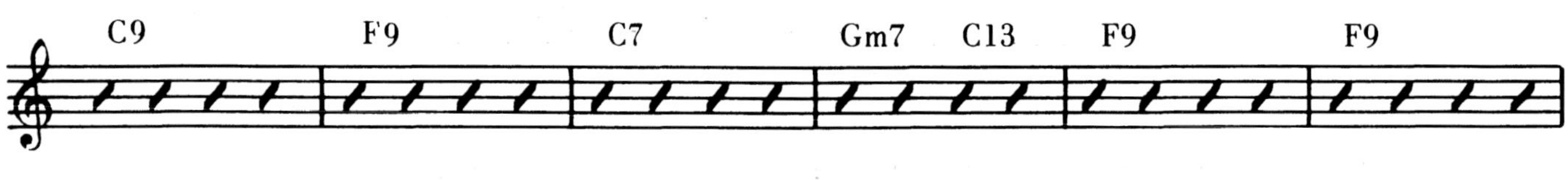

NOTE: Try to sustain lead notes from one chord to the next. For example, C9 to F13, sustain the G on top.

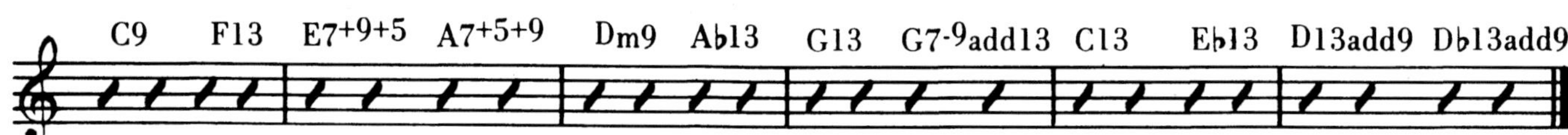

MINOR chords connect the subdominant chord to the tonic chord:

ALL chords may be connected by moving into the chord from a half-step (one fret) above or below:

Here is a blues to illustrate the half-step (one fret) connection principle. The whole thing can be played using this one fingering:

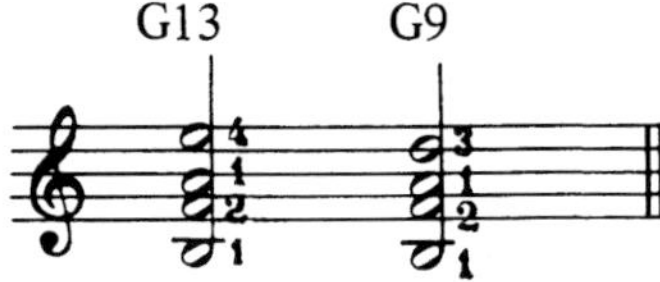

Use other fingerings if you like. Try Am7 or A7+5±9 in the 9th measure.

These are more than just one-fret "slurs." The "pickup" chord is D7+5+9, moving down to G13 and G9 in the 1st measure. The final chord in that measure is G7+5±9 or D♭13/D♭9. Analyze these chords:

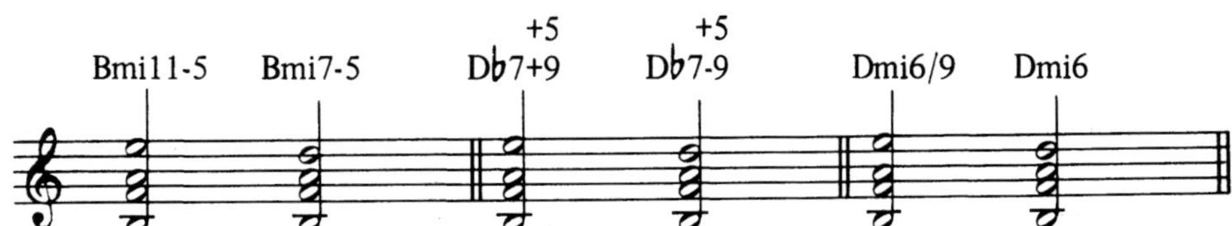

Back-Cycling

Another way to add harmonic interest to a chord pattern is to "back-cycle" through the order of dominants (cycle of fifths). This should illustrate:

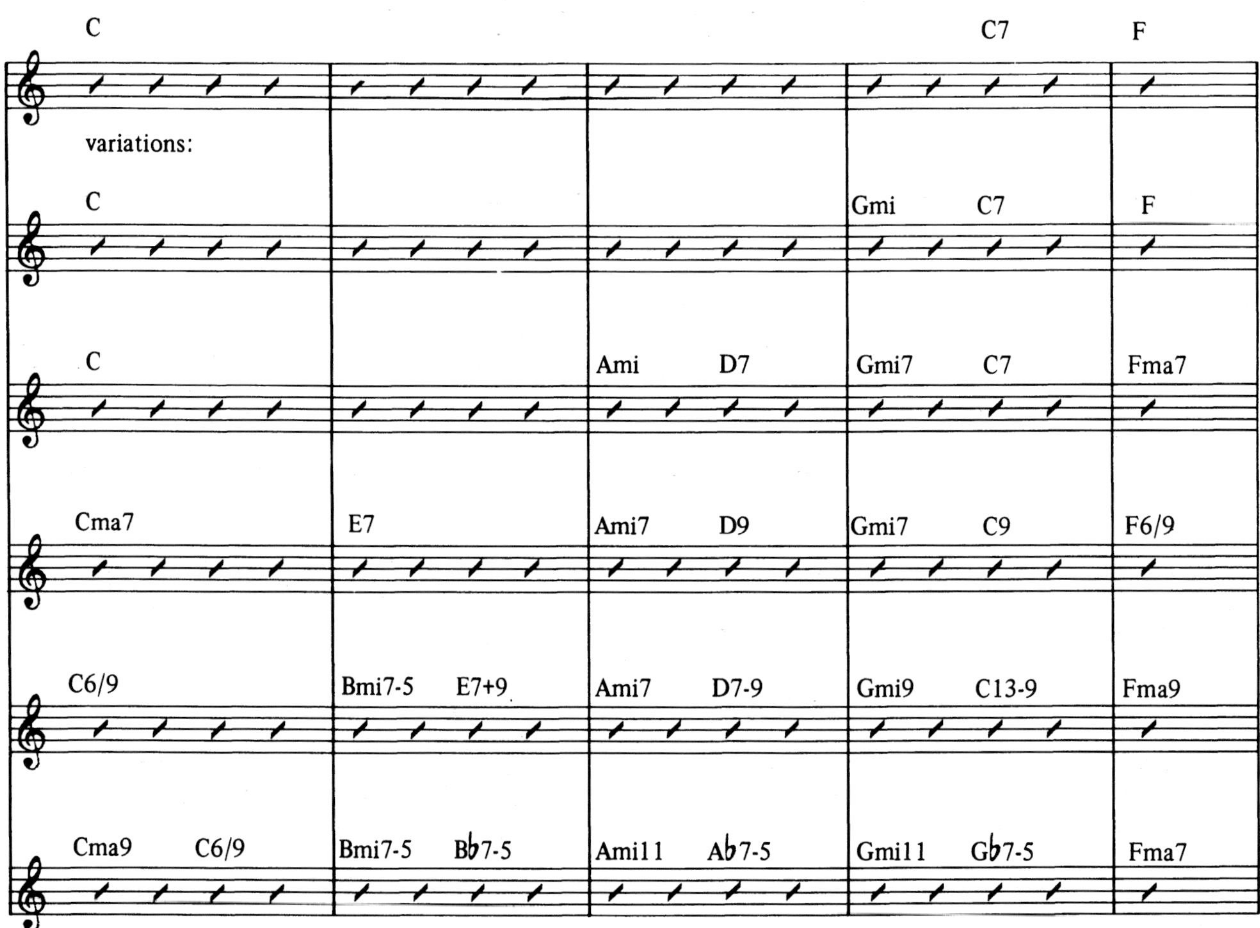

NOTE: The principles of chord embellishment, substitution and connection are THEORETICALLY applicable to any given chord pattern. You'll find that some of them work nearly all the time, and some others less frequently. Try to use them in songs, and LISTEN! Your ear will tell you when it's right.

Symmetric (Chromatic) Chords

Most chords can be moved up or down the fingerboard in almost any interval (half-steps, whole-steps, major or minor thirds) PROVIDED that the final chord in the symmetric sequence resolves properly into the following chord.

This study uses a single fingering throughout:

Analyze the chords below. The top four tones in each are identical. Depending upon the bass-line used, the study above could be played against C7, Gm, G♭7 or Em chords.

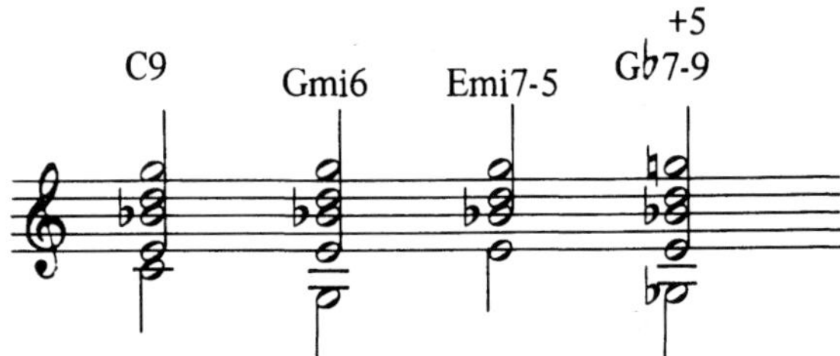

If that study were played against a C7 chord, the bass-line could move symmetrically with the chords, or just pedal a "C" note:

For the same chord (C7-5) the G♭ bass note could move up with the chords, or be sustained as a pedal tone in the rhythm section:

"Diminished" Chords

You know that a Diminished 7th chord moves up or down the fingerboard in minor third intervals. The same is true of ANY chord which has a "diminished" character (7-9, 7-5, 13-9, 7+5-9, etc.)

C7-5-9 up and down in minor thirds:

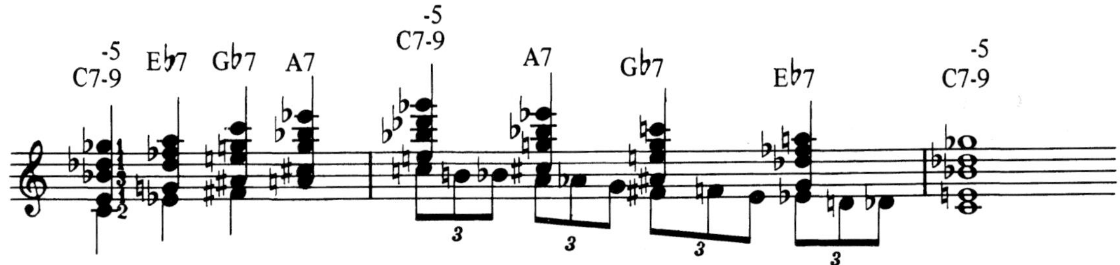

The "C7" chord in the study above could resolve into an F chord at any of the "C7" points, or from either of the "G♭7" points. The "E♭7" and "A7" chords would not resolve well into F.

You needn't limit the symmetric motion to minor thirds. In the next study, F7-9 moves quite a lot before resolving into B♭7-9:

Add appropriate bass-notes to hear the true chord sound.

The next study is basically B7 to E7 to A7 to D7:

In symmetric harmony, the chords move from one "good" point to another. What takes place between those points is up to your ear.

F13 up in minor thirds:

Try the same thing with F13 - 9:

F7+5+9 or B13 down in minor thirds. Resolve F7 into B♭, B13 into E:

Dm7 to G7 to C:

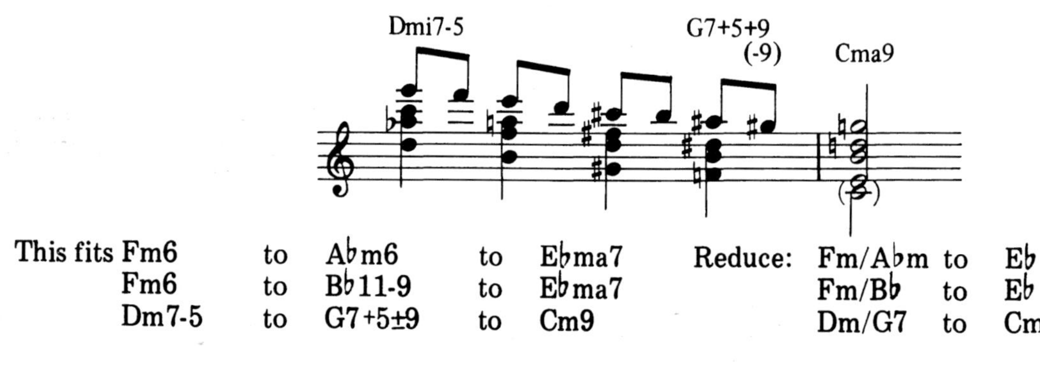

This fits Fm6	to	A♭m6	to	E♭ma7	Reduce:	Fm/A♭m	to	E♭
Fm6	to	B♭11-9	to	E♭ma7		Fm/B♭	to	E♭
Dm7-5	to	G7+5±9	to	Cm9		Dm/G7	to	Cm

Fm7/B♭7 to E♭ or Dm7/G7 to Cm:

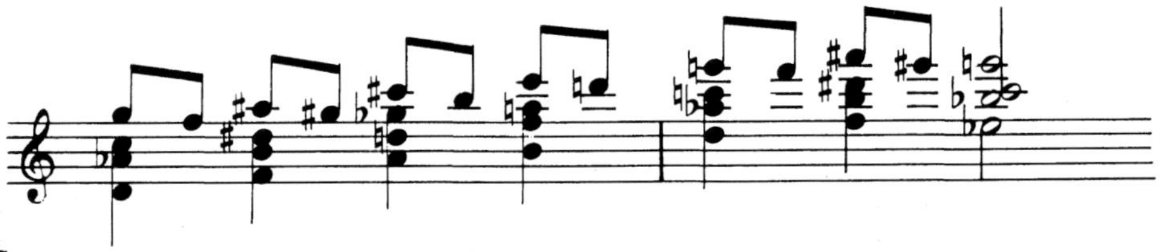

Dm7/G7 to C:

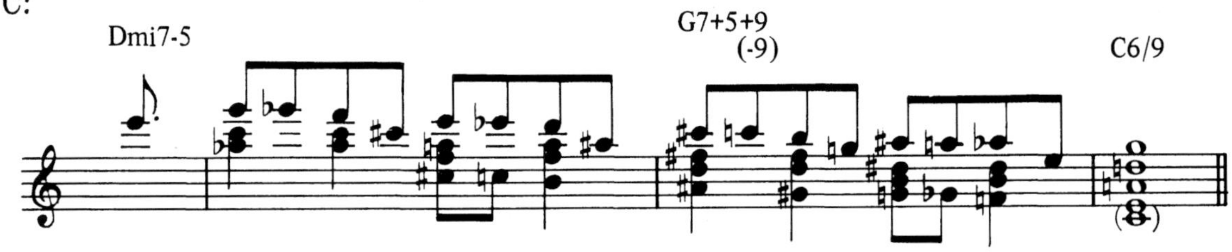
Dmi7-5
G7+5+9
(-9)
C6/9

D7 to G:

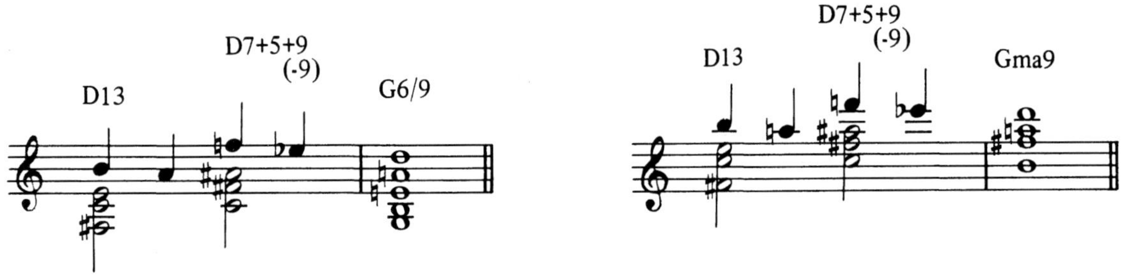
D13
D7+5+9
(-9)
G6/9
D13
D7+5+9
(-9)
Gma9

A♭7 to D♭:

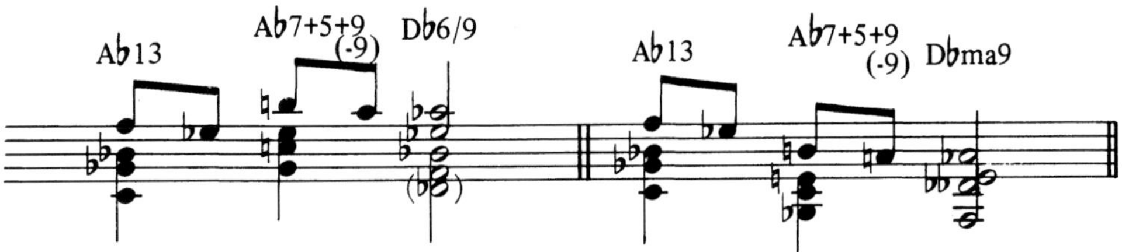
A♭13
A♭7+5+9
(-9)
D♭6/9
A♭13
A♭7+5+9
(-9)
D♭ma9

This study uses an E♭m triad moving symmetrically down in minor thirds. It could fit E♭m, C7, G♭7, Cm or A♭7 Chords.

C7-5-9 down in minor thirds:

re-phrased:

variation:

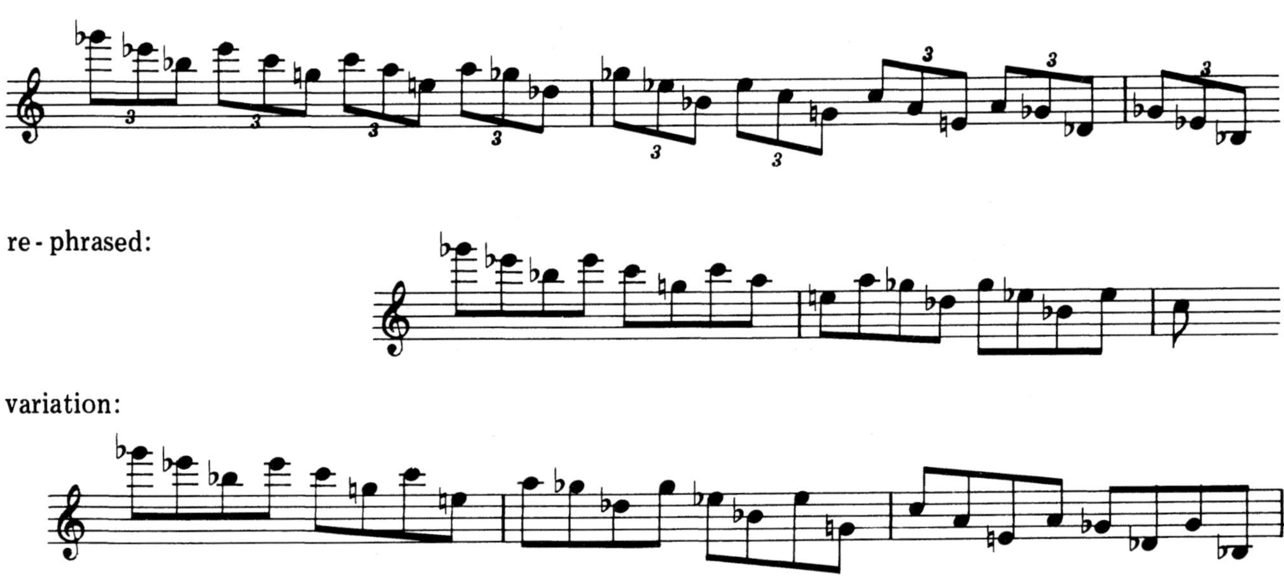

These are just a few ideas, to help illustrate the point. The guitar is built a certain way, and lends itself to this kind of chordal thinking. Experiment until you get the feel of it. Your ear will tell you when it's right.

Major Chord Forms

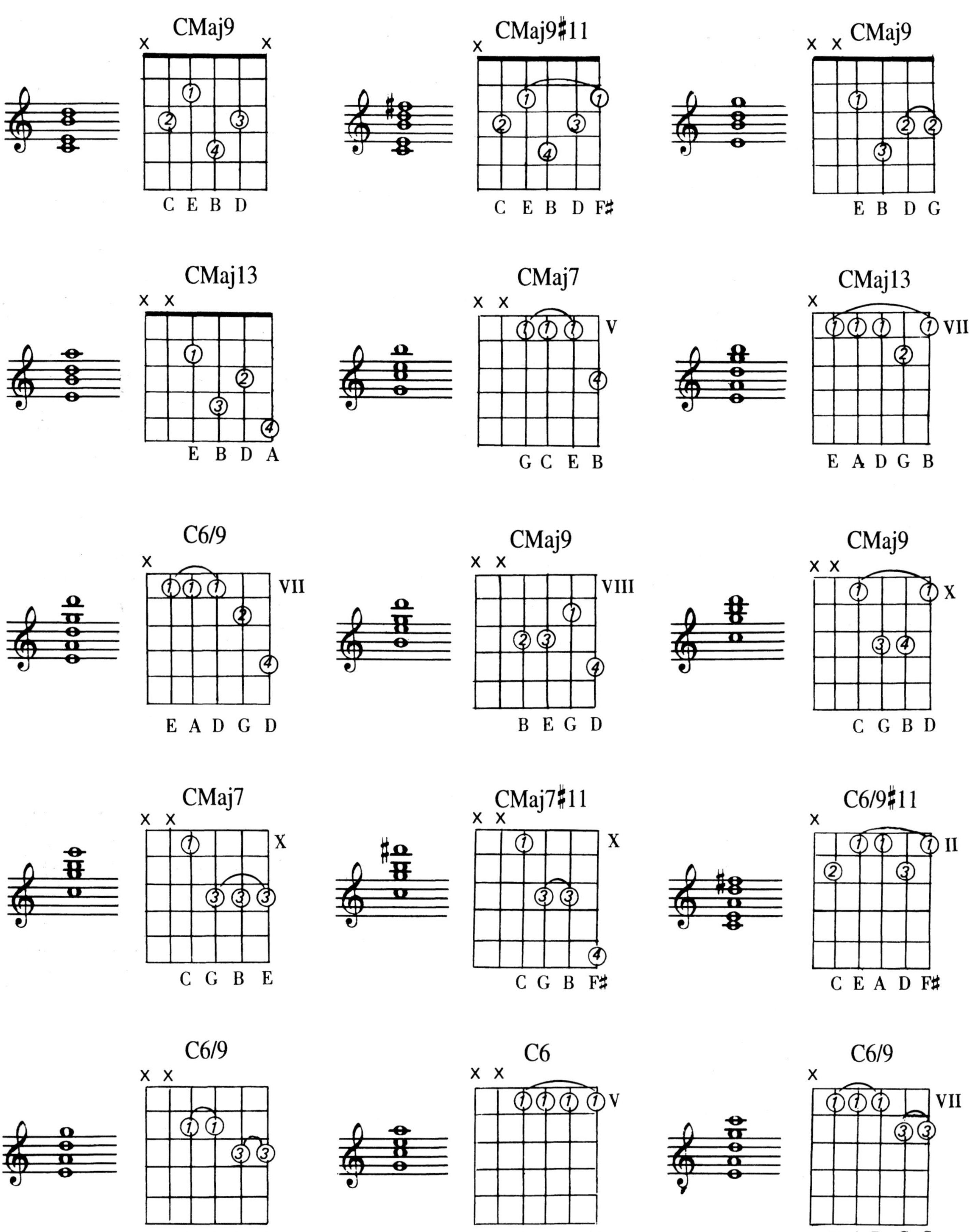

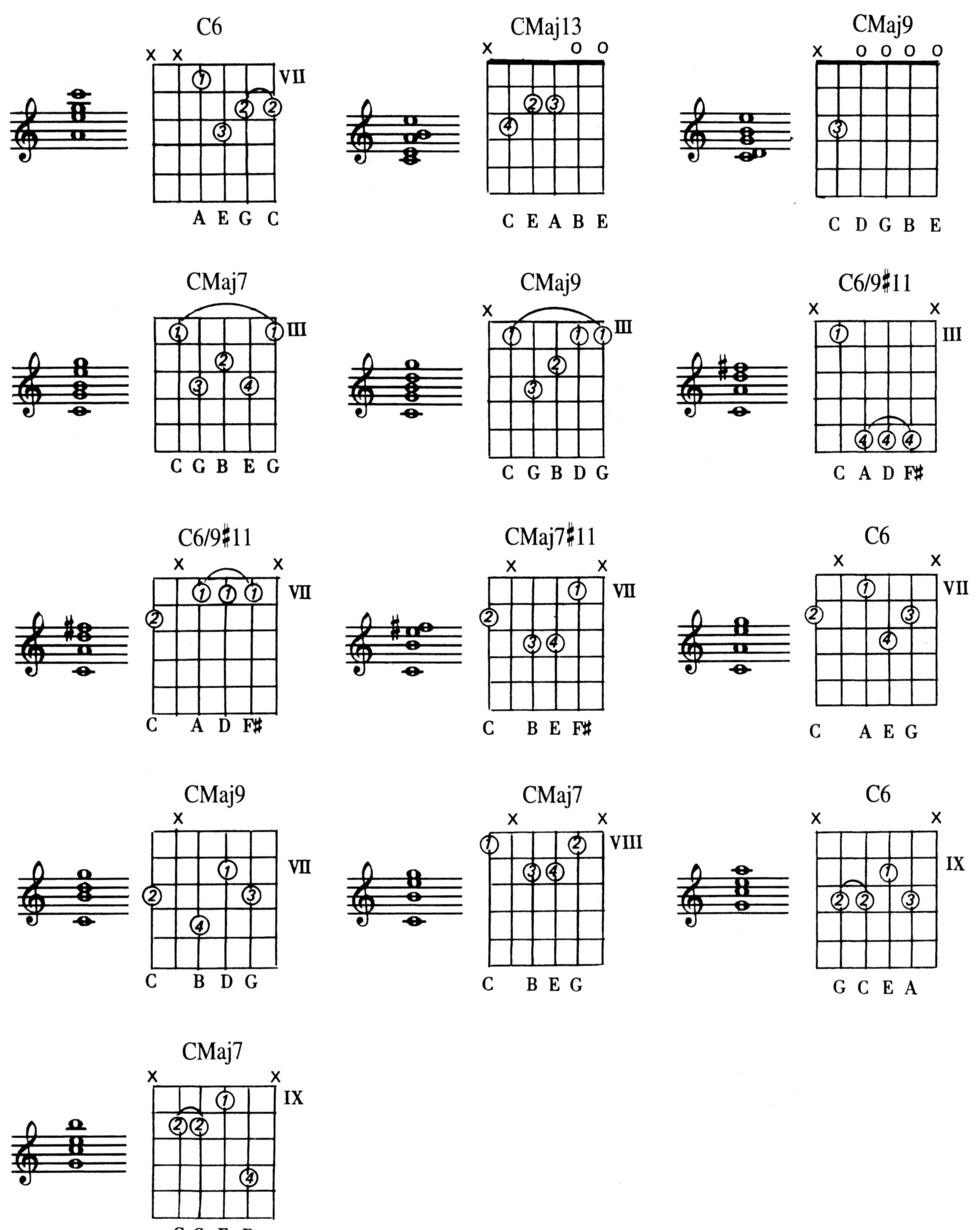

C6
VII
A E G C
CMaj13
C E A B E
CMaj9
C D G B E
CMaj7
III
C G B E G
CMaj9
III
C G B D G
C6/9♯11
III
C A D F♯
C6/9♯11
VII
C A D F♯
CMaj7♯11
VII
C B E F♯
C6
VII
C A E G
CMaj9
VII
C B D G
CMaj7
VIII
C B E G
C6
IX
G C E A
CMaj7
IX
G C E B

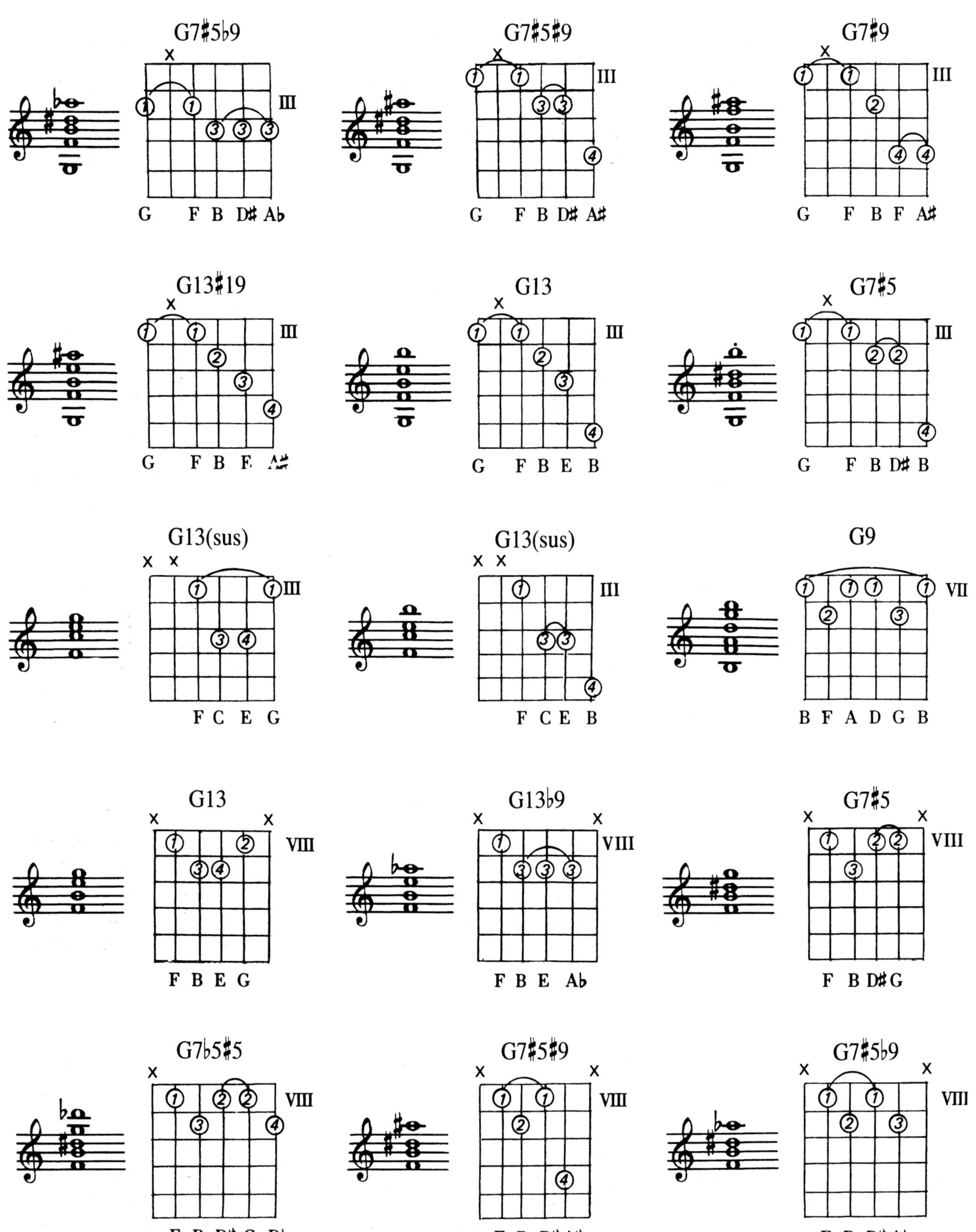
G7♯5♭9
III
G F B D♯ A♭
G7♯5♯9
III
G F B D♯ A♯
G7♯9
III
G F B F A♯
G13♯19
III
G F B E A♯
G13
III
G F B E B
G7♯5
III
G F B D♯ B
G13(sus)
III
F C E G
G13(sus)
III
F C E B
G9
VII
B F A D G B
G13
VIII
F B E G
G13♭9
VIII
F B E A♭
G7♯5
VIII
F B D♯ G
G7♭5♯5
VIII
F B D♯ G D♭
G7♯5♯9
VIII
F B D♯ A♯
G7♯5♭9
VIII
F B D♯ A♭

Seventh Chord Forms

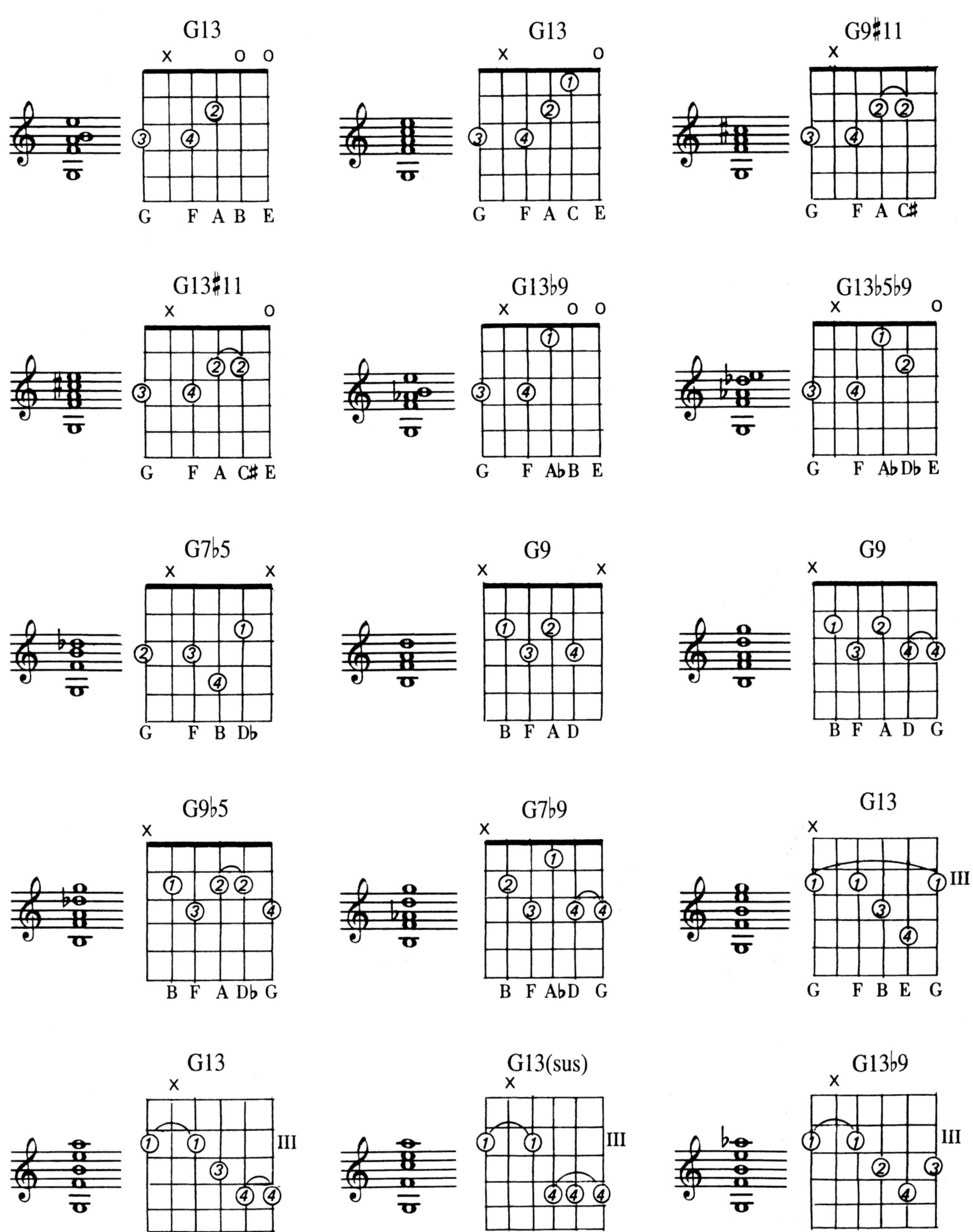

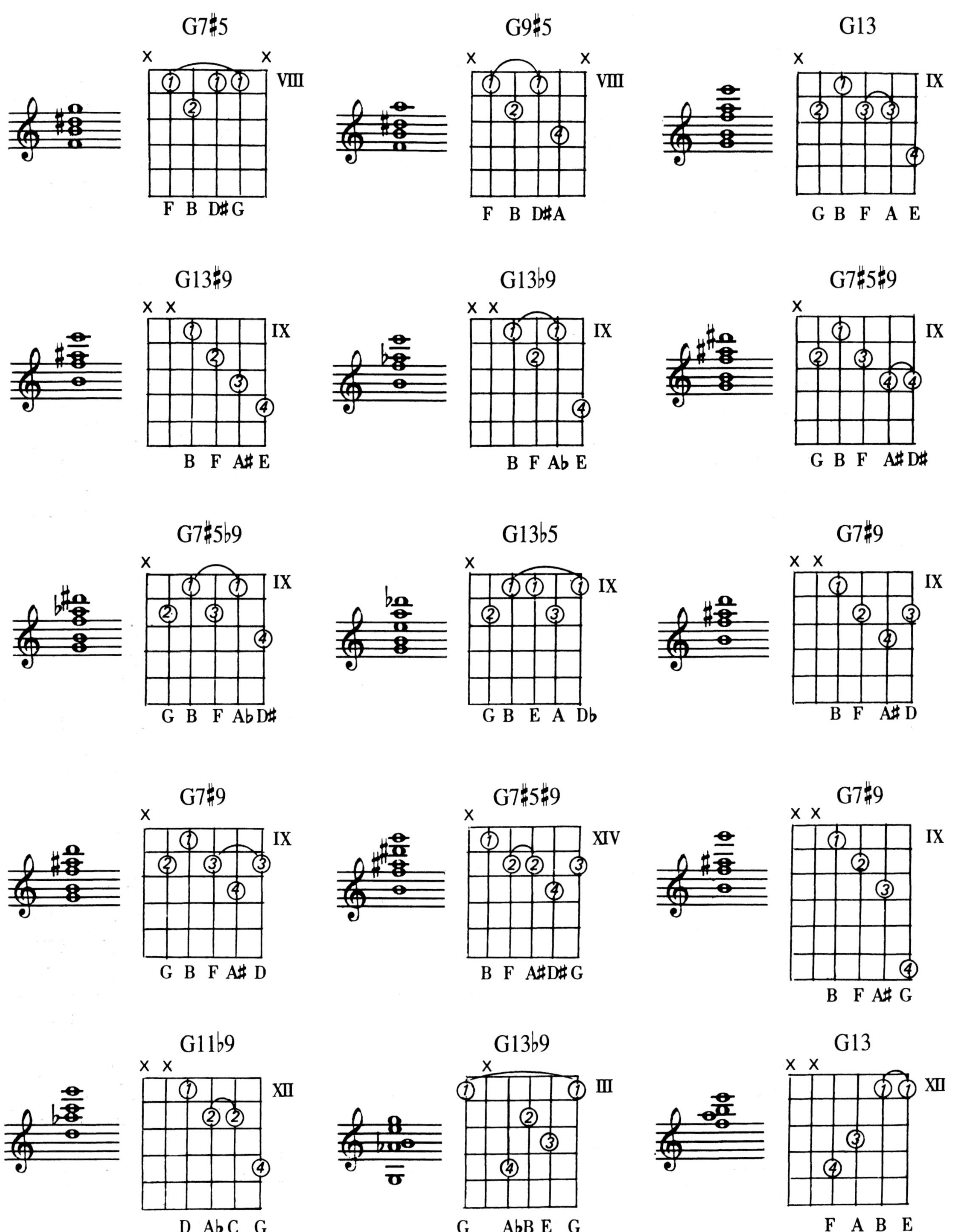
G7♯5
VIII
F B D♯G
G9♯5
VIII
F B D♯A
G13
IX
G B F A E
G13♯9
IX
B F A♯ E
G13♭9
IX
B F A♭ E
G7♯5♯9
IX
G B F A♯ D♯
G7♯5♭9
IX
G B F A♭D♯
G13♭5
IX
G B E A D♭
G7♯9
IX
B F A♯ D
G7♯9
IX
G B F A♯ D
G7♯5♯9
XIV
B F A♯D♯ G
G7♯9
IX
B F A♯ G
G11♭9
XII
D A♭C G
G13♭9
III
G A♭B E G
G13
XII
F A B E

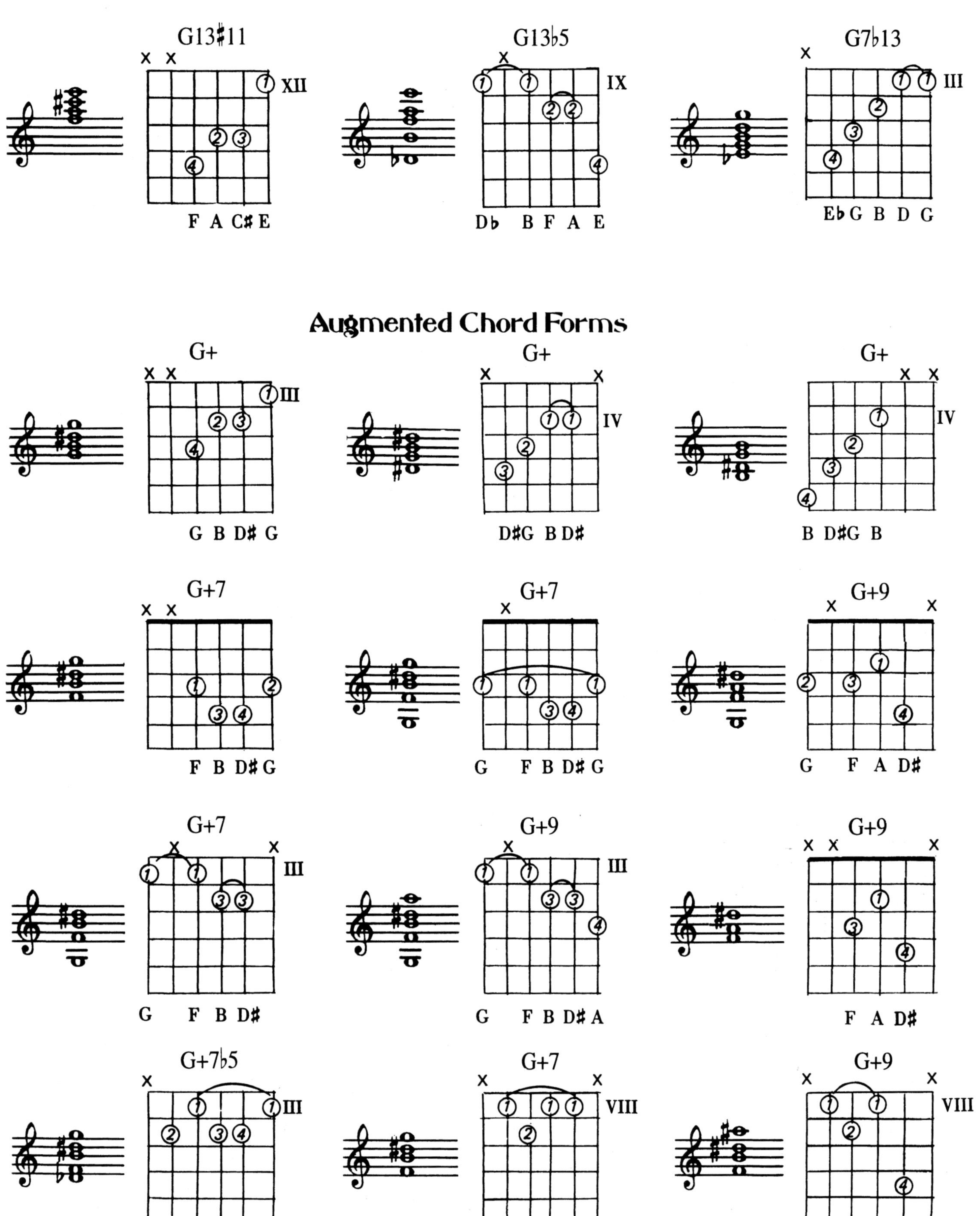
G13♯11
XII
F A C♯ E
G13♭5
IX
D♭ B F A E
G7♭13
III
E♭ G B D G
Augmented Chord Forms
G+
III
G B D♯ G
G+
IV
D♯G B D♯
G+
IV
B D♯G B
G+7
F B D♯ G
G+7
G F B D♯ G
G+9
G F A D♯
G+7
III
G F B D♯
G+9
III
G F B D♯ A
G+9
F A D♯
G+7♭5
III
D♭F B D♯ G
G+7
VIII
F B D♯ G
G+9
VIII
F B D♯ A♯

G+7♭5♯9

VIII
F B D♯ A♯ D♭

G+7♯9

III
F B D♯ A♯

G+7

II
F B D♯ G

G+7♭5

D♯ A D♭ G

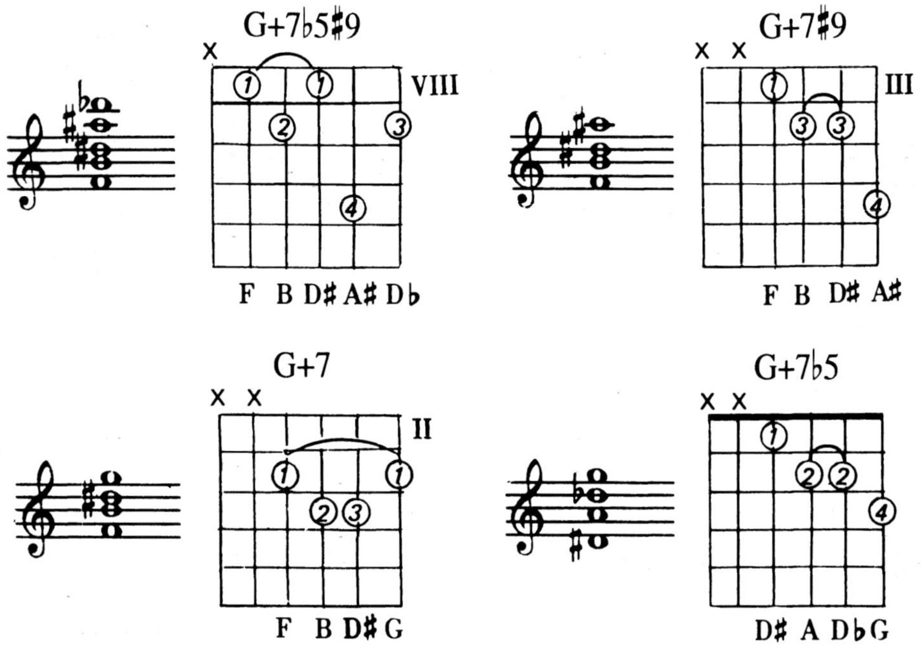

Minor Chord Forms

Cm7

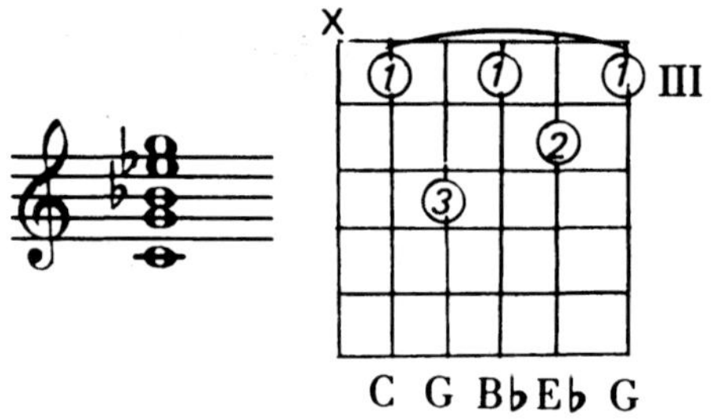

III
C G B♭ E♭ G

Cm7

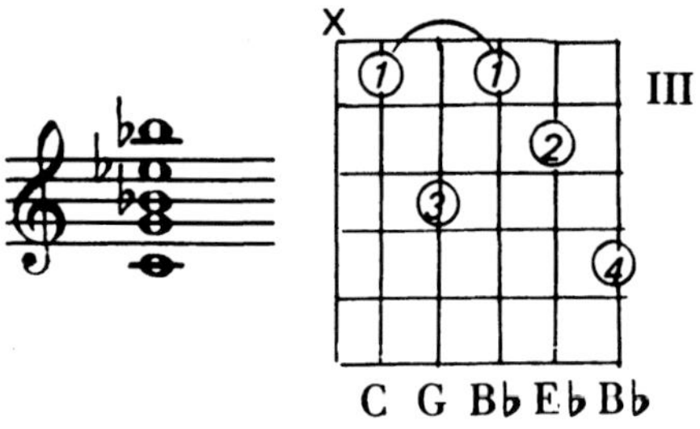

III
C G B♭ E♭ B♭

Cm13

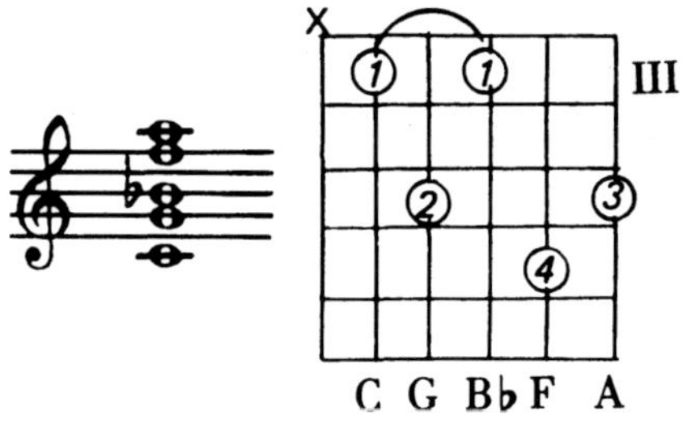

III
C G B♭ F A

Cm11

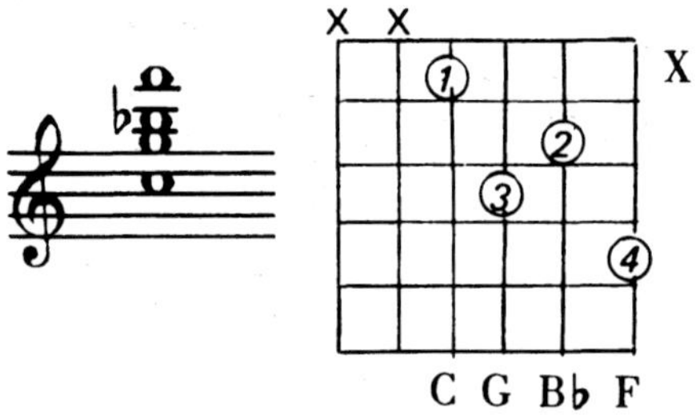

X
C G B♭ F

Cm7

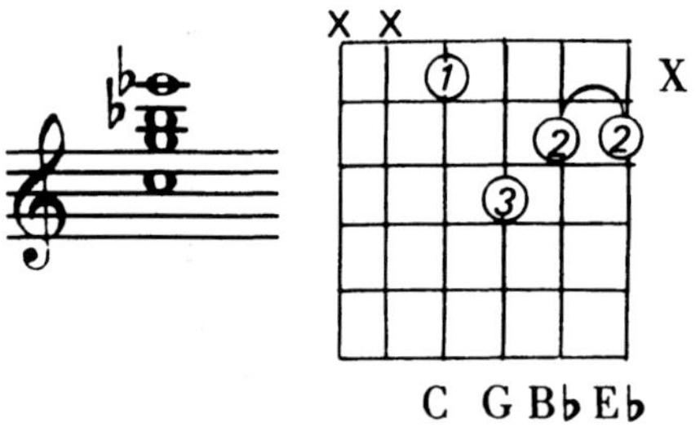

X
C G B♭ E♭

Cm9

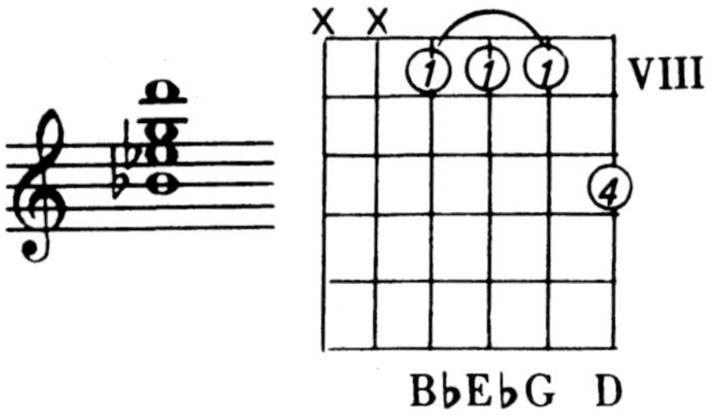

VIII
B♭ E♭ G D

Cm7

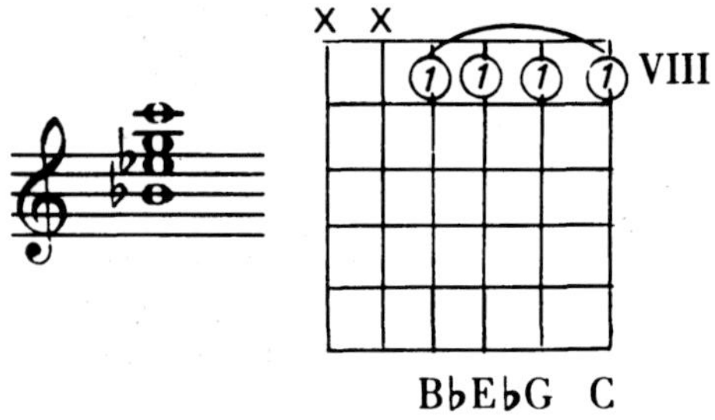

VIII
B♭ E♭ G C

Cm7

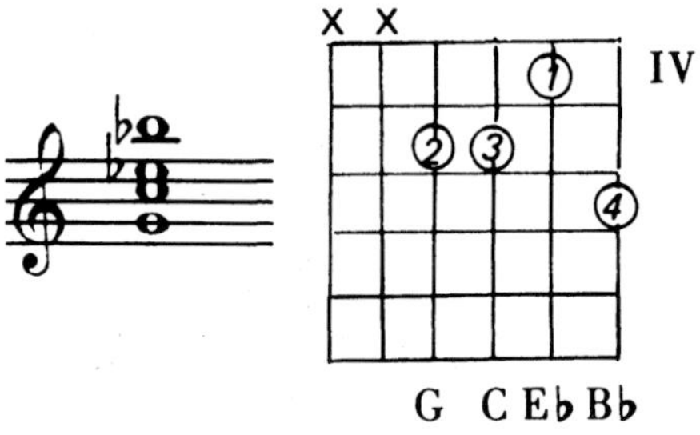

IV
G C E♭ B♭

Cm11

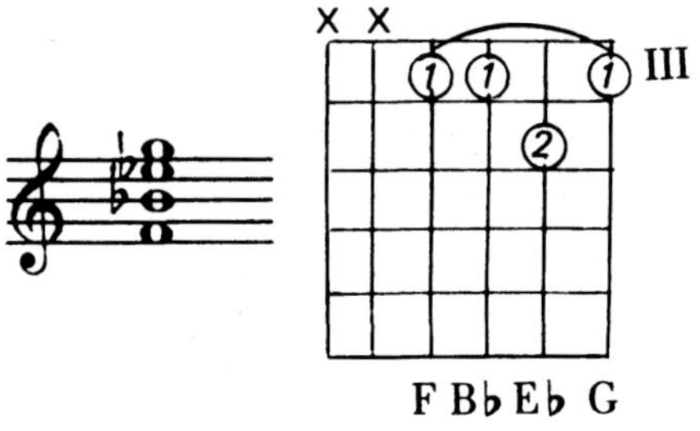

III
F B♭ E♭ G

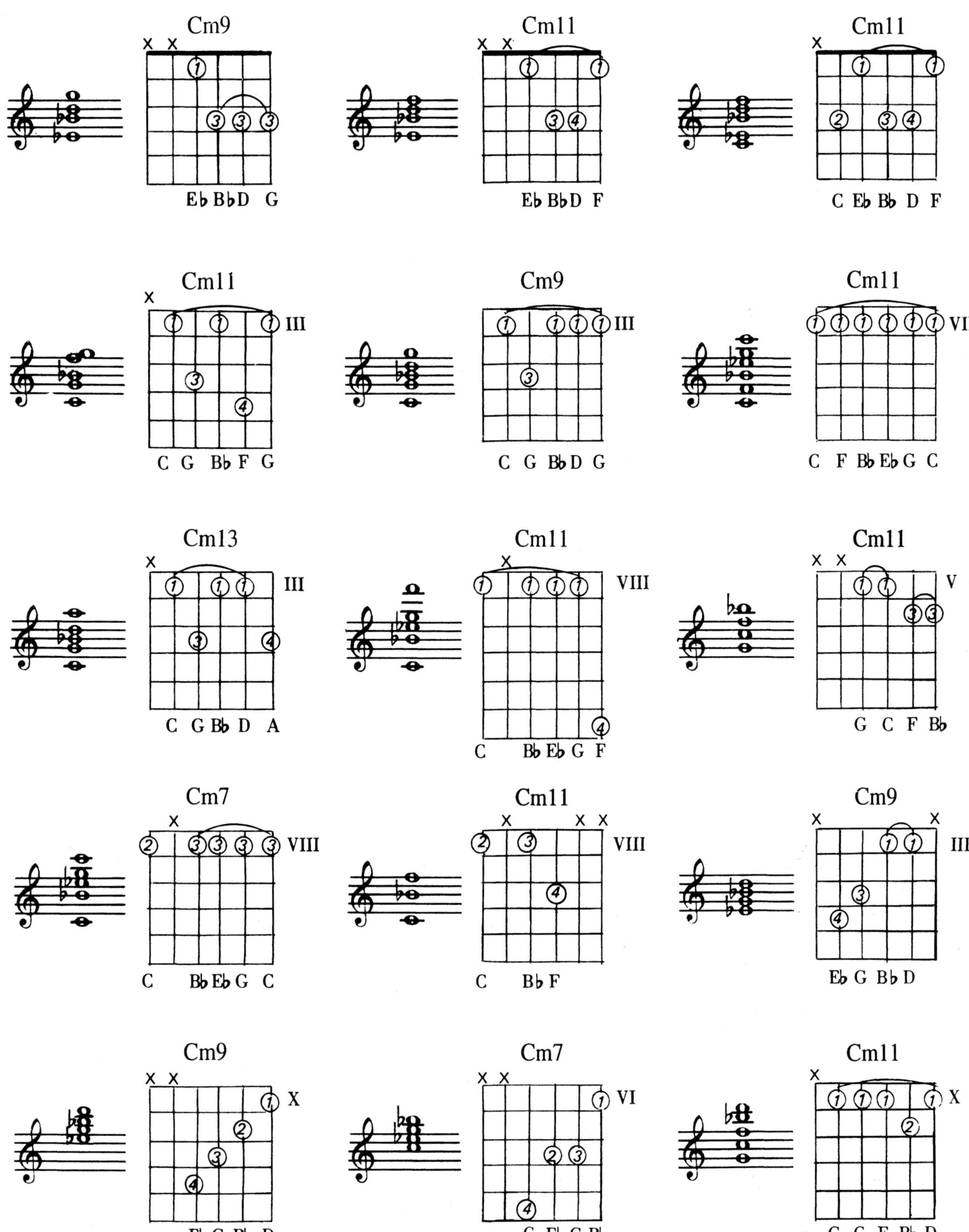
Cm9
Eb Bb D G
Cm11
Eb Bb D F
Cm11
C Eb Bb D F
Cm11
III
C G Bb F G
Cm9
III
C G Bb D G
Cm11
VIII
C F Bb Eb G C
Cm13
III
C G Bb D A
Cm11
VIII
C Bb Eb G F
Cm11
V
G C F Bb
Cm7
VIII
C Bb Eb G C
Cm11
VIII
C Bb F
Cm9
III
Eb G Bb D
Cm9
X
Eb G Bb D
Cm7
VI
C Eb G Bb
Cm11
X
G C F Bb D

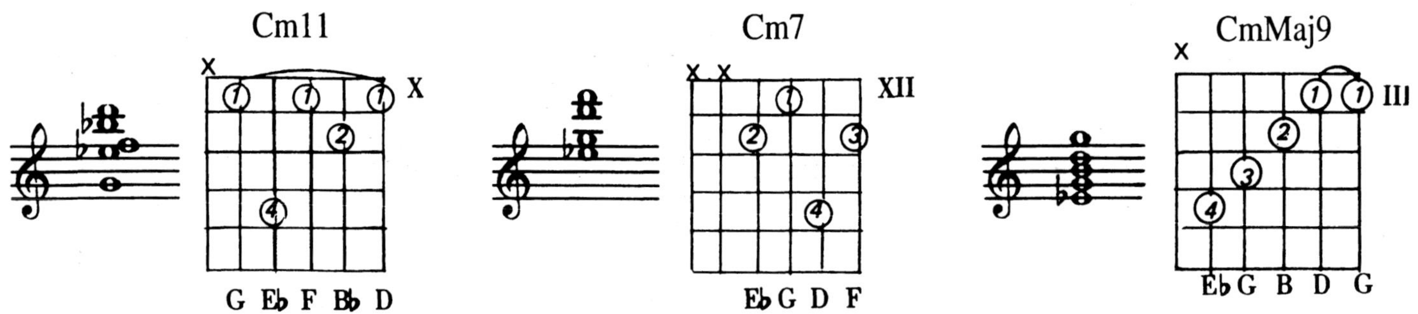

Diminished Chord Forms

C°/F♯°

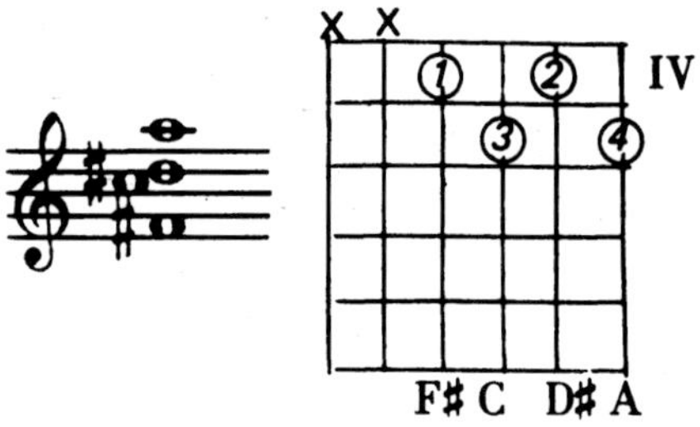

X X

IV

F♯ C D♯ A

C°

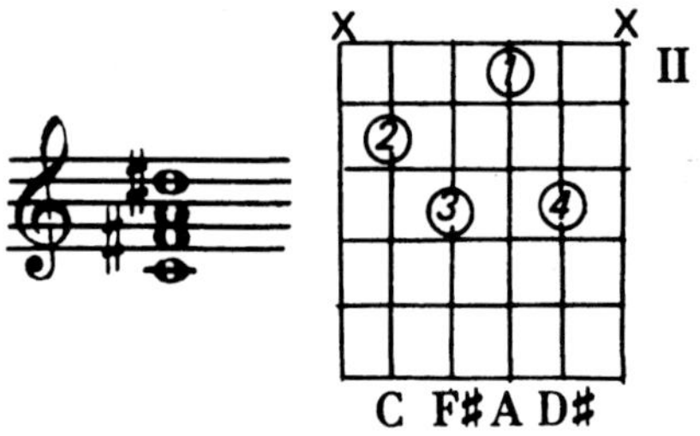

X X

II

C F♯ A D♯

A°

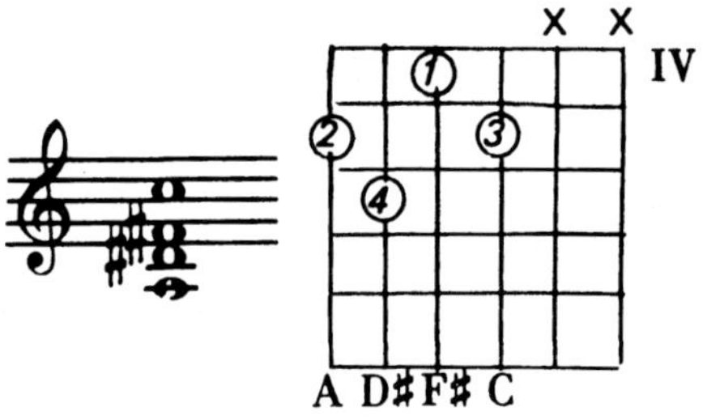

X X

IV

A D♯ F♯ C

C°(♯5)

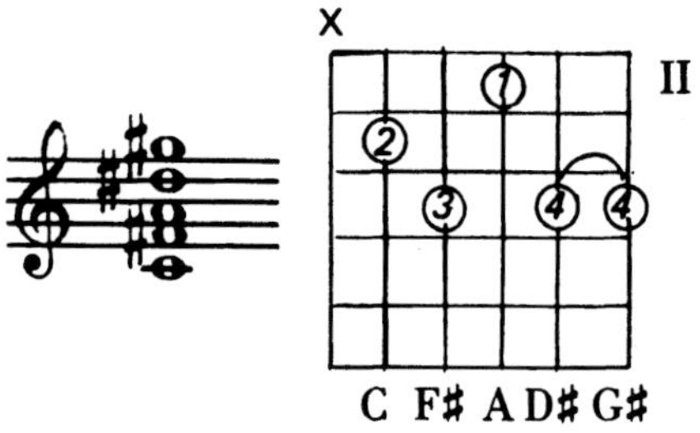

X

II

C F♯ A D♯ G♯

C°

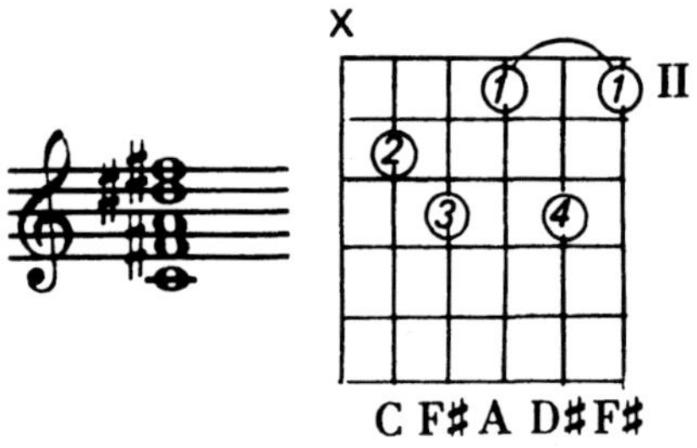

X

II

C F♯ A D♯ F♯

F°

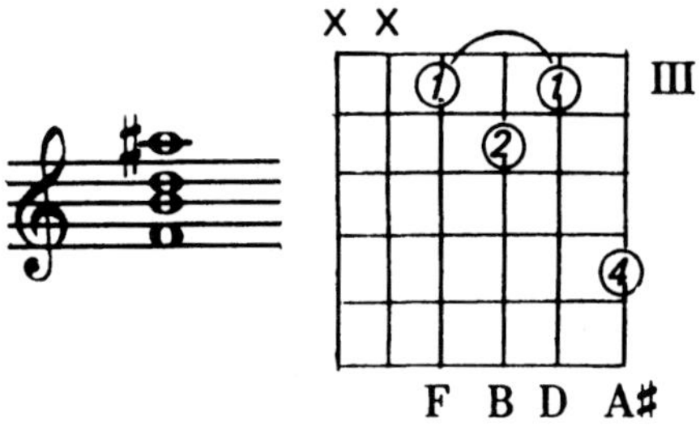

X X

III

F B D A♯

B°

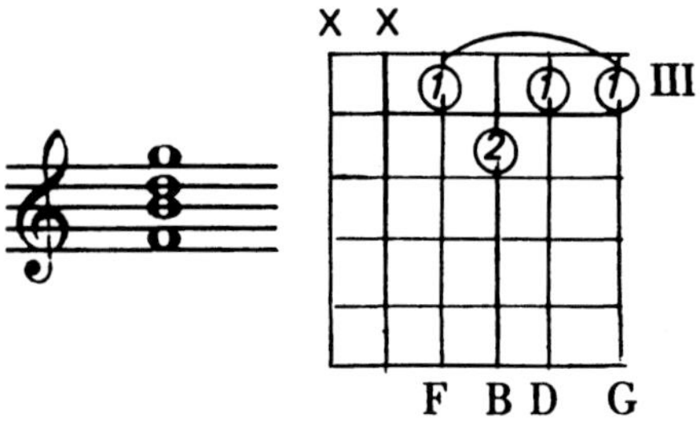

X X

III

F B D G

F°

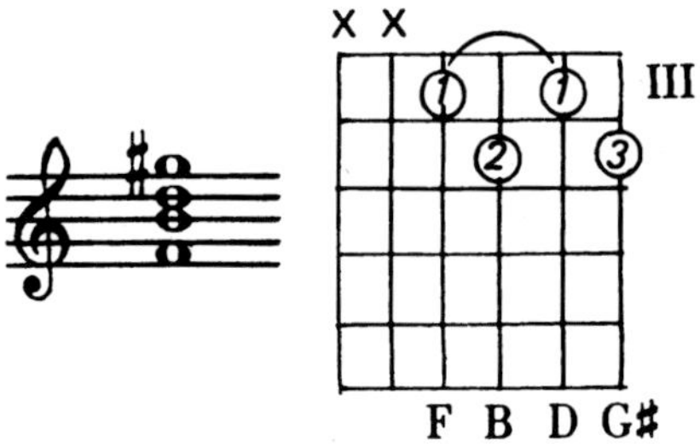

X X

III

F B D G♯

G♯°/G7♭9

X X

III

G♯ B D G

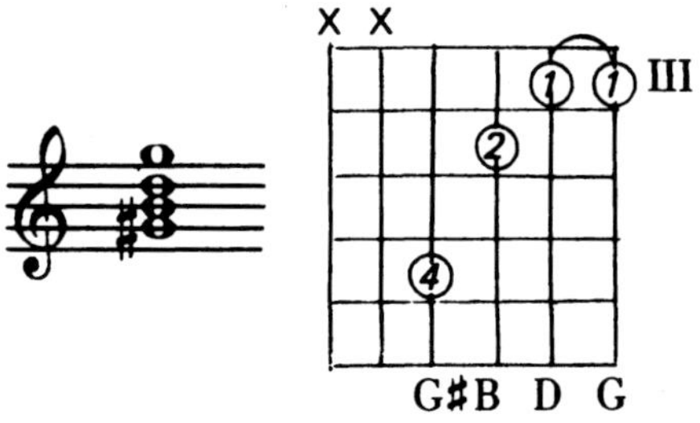

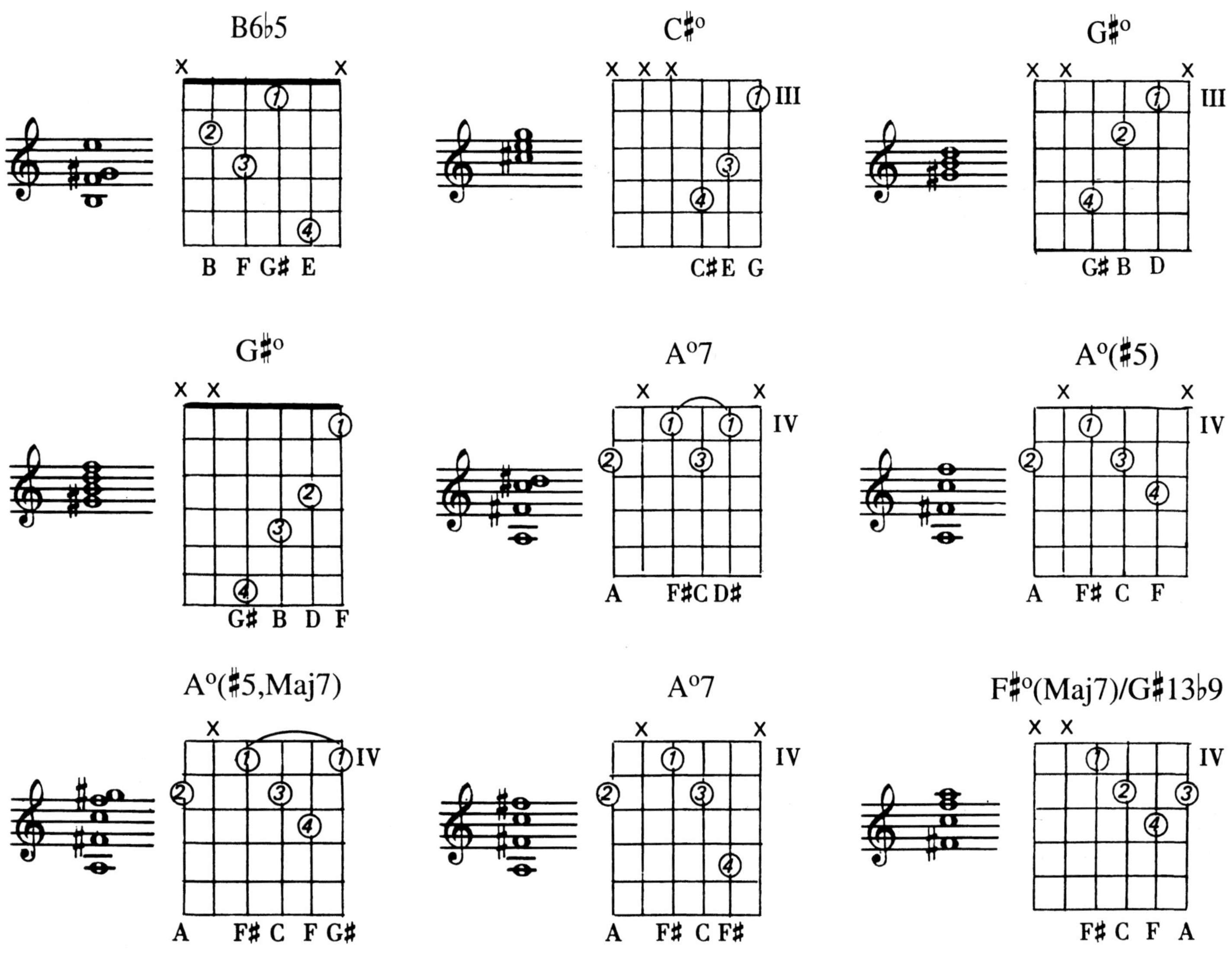
B6♭5
X X
B F G♯ E
C♯°
X X X
III
C♯ E G
G♯°
X X X
III
G♯ B D
G♯°
X X
G♯ B D F
A°7
X X
IV
A F♯ C D♯
A°(♯5)
X X
IV
A F♯ C F
A°(♯5,Maj7)
X
IV
A F♯ C F G♯
A°7
X X
IV
A F♯ C F♯
F♯°(Maj7)/G♯13♭9
X X
IV
F♯ C F A

Minor Seventh Flat Fifth Chord Forms

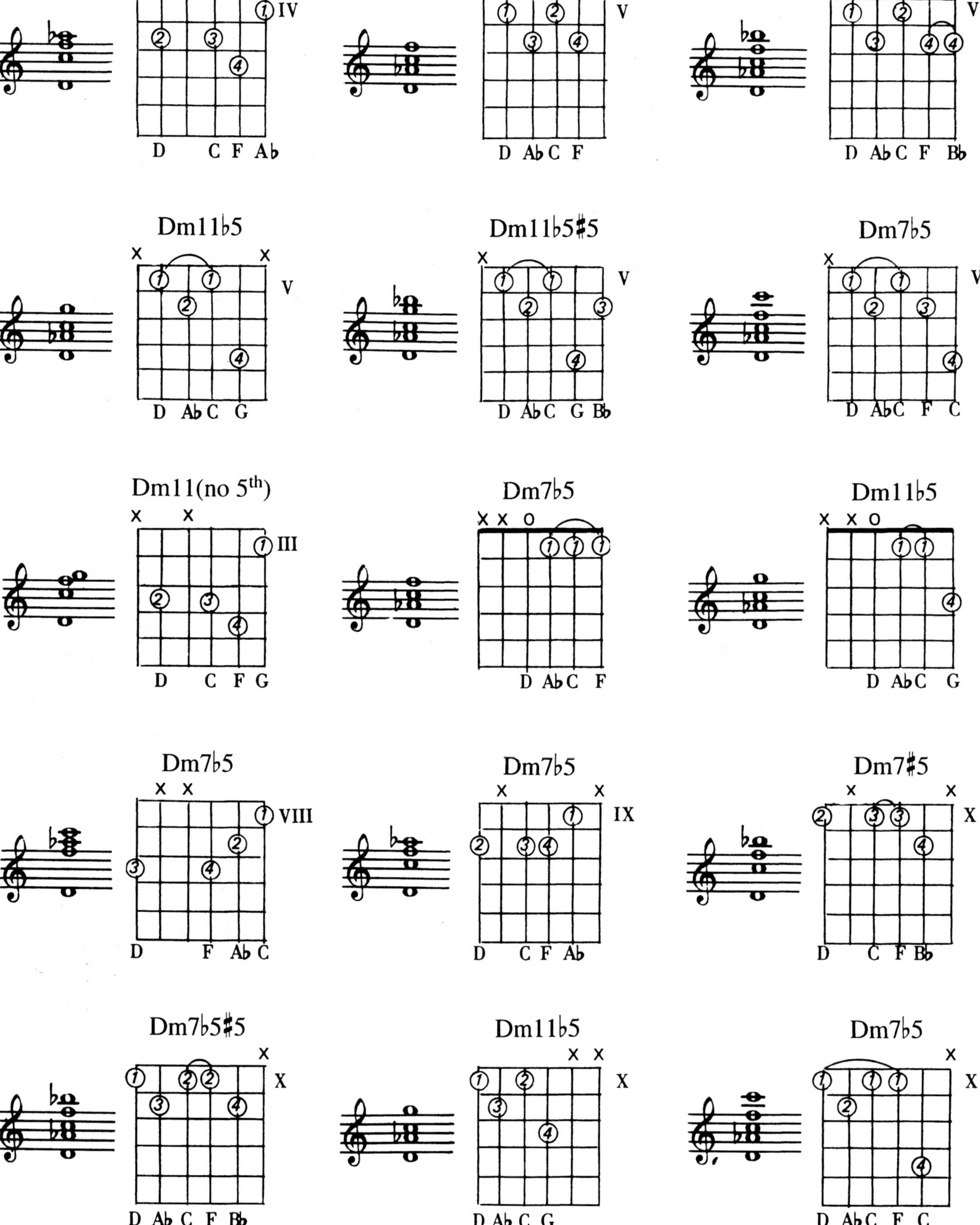

CHORD PASSAGES

These are examples of chordal movements.

MAJOR SOUNDS: The first four chords illustrate movement in "C". The fifth chord is G13b5 (or Db7+9b5) which resolves into Cma9.

MINOR SEVENTH TO SEVENTH SOUNDS: First four chords illustrate movement in Dm7, resolving into Ab13 to G13.

SEVENTHS: The first three chords illustrate movement around G7. The next four chords illustrate a substitute turnaround back to G13, followed by a cycle seventh movement.

DIMINISHED SOUNDS: Resolve the last chord in this sequence into any chord. For example: (1) Dm7 – G7 – Cma7, or (2) Em7 – Eb9 – Dm9 – Db9.

MINOR SEVENTH FLAT FIFTH TO SEVENTH SOUNDS: A7b9 to Dm7b5 resolving finally to G aug.

MINOR SEVENTH FLAT FIFTH TO AUGMENTED SOUNDS: Dm7b5 chords to G aug. Notice the chords used to obtain these sounds.

DIMINISHED PASSAGE: Use of diminished chords for seventh flat ninth chord movement, utilizing the basic pattern of A7 – Dm – G7 – C.

AUGMENTED SOUNDS: The first six chords are basically G aug. Movement is used chromatically to get to the basic cycle (A7 – D7 – G).

Major Sounds

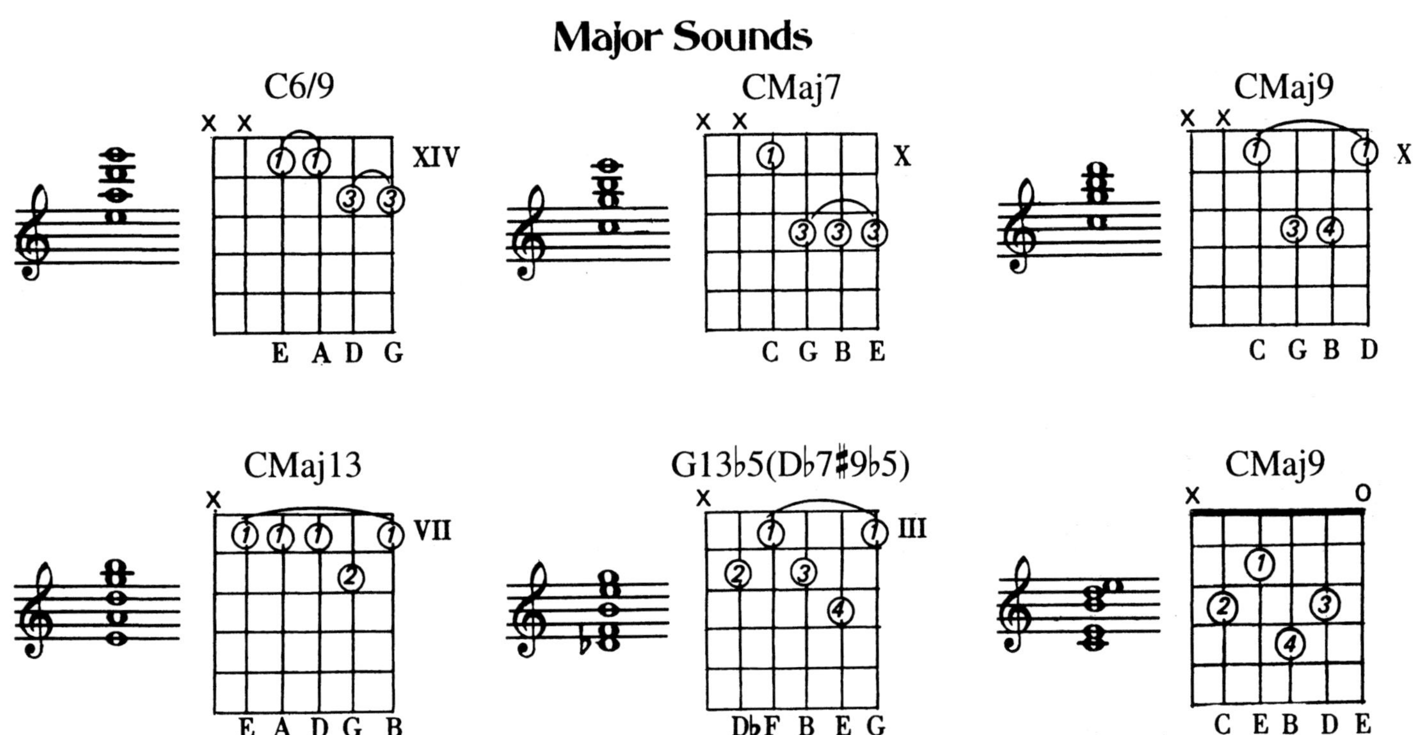

Minor Seventh to Seventh Sounds

Dm11
X X
XII
D A C G

Dm9
X X
X
C F A E

Dm11
X X
VII
A D G C

Dm9
X X
III
F C E A

A♭13
X X
IV
A♭ G♭ C F

G13
X X
III
G F B E

G13
X X
IX
B F A E

A♭13
X X
X
C G♭ B♭ F

G13
X X
IX
B F A E

F13
X O
V
A G C♯ F C

Dm7sus
X X
V
D A C G

A♭7♯5
X
IV
A♭ G♭ C E

G13

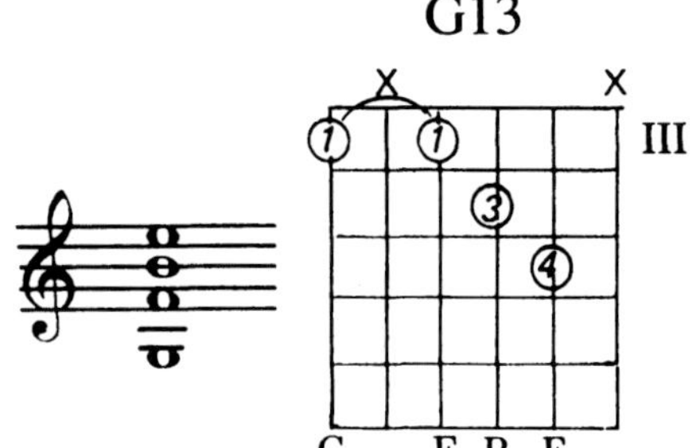

Sevenths Substitutions

E7♯9
VI
E G♯ D G

A7♯5♯9
V
A G C♯ F C

D7♯9
IV
D F♯ C F

G7♯5♯9
III
G F B D♯ A♯

Diminished Sounds

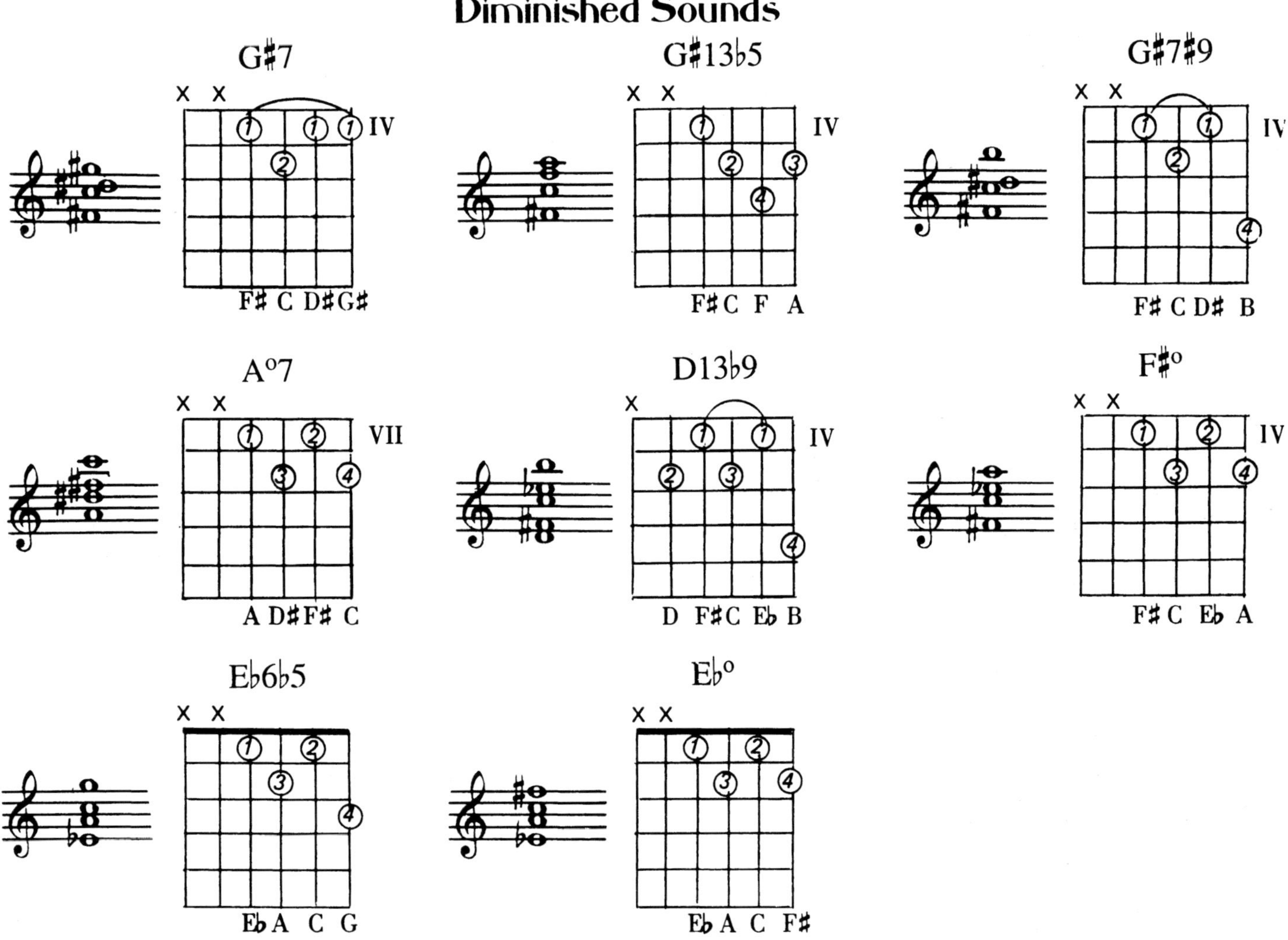

Minor Seventh Flat Fifth to Seventh Sounds

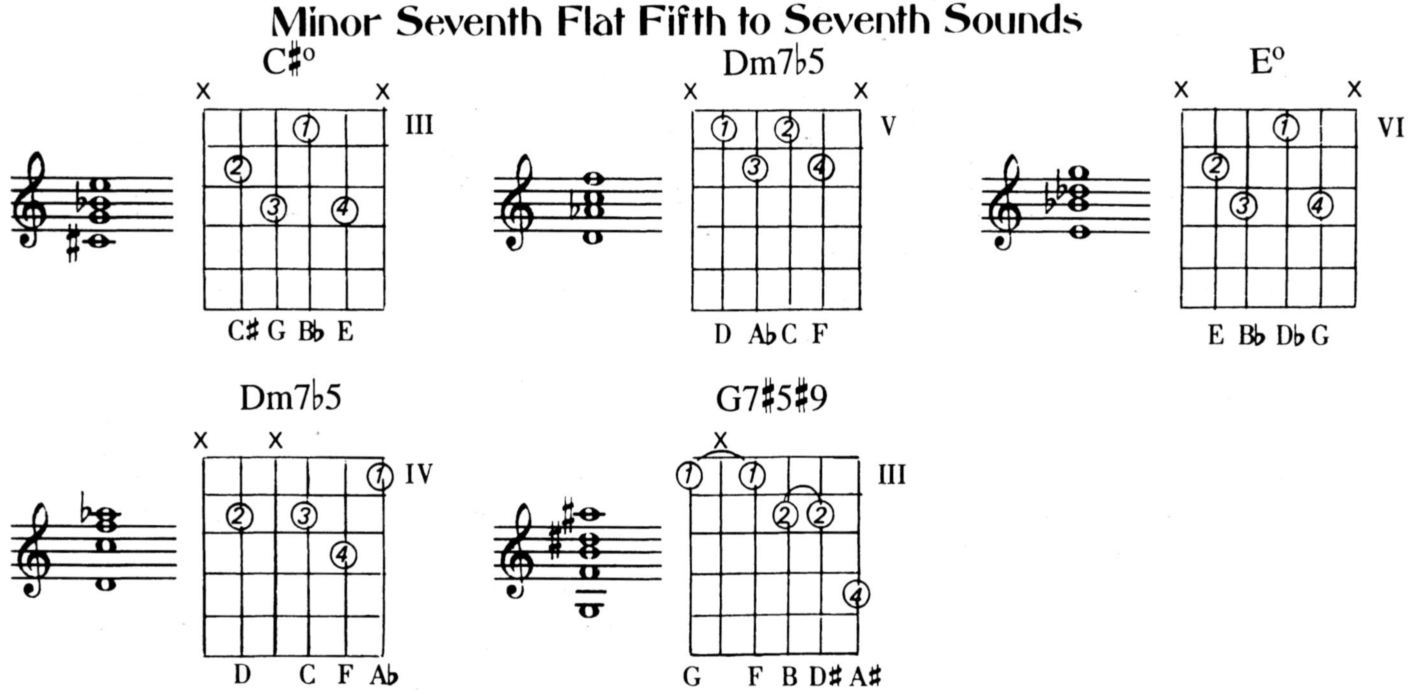

Minor Seventh Flat Fifth to Augmented Sounds

Dm11♭5
X X
XII
D A♭ C G

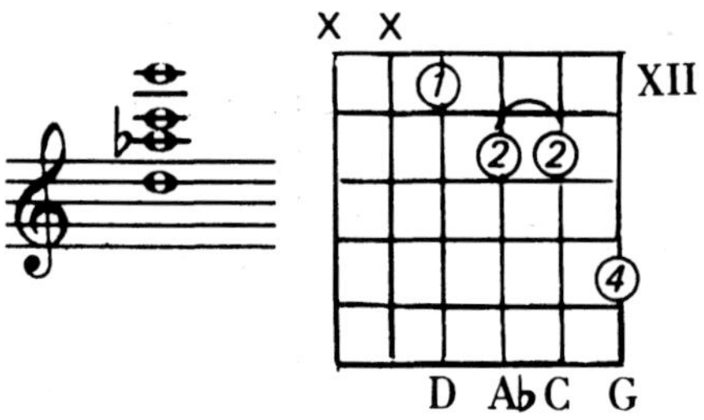

Dm7♭5
X X
XII
D A♭ C F

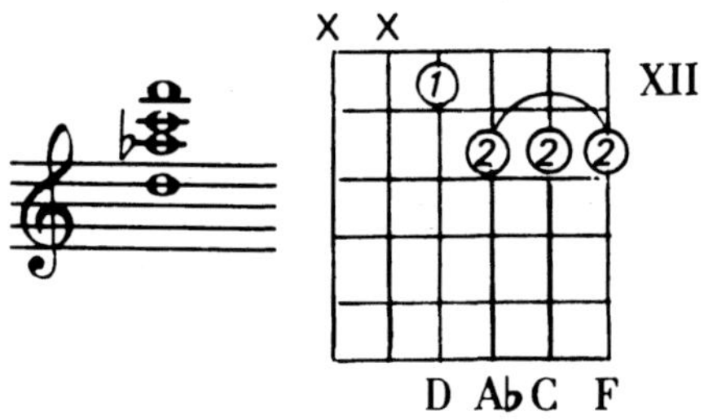

E♭6/9
X X
X
C F B♭ E♭

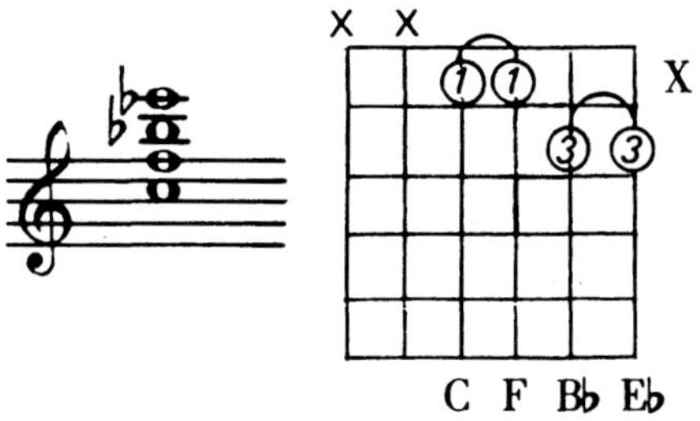

B♭13
X X
VI
A♭ D G C

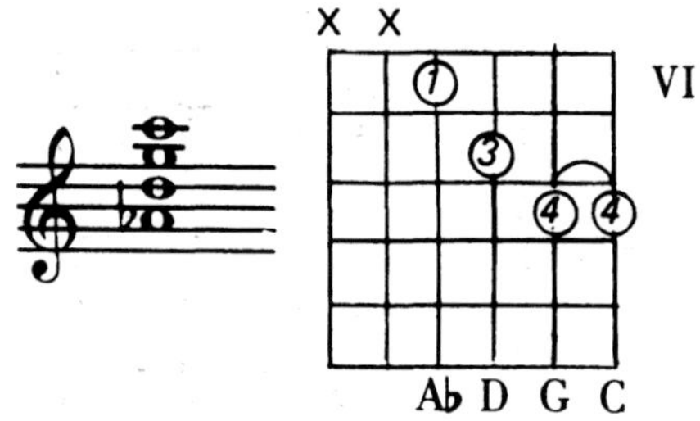

Dm7♭5♯5
X
V
D A♭ C F B♭

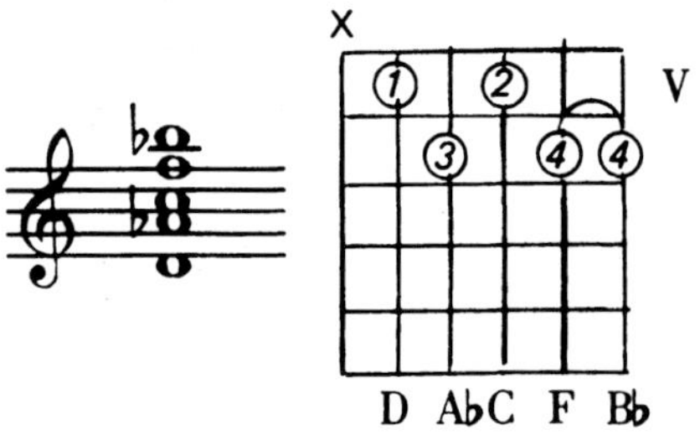

Dm7♭5
X X
IV
D C F A♭

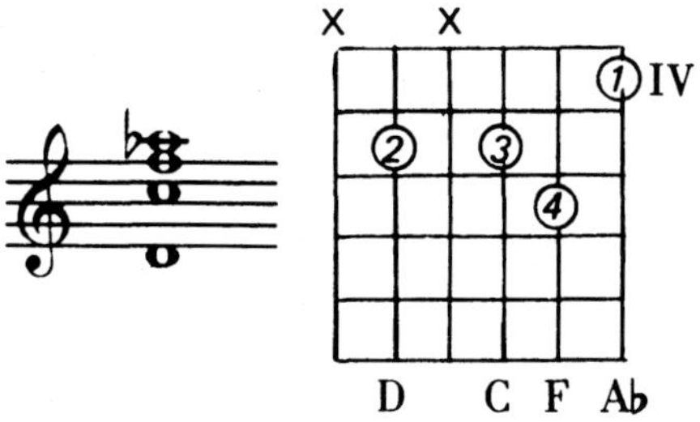

G7♯5
X
III
G F B D♯ G

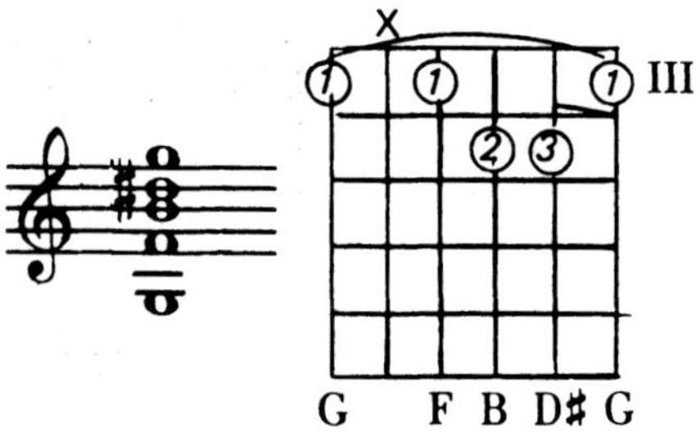

Diminished Passage

Augmented Sounds

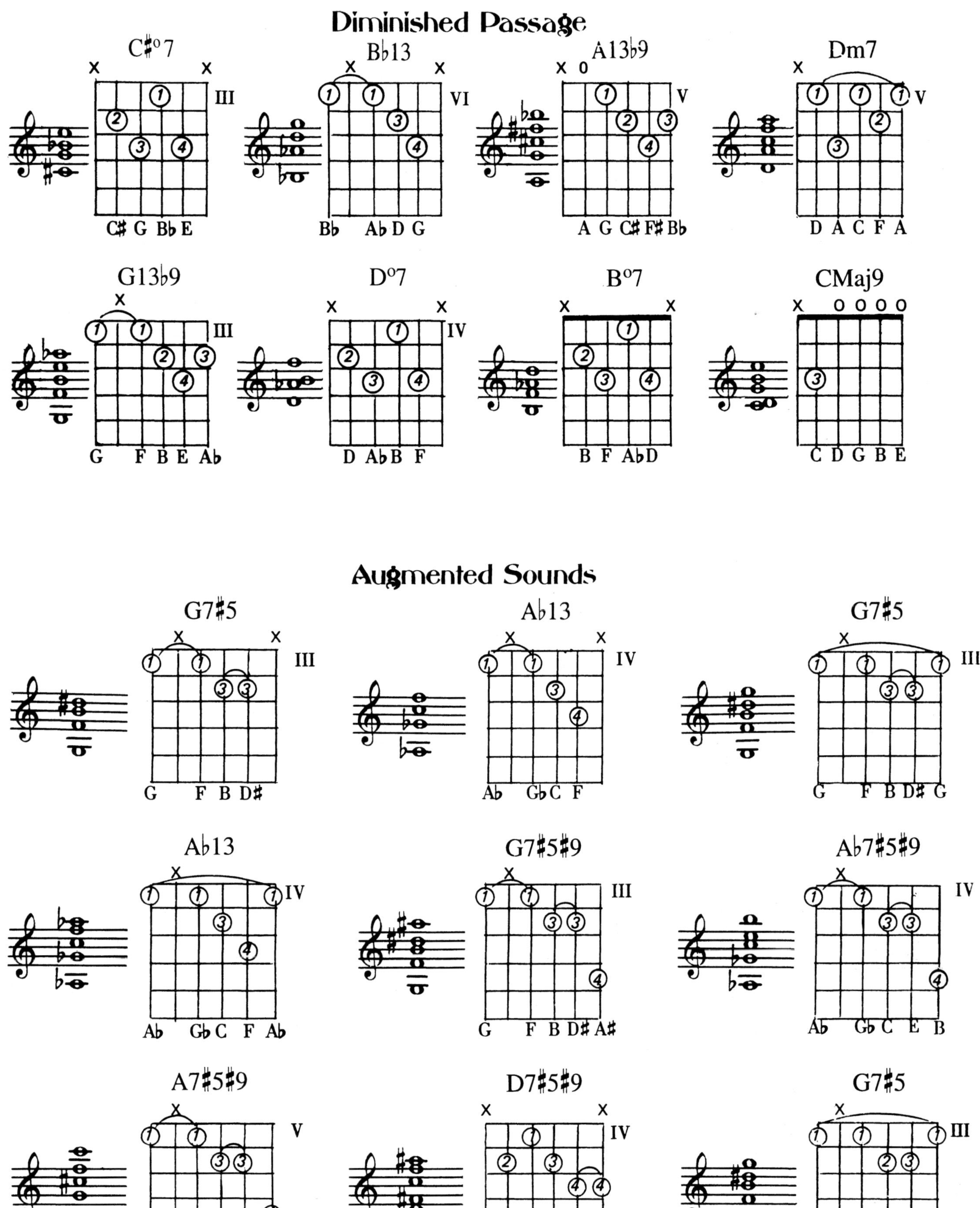

NEIGHBORING CHORDS

1. **Neighboring chords** is an exercise that will enhance your ability to make smooth chord changes by simply changing the position of one finger.

    a. Use three notes per chord.

    b. Work in groups of three chords using this pattern:

EXAMPLE: C7 (the V chord) to C M 7 (the I chord) to F M 7 (the IV chord).

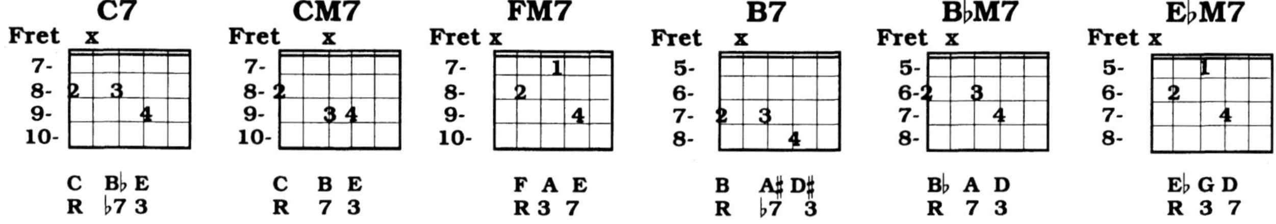

2. Play the following group of chords using the fingering patterns as shown.

    a. Then play a line over the chords.

    b. Tape record the chords you play, then vary the lines you play over the chords.

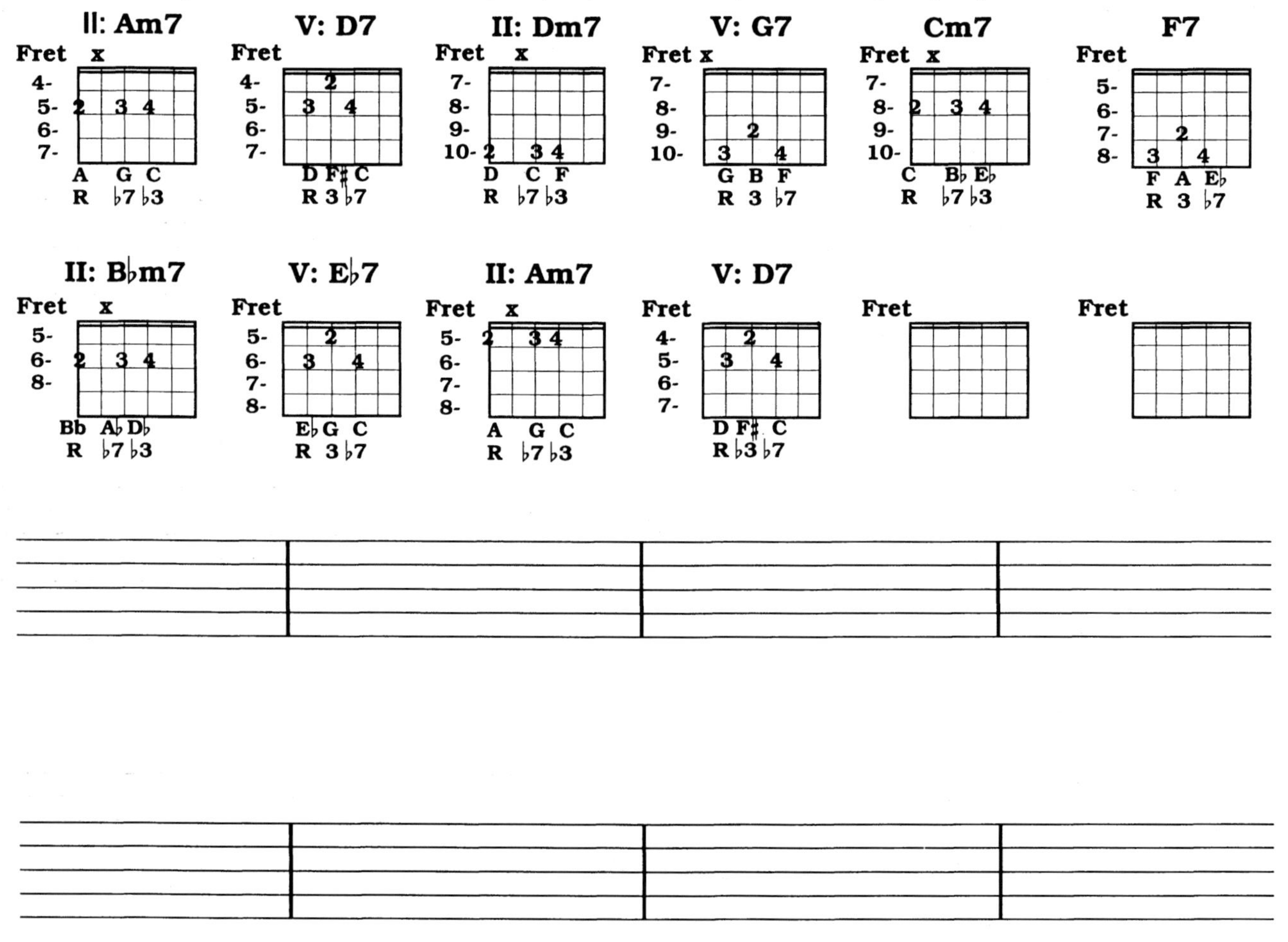

NEIGHBORING CHORDS (cont)

3. Following the pattern of Step 2. On the preceding page, use any II - V progression your own pattern, using three notes per chord.

a. On the staff lines, write out the notes that you have hummed in developing a melodic motif.

Fret II Fret V Fret II Fret V Fret Fret

Fret Fret Fret Fret Fret Fret

HOW TO PLAY A MOVING BASS LINE

Perhaps the signature of **Joe Pass** is his unequaled skill in playing a moving bass line. He began developing this technique as a teenager when he played in a dance band in Pennsylvania. The band leader was often without a bass player, and Joe would play bass lines on his guitar.

Fortunately for Joe, this demand from his band leader turned out to be one of his most sought after and admired techniques from aspiring guitarists, as well as his audiences in general.

While Joe tells us this is an easy technique, it only becomes "easy" after you work diligently and pay close attention to his suggestions.

JOE PASS QUOTE:

"If you can't play a bass line that's musical, you're not allowed to play that way."

To become a player who *can* play a musical bass line, do the following:

1. Play one bar of G7 (the V chord in the key of C), then one of C 7.

2. Now play a bass line, starting on a note that is in the chord you are playing.

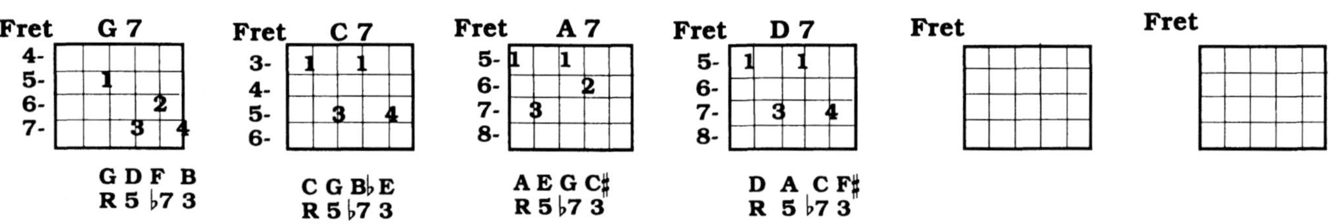

3. Play four beats (4/4 time) per measure using the notes of the G7 chord. But remember:

4. That the 5th note you play, or the **1st** note of the next measure, is to **begin** with the **Root** of the next chord named.
ie: Under Step 2., G7, you play the notes G - D - F - **B** (which is a half-step from the Root of the next measure and chord, **C**;) C7, you play **C** - G - E - **B♭** (which is a half-step from the Root of the next measure and chord, **A**;) A7 and so on.

5. Then go back to the G7 chord and play notes in a different pattern, except that the 4th note of the measure is to be a half-step away from the first note of the next measure.

6. **It is important to remember that bass lines are linear.**

7. **It is also important to note that the notes that define a line as a linear bass line must always be a half-step above or below the note of the next measure that has a new chord.**

8. Comping on a bass line is done by playing a shuffle rhythm on every other beat (1 and 3) followed by plucking the bass line on the 2nd and 4th beats.

9. A Blues Pattern you can use to practice the Moving Bass Line may look like this: (Measure numbers above the chord names.)

1 2 3 4 5 6 7 8 9 10 11
G 7 / C 7 / G 7 / Dm7 G 7 / C 9 / G 7 / C 7 / F 7/ E 7 / Am 7 / E♭9 /
12 (Turnaround) D 7 / [G 7 - E 7 - A 7- D 7]
Repeat from G 7.

PART TWO

MELODY

SCALES

JOE PASS QUOTE

The purpose of learning scales and arpeggios is to coordinate the right and left hands and to know where the intervals are. To learn how to hear the sounds (intervals), play slowly. Make your notes consistent, even.

When a note is unclear, a problem area, go to it and repeat it until you clear it up. This is a good way to practice.

"Play the scale from the beginning of the chord and stop when you play the last note of the chord you are playing. Then play the chord again. Play the chord before you play the scale so that you hear how it is suppose to sound. By playing the notes that way, you will have created a *line*, rather than just having played a scale."

MAJOR SCALES

There are seven notes in the **Major Scale** before the octave note is repeated. The **C Major Scale** reads:

C	D	E	F	G	A	B	C
1	2	3	4	5	6	7	8

Write out another **Major Scale:**

Write out another **Major Scale:**

Write out another **Major Scale:**

MINOR SCALES

There are three **Minor Scale** types: 1) the **Melodic Minor Scale**; 2) the **Harmonic Minor Scale**; 3) and the **Natural Minor Scale**.

The **C Melodic Minor Scale** is:

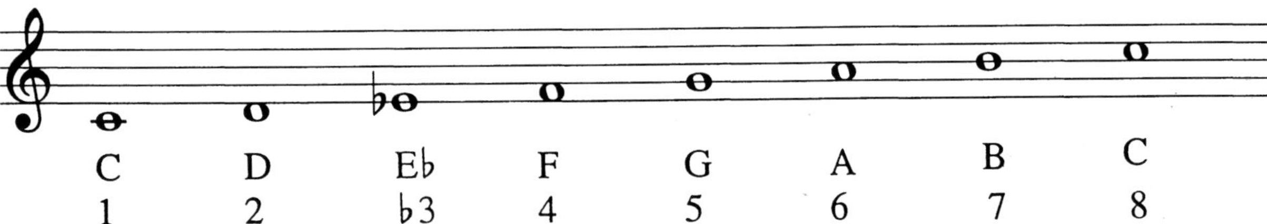

The **C Harmonic Minor Scale** is:

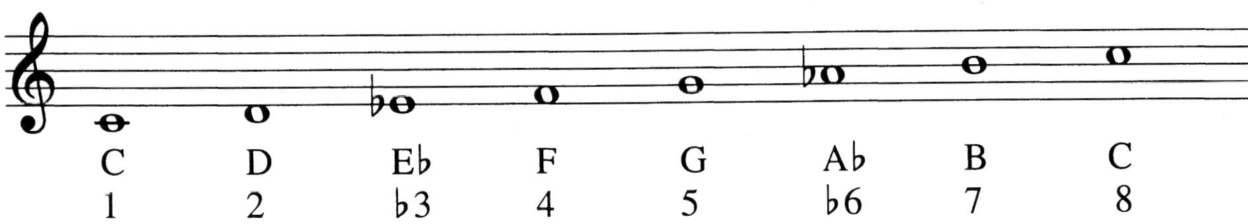

The **C Natural Minor Scale** is:

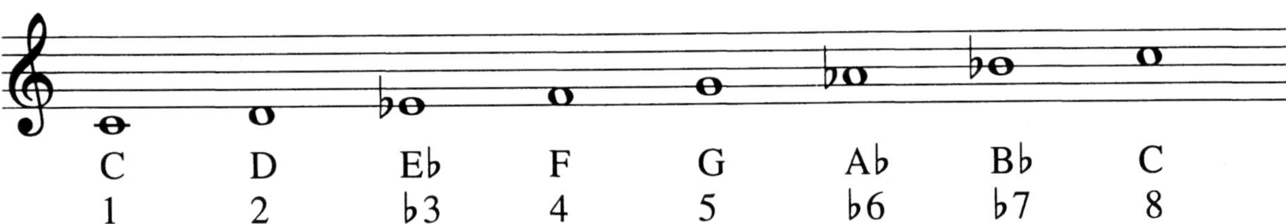

Write out another **Melodic Minor Scale:**

Write out another **Harmonic Minor Scale:**

Write out another **Natural Minor Scale:**

DOMINANT SCALES

Three of the most frequently used **Dominant Scale** types are: 1) the **Dominant Scale**; 2) the **Lydian Dominant Scale**; 3) and the **Fifth Mode Harmonic Minor Scale**.

The **C Dominant Scale (also called the C-Mixolydian mode)** is:

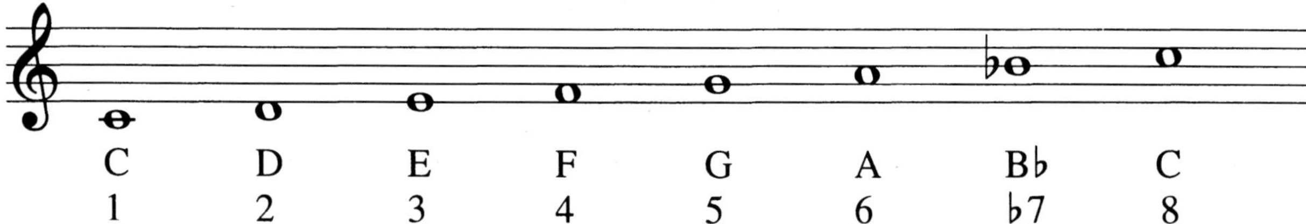

The **C Lydian Dominant Scale** is:

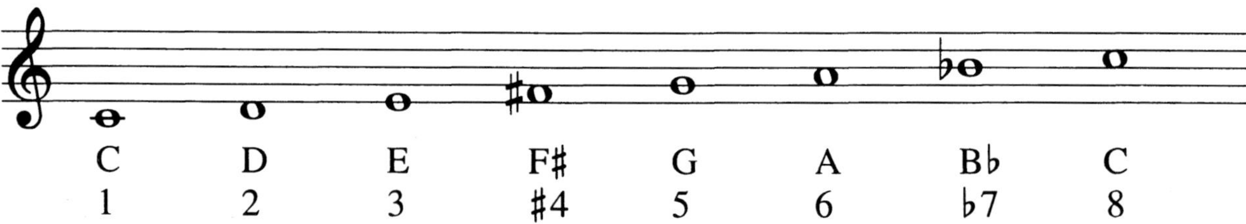

The **C Fifth Mode Harmonic Minor Scale** is:

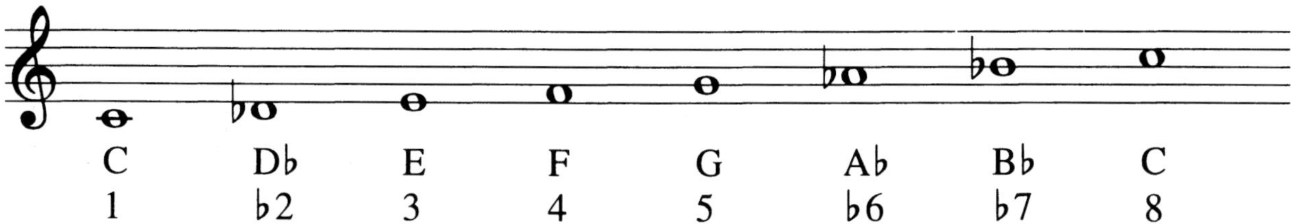

Write out another **Dominant Scale:**

Write out another **Lydian Dominant Scale:**

Write out another **Fifth Mode Harmonic Minor Scale:**

ALTERED DOMINANT 7TH SCALES
or SUPER-LOCRIAN SCALE

This scale is known by many names, but the **Altered Dominant 7th Scale** or the **Super-Locrian Scale** are most often used.
The key of C is written out for you. Following the **C Altered Dominant 7th Scale** natation, fill in the four other scales found on this page.

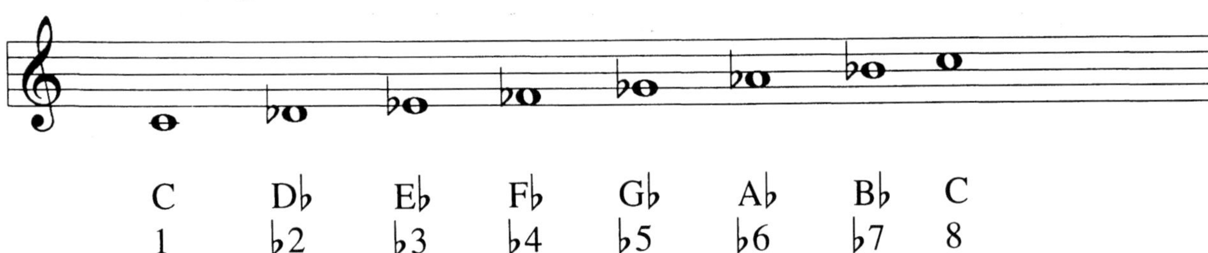

Key of A♭

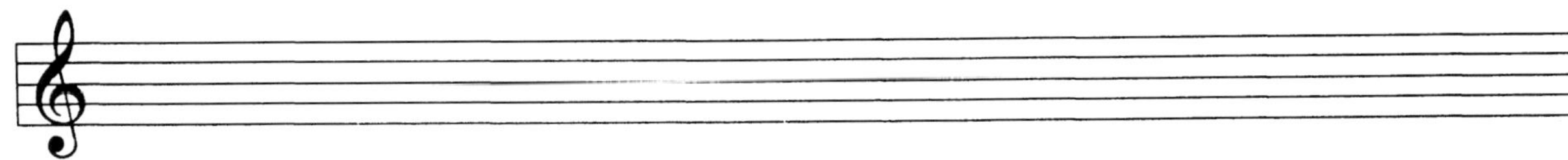

Key of B♭

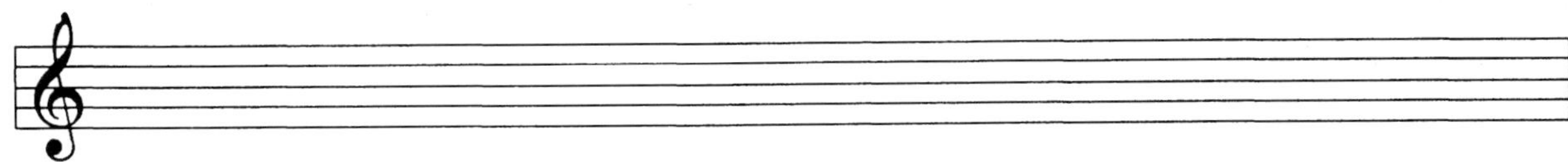

Key of E♭

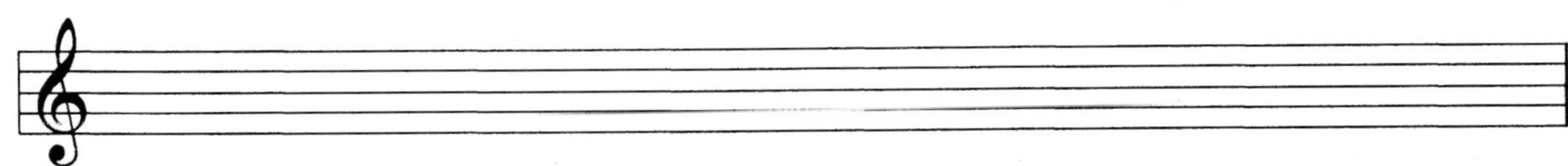

Key of G

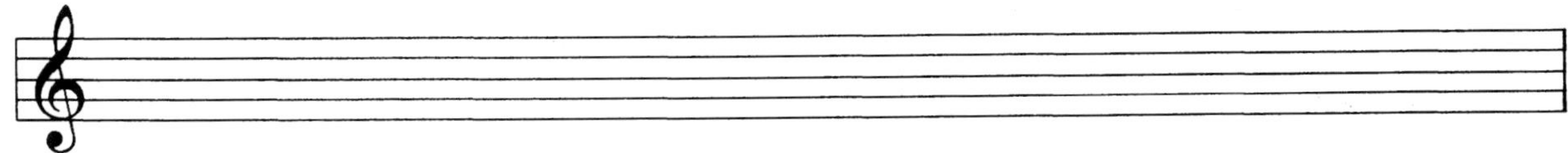

WHOLE-TONE SCALES

There are only two **Whole-Tone Scales**: six notes in one set; six notes in the other.

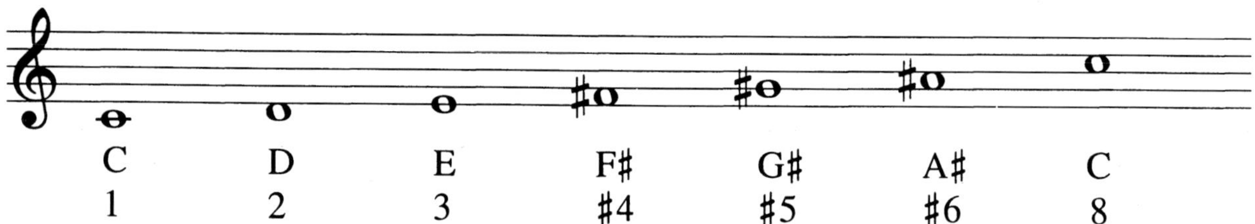

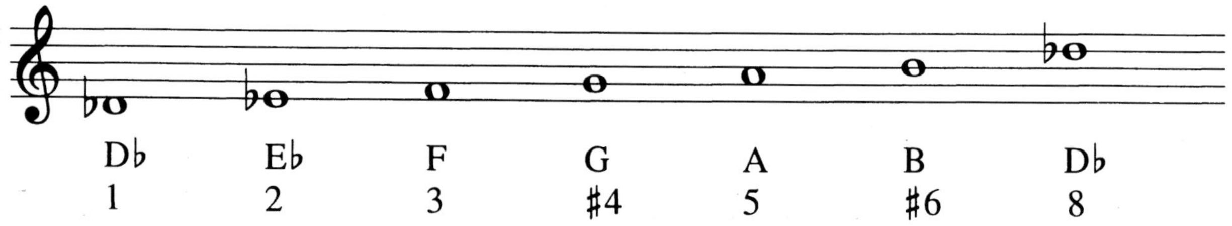

DIMINISHED SCALES

The **Diminished Scale** is sometimes referred to as the *Eight-Tone Scale*.
The **C Diminished Scale** reads this way:

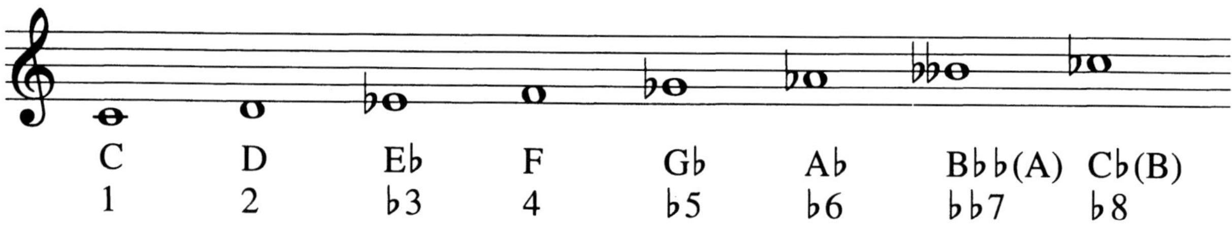

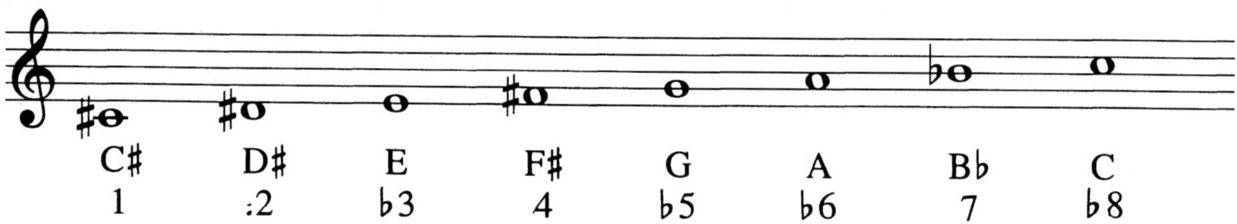

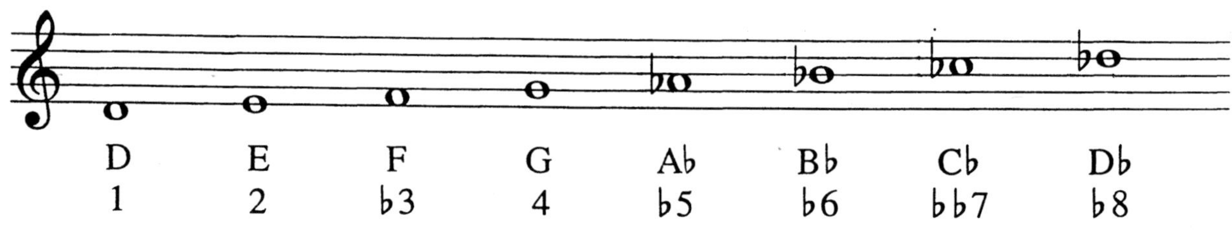

HALF-DIMINISHED SCALES

The **Half-Diminished Scale** is also called the *Locrian Scale.*

The **C Half-Diminished Scale** is:

C	D♭	E♭	F	G♭	A♭	B♭	C
1	♭2	♭3	4	♭5	♭6	♭7	8

Write out another **Half-Diminished Scale:**

Write out another **Half-Diminished Scale:**

Write out another **Half-Diminished Scale:**

Write out another **Half-Diminished Scale:**

BLUES SCALES

Typically, there are six notes in the **Blues Scale** (The 1 or R of the scale, in this case C, begins and ends the scale but is only counted as one note, rather than two). It's an option to think of the ♯4 as a ♭5.

The **C Blues Scale**:

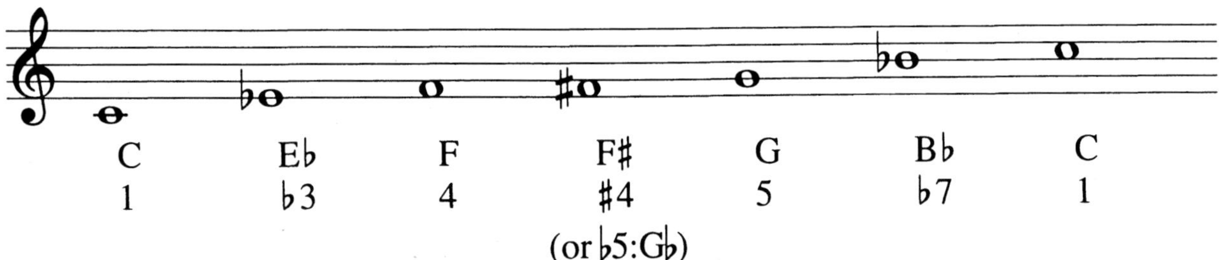

Write out any **Blues Scale** here:

Write out another **Blues Scale** here:

Write out another **Blues Scale** here:

Write out another **Blues Scale** here:

JUDE'S BLUES

by Joe Pass © 1989

HOW TO PRACTICE THE BLUES

1. IMPROVISING ON A G 7 CHORD (The V chord in the key of C is the G 7 chord, or Dominant 7 chord, is often referred to as the "blues" chord.) You can play any of the dominant scale notes but you have to land on any strong tone of the chord at the end of a measure. The strong tones of a dominant 7th chord are the R, 5, ♭7 and 3. Write out your own Blues line in the 8 measures below:

2. PLAY EVERY CHROMATIC NOTE IN THE SCALE and then use these notes in your improvising motifs. Resolve to any of the key (strong) tones. You can play any notes of the scale.
JOE PASS: "BUT YOU HAVE TO PLAY SOMETHING MUSICAL, NOT JUST SCALES."
A motif, or musical design comes from one idea you have and then developing it; that is, repeat an idea in various places. You can use this method in any song. Write out your Blues line in the measures below:

JOE PASS "HOW TO" SUGGESTIONS

As one who has purchased many guitar books over the years looking for the one magical book which will unlock the mystery as to how to improvise, none gave me answers as much as did the few hours in the Jazz Masters Class with Joe Pass.

Trying to recreate the kind of excitement and "aha" learning experiences that my fellow colleagues and I had in that class is what is contained on the next few pages. Here is where Joe really came through in exemplary form for us students.

He came up with one idea after the other for making practice fun, improvising (almost) easy, and learning scales, an enthusiastic exercise in fruition, rather than futility. After employing these practice sessions, I hope you will agree.

We put these practice ideas toward the end of the book, as they are dependent upon your knowing something about chords and scales. Enjoy them!

HOW TO PRACTICE SCALES

FROM JOE PASS:
"If you want to play fast, you have to practice slow...slow and even. You have to think fast in order to play fast."

To get the *legato* (smooth and even) feeling, use hammer-ons, slurs and pull-offs. Practice these fretboard techniques while you are learning scales and chords.

1. **Scales teach you where the intervals are.** To learn scales:
   a. Play any chord first.
   b. Then play the scale that fits it.
   c. Play two octaves per scale.

For example: play a C Major 7th chord:

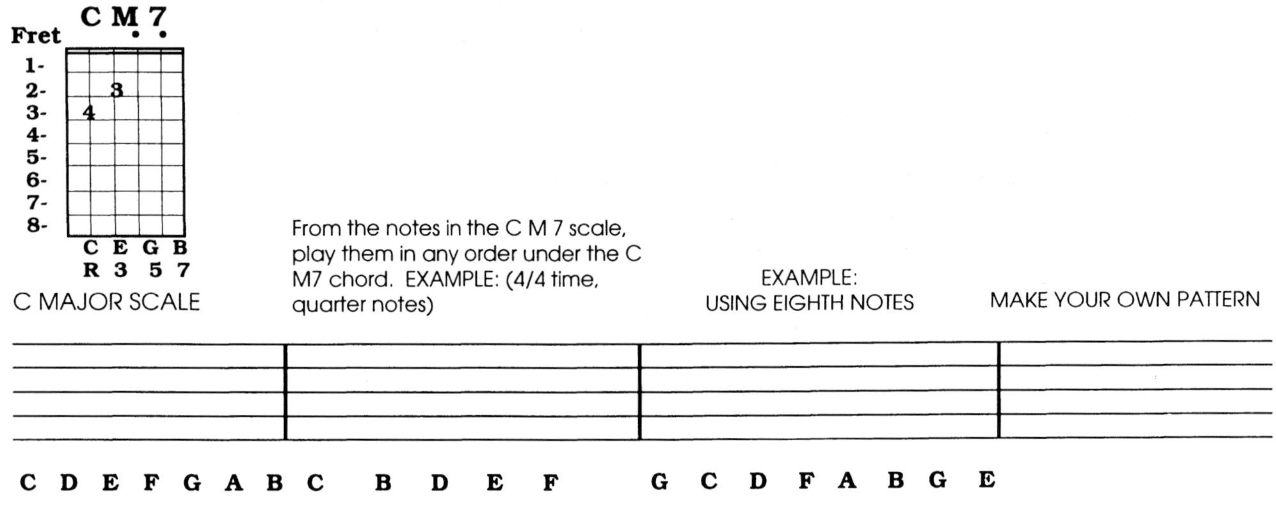

HOW TO PRACTICE SCALES (cont)

d. Learn intervals in the scale as a way to vary the way to practice. That is, instead of playing as the scale is spelled, C-D-E-F-G-A-B-C, play the R of the C Major 7 chord, C; then the 5th, G; next the 7th, B and finally the 3rd, E. Make up your own patterns.

REMEMBER TO PRACTICE SCALES AND CHORDS IN ALL KEYS. HEARING THE SOUNDS OF THE NOTES IN THEIR DIFFERENT SETTINGS IS KEY TO PLAYING AND IMPROVISING WELL.

CM7

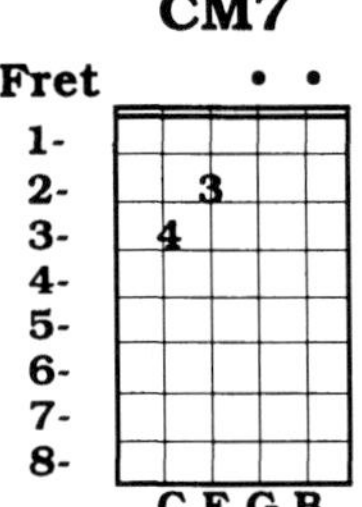

C E G B
R 3 5 7

C MAJOR SCALE

From the notes in the C M7 scale, play them in any order under the C M7 chord. EXAMPLE: (4/4 time, quarter notes)

C D E F G A B C C G B E

EXAMPLE:
USING EIGHTH NOTES

C G B E F B E C

MAKE YOUR OWN PATTERN

e. Make up exercises in the scale by varying tempos; that is, the pace which the song is to be performed. Use whole notes, half notes, quarter notes, etc.

f. Practice scales at least 30 minutes per day.

2. Play one key all the way through, from C through B.

a. Next, play the same scale chromatically.

b. Then play five notes per string in the same scale.

3. Pick a note from the first or second strings.

a. Then put chords to it. Play chords that have their Roots in the bass -- on the 5th or 6th strings.

HOW TO PRACTICE SCALES (cont)

b. **Make at least five different chords per note.** See the examples below. You fill in the notes.

CM7 Cm7 C•7 C7 C7+5 C13

Fret 1- 2- 3- 4- 5- 6- 7- 8-

C E G B
R 3 5 7

C MAJOR SCALE

C D E F G A B C

From the notes in the C Major scale, play them in any order under the C M7 chord. EXAMPLE: (4/4 time, quarter notes)

Do the same for another chord you wrote.

Do the same for another chord you wrote.

c. Play the related scale of the chord you have chosen up to the top note that you have selected for this exercise.

d. Repeat 3 a - c with each new chord and scale you find that ends on your chosen note.

e. This exercise develops your ear to hear sounds that chords make.

_ M7

Fret 1- 2- 3- 4- 5- 6- 7- 8-

_ MAJOR SCALE

From the notes in the _ M7 scale, play them in any order under the _ M7 chord. EXAMPLE: (4/4 time, quarter notes)

EXAMPLE:
USING EIGHTH NOTES

MAKE YOUR OWN PATTERN

HOW TO PRACTICE SCALES (cont)

_ M7

Fret
1-
2-
3-
4-
5-
6-
7-
8-

_ MAJOR SCALE

From the notes in the _ M7 scale, play them in any order under the _ M7 chord. EXAMPLE: (4/4 time, quarter notes)

EXAMPLE:
USING EIGHTH NOTES

MAKE YOUR OWN PATTERN

_ M7

Fret
1-
2-
3-
4-
5-
6-
7-
8-

_ MAJOR SCALE

From the notes in the _ M7 scale, play them in any order under the _ M7 chord. EXAMPLE: (4/4 time, quarter notes)

EXAMPLE:
USING EIGHTH NOTES

MAKE YOUR OWN PATTERN

Good improvising is humming or singing a melody in your mind while simultaneously playing that melody on the guitar. The sound must be in your ear and in your hand.

One of the goals of this part of the book is to provide you with some basic skills in coordinating the ear/hand relationship. More importantly, the studies and solos are designed to acquaint your ear with more MODERN sounds than are normally included in guitar books. You may have to do a lot of thinking and listening, but with a little effort you can force your ear into new harmonic ground faster than the normal process of on-the-job experience would take you there.

Every study should be transposed to all keys, and played in all possible fingerings and positions on the fingerboard. Studies which cover a range of one octave should be extended to two-octave or three-octave figurations, etc. Work them into your own music, improvise only after learning the patterns. Think in terms of SOUNDS always.

Chord Scales

Scale of G major:

Altered to fit G7 chord:

Chord scales are formed by altering the root scale to conform to the SIGNIFICANT chord tones. When playing against a G7 chord, the G major scale is altered to include the 7th (F), rather than the ma7th (F♯). The chord scale of G7-5 would be altered to include the flat 5th (D♭).

The G7 chord scale contains no sharps or flats. It is equivalent to the scale of C major. Within certain limitations, the C major scale fits the sound of all the following chords:

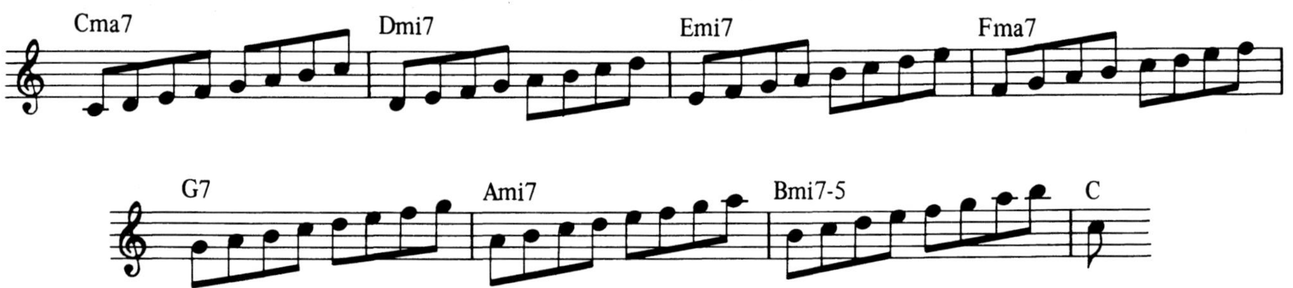

Analyze each measure carefully. It will become apparent that the scale of C major does not ALWAYS apply to every chord shown in the example. A breakdown follows:

First measure fits C, C6, Cma7, Cma9, C6/9

Second measure fits Dm, Dm7, Dm6, Dm9, Dm11. These sounds apply to any "Dm" chord going to G7 and C.

Third measure fits Em7 when used as Secondary Relative Minor substitute for C. If the chord were Em6 or Em9 the scale would include F♯ and C♯ (D major scale.)

Fourth measure fits any F chord (F6, Fma7) used as a substitute for Dm. For a true "F major" sound, the scale would include B♭(F major scale.)

Fifth measure fits G7, G9, G11, G13. All the unaltered "G7" chords going into C major.

Sixth measure fits Am, Am7, Am9 when used as substitutes for C. For Am6 the scale would include F♯ (G major scale.)

Seventh measure fits Bm7-5 going into E7(+5-9) and Am. For this chord, use (a) the Am natural minor scale (same as C major scale) or (b) the Am harmonic minor scale.

Am harmonic minor scale fits these chords:

Combining the minor scales produces results like this:

Minor chord scales may resolve into major chords:

The reverse of that is often (but not always) true. Dm9 and G13, for example, each contain the MAJOR 3rd of C. While those chords may be resolved into a Cm chord, the line will imply a stronger minor sound if they include the MINOR 3rd (E♭). That is, G7+5 to Cm is a more minorsounding resolution than G13 to Cm.

Minor chord scales are easy to form, if you keep in mind HOW the chord is being used. Notice the different chord scales used for Am in this study:

C major (Am natural minor) scale

F major scale (Am is secondary relative minor to F)

G major scale

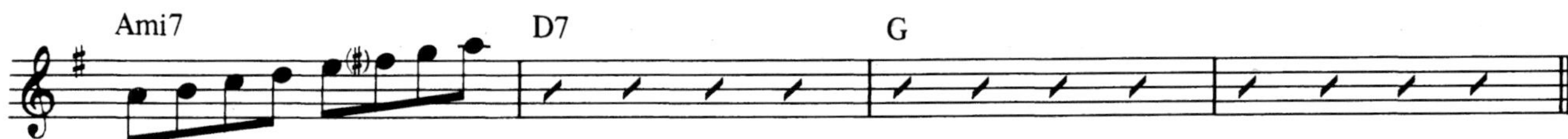

Am harmonic minor scale

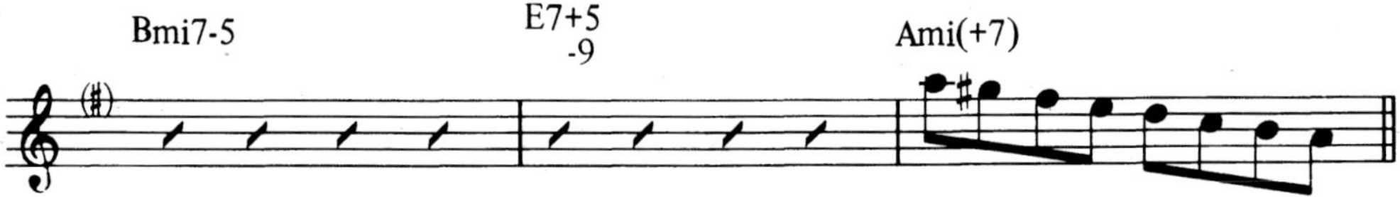

Gm harmonic minor scale

Gm natural minor (B♭ major) scale

(Ascending) Cm melodic minor scale (Cm6=Am7-5)

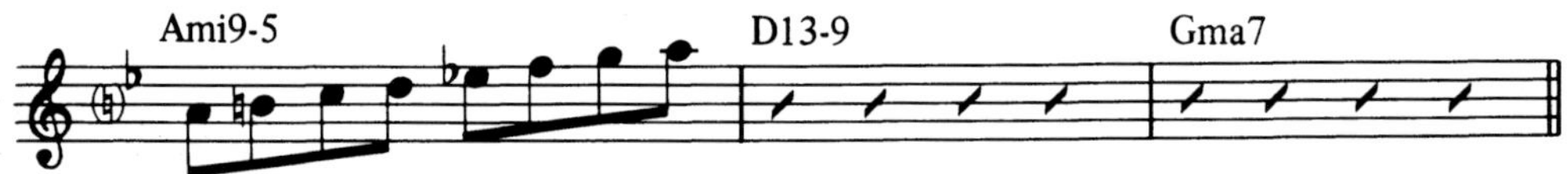

The F♮ in this last example could be played as F♯, to sound like the major 3rd of D7 and the major 7th of G.

This study illustrates the implied chord-sounds in the C major scale. The scale, played from "C" to "C", sounds like C, Cma7, C6. Played from "D" to "D" it sounds like Dm, Dm6, Dm7, etc.

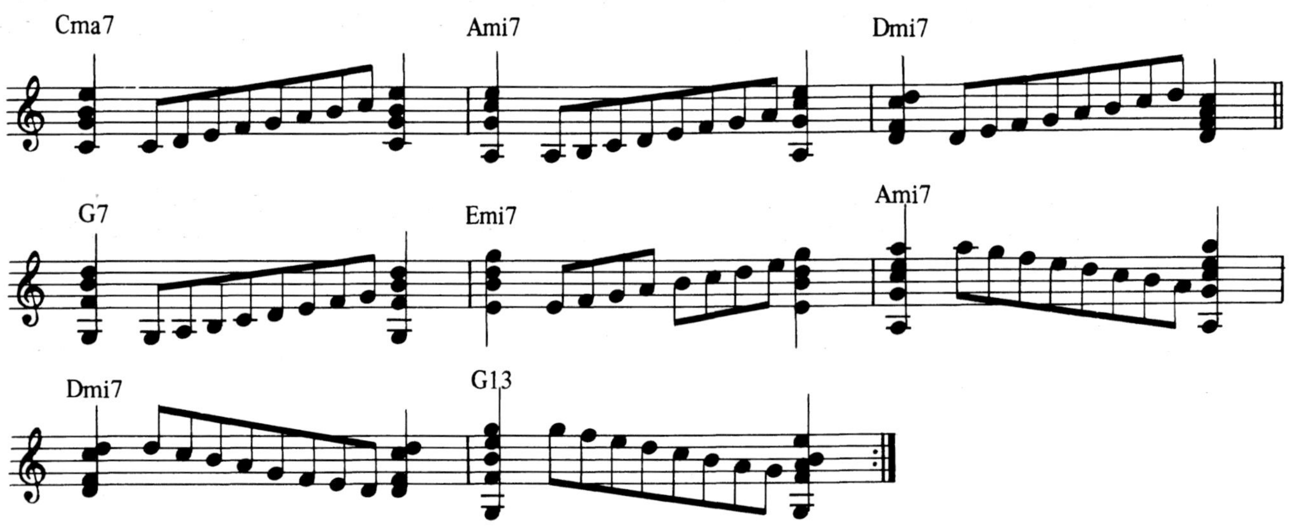

Below is a standard chord progression, showing the proper chord scales.

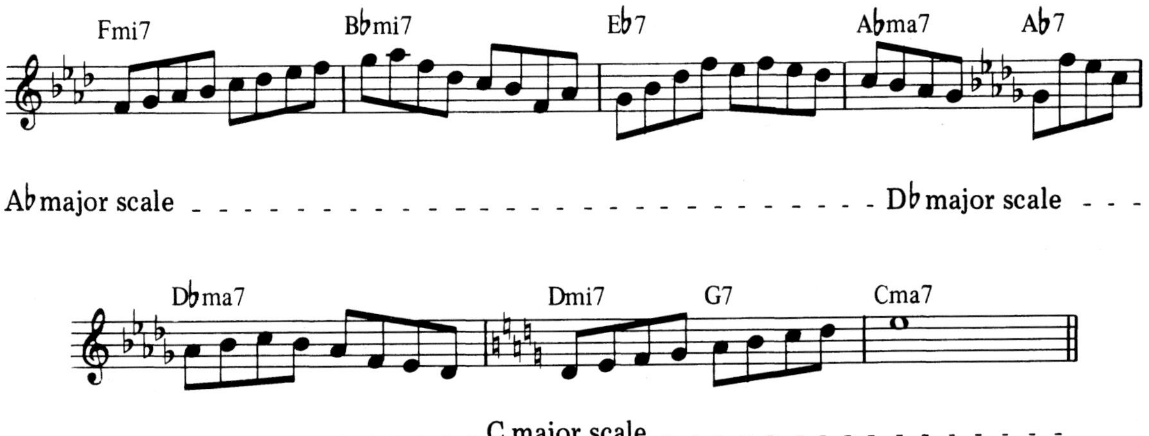

In the first measure above, the Fm7 chord could also be played using D♮ instead of D♭. (Scale of E♭major).

Another example. In this study, the A7 chord in the 6th measure could be played using the Dm harmonic minor scale. That sounds more like A7+5-9:

NOTE: Thinking in terms of "equivalent" scales is fine for study purposes, while your ear is learning to "hear" chord scale sounds. When improvising, you should be aware of the chords as separate entities because (as later studies will show) there are certain sounds that might fit one kind of chord (seventh) but not all others (major or minor).

The practical value of these equivalents is that while you may be THINKING of G7, for example, your left hand works in the familiar habit patterns of the C major scale.

Altered Scales

In the same way that chords can be altered (+5, -5, +9, -9 etc.) the chord scales may also be altered to include those sounds. The following studies move from a "pure" G7 scale to some more modern sounds.

G7 without leaving the chord

This uses both F♯ and F♮ to heighten the "seventh" feeling:

Here the sharp 5th (D♯) is added:

G7 with passing tones (±5, ±9, ma7)

G7-5

G7-5 G7-5

G7(±5, ±9)

G7-5+9 (-9) G7+5(+9) (-5-9)

Whole tones for G7+5, G7-5

+5 G7-5

Combination: whole tones and +9, -9

G7+5(+9) (-5-9) +5

G7+5+9

G7+9 G7+5 G7-5

G7±5 ±9

G7+5(+9) (-5-9)

Keep your thinking simple on these. Each study has a certain sound of its own, but they are all basically G7 sounds. Think G7.

If some of these sound a little strange, go ahead to the Ear Training studies, come back and try these later.

Ear Training

Most scale studies tend to take the ear away from the basic chord sound. In the following example, only the C major scale is used, but it SOUNDS as if the chords were moving from C to Dm7, Em7, F, etc.

That same scale pattern may be played this way:

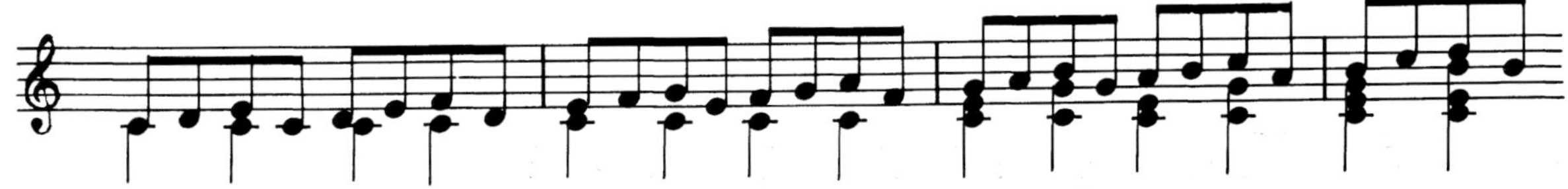

It isn't necessary to play the notes exactly as they appear above. Just try to keep hearing the chord root, C.

Another good study for ear training (and developing chord scales) is this one:

Use B♭ in that last measure and play C9. Then play up to E♭ and play C7+9, and so on.

A variation on the same idea:

Minor scales may be practiced in the same way, but there are three kinds of minor scales. Their differences involve the 6th and 7th scale tones:

NATURAL minor scale (Cm)

HARMONIC minor scale (Cm)

MELODIC minor scale (Cm)

In the following studies, the 6th and 7th scale tones may be played as flats or naturals. The notes which can be played both ways are marked with a "natural" sign in parenthesis (♮):

Each line shows a chord, its scale and arpeggio. Recommended practice sequence: chord, scale, chord, arpeggio, chord. Transpose to all keys, fingerings and positions.

MAJOR CHORDS:

SEVENTH CHORDS:

There are many variations possible in altered 7th chord scales. A few examples are shown below. Don't spend too much time on these until you've finished the more basic chord scales and arpeggios.

This sounds more modern than the "pure" C7-5 scale above. This includes the sharp and flat 5th and 9th:

Even more modern sounding. End on different chords for variety:

MINOR CHORDS:

Notes preceded by a "natural" sign in parenthesis (♮) may be played as ♭ or ♮ . Try all combinations.

SCALE CHORD ARPEGGIO

Cmi

Cmi+7

Cmi7

Cmi6

Cmi9

Cmi11

Cmi7-5

Cm7-5 normally progresses to F7 and B♭ or B♭ m. Use the natural minor scale (same as D♭ major) or the harmonic minor scale. Experiment with the optional scale tones marked below:

When in doubt about the variations in altered minor scales, think of where the chords are progressing. Below are three versions of a Cm7-5 chord scale (note key signatures):

Line 1 uses the B♭ m harmonic minor scale. Line 2 uses the natural minor scale (same as D♭major). In each of these two lines, the F7 chord might be played as F7+5-9.

Line 3 uses the B♭major scale, but G is flatted to conform to the chord sound. The F7 chord might be played as F13-9.

In the following study, line 1 uses B♭natural minor scale, moving into F7+5±9 and B♭m.

The "D" note in line 2 may be played as D♭(B♭harmonic minor scale) or as D♮, going into F7 and B♭ major.

Start and end these studies on different notes or beats for variety. Here are five variations on the same phrase:

Whole Tone Scales

Whole tone scales may be played over any ♯5 or ♭5 chord. Analyze the "C" whole tone scale below:

chord tone:

That scale fits C7+5, C7-5, C+ or C9±5 chords. When the ♯9 and ♭9 are used in combinations with whole tone passages, they fit ALL the "C7" chords: C7+5-9, C13-5-9, C7+5+9, etc.

The next four examples fit G+, G7+5, G7-5 or basically any "G7" chord:

Whole tones move chromatically through dominant passages:

Whole Tone Blues

Improvise some whole tone combinations in the blank measures, above.

Chord Resolutions

Here are four studies showing the resolution of G7 into C (or C7). Line 4 can go to Cm if the last note is changed to E♭. Lines 1 and 3 could also stay in G7. Try to play the chords with the melody, to help your ear.

"Lead-In" Notes

In the transition from one chord scale to another, there is a "lead-in" note which signals the point of departure from the preceding chord, and implies the sound of the chord to follow.

In each of these examples, the "lead-in" is the first note in the second measure:

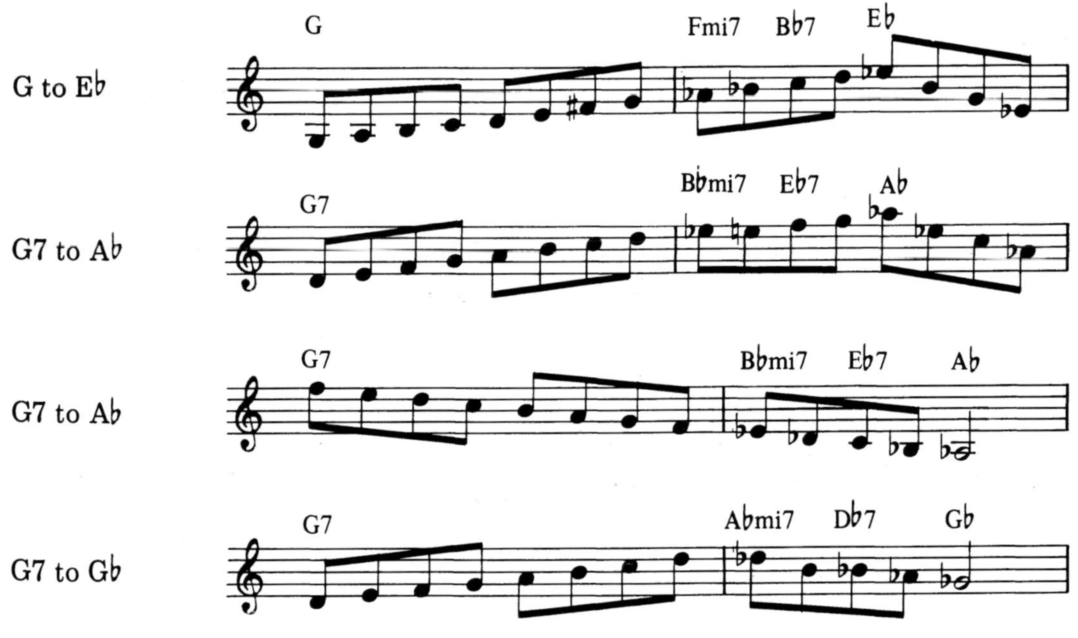

See what you can do by changing one or two notes:

G7 to B♭7

G7 Fmi7 B♭7

Flat B, E and A in the first measure (above) for Fm7 to B♭7

G7 to B♭7 (End on different chord tones for B♭7 - 9, etc.)

G7 to B♭7 (Try using B♭, E♭, A♭ in the first measure for Fm7 to B♭7)

This same phrase appears in the 3rd and 4th measures, below:

Extend these into longer lines. The last example (above) begins this next extension:

The same (or similar) phrase may be repeated through the chord changes.

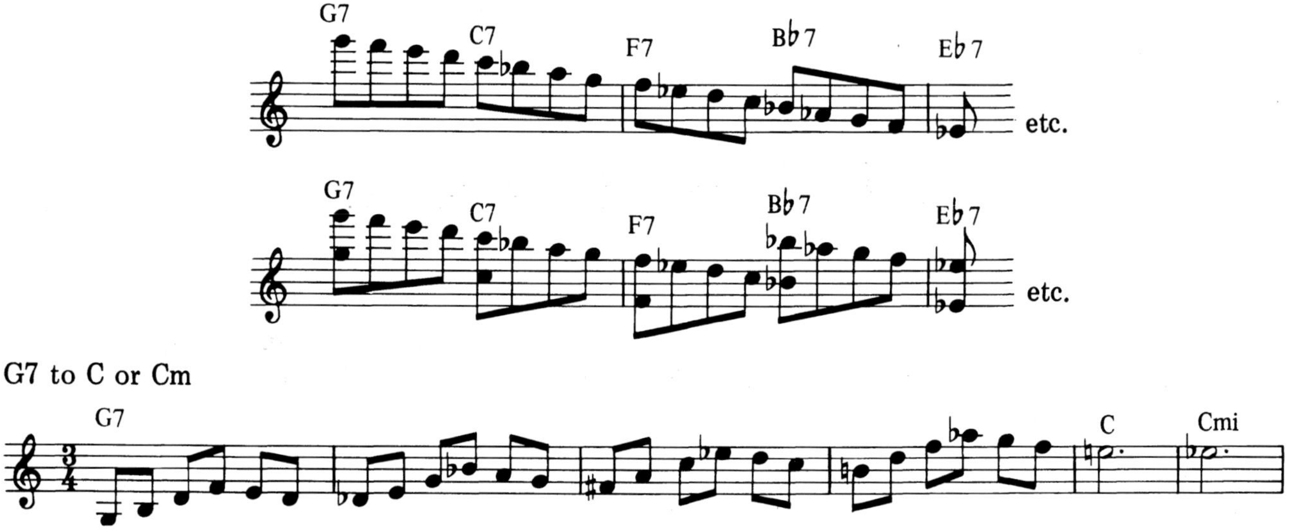

Diminished Lines

Here are five practice patterns, ascending and descending. The first two use only the tones of the diminished seventh chord. The last three involve "slurs" into those tones from a half-step away:

Diminished Substitutes

Notice the similarity between G7-9 and A♭° . Every 7-9 chord is (with root omitted) equivalent to a diminished chord one half-step higher. That is, diminished-sounding scales may be applied to 7-9 chords, and vice-versa.

Below is a common chord pattern, using 7-9 substitutes for the diminished chord. Note use of ♯5 in those chords.

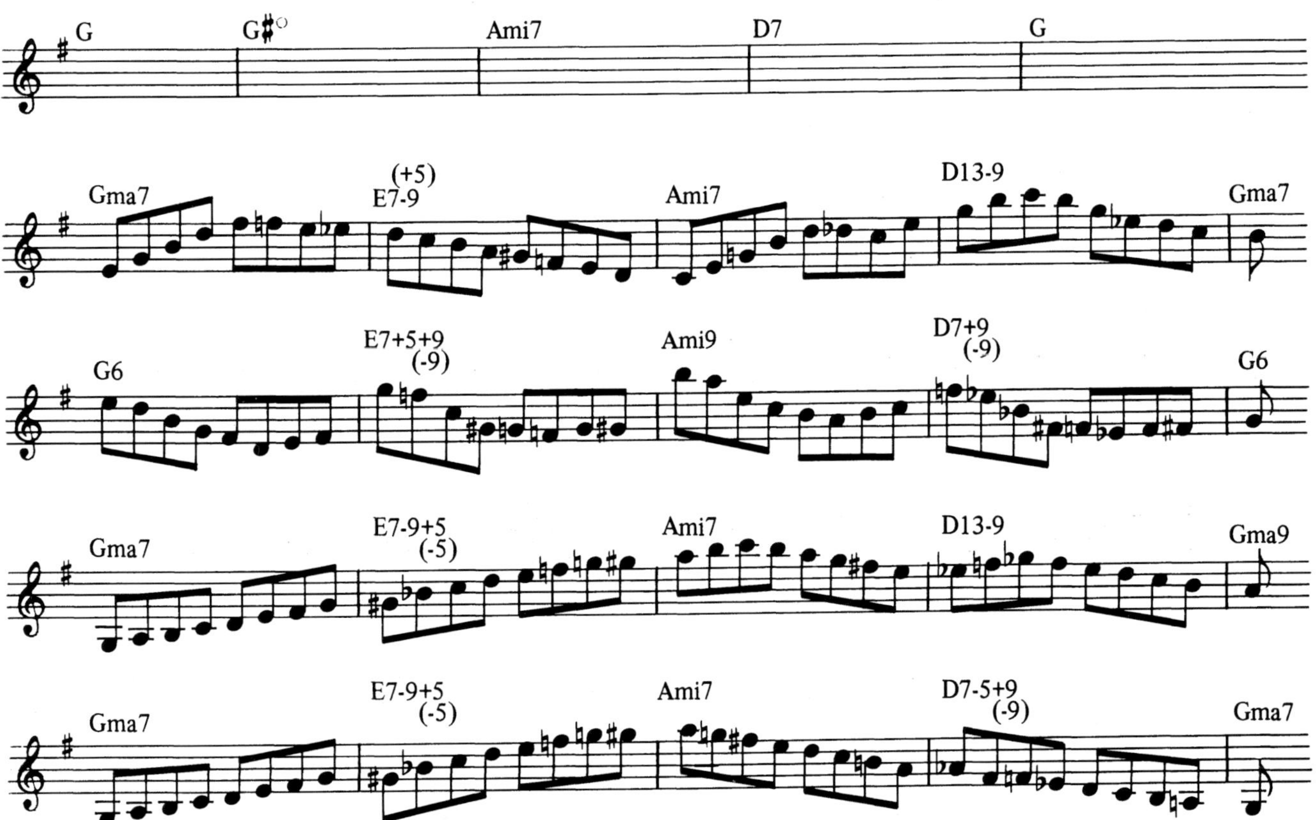

Three more variations on the same pattern (G to G#° to Am7 to D7). Note the use of A7+9 for Am7:

Some 16th-note variations on the first two measures:

In this study, E7 becomes Bm7-5/E7-9. This gets pretty far away from the original "diminished" sound, but may be used with discretion:

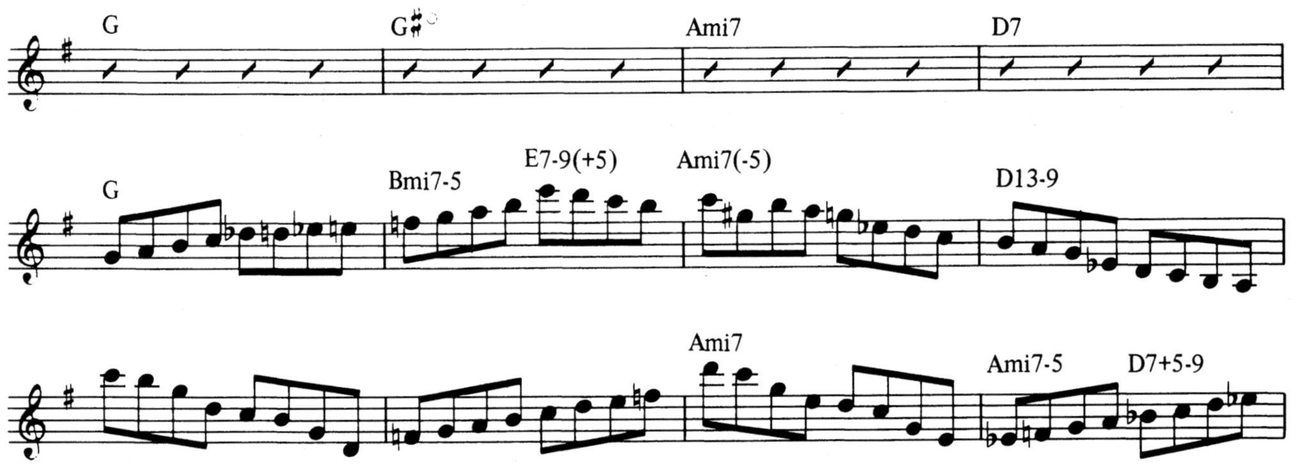

Chordal Thinking

The chord shown above is Cm7-5. It is also E♭m6 or A♭9 with root omitted.

When playing a line against that chord you can THINK in Cm:

or think in A♭: (note key signature)

or in E♭m:

Depending upon where the chord is progressing, you can THINK in terms of what is most familiar to you. Resolve Cm7-5 to F7-9/B♭m. Resolve A♭9 to D♭, and E♭m6 to A♭7/D♭.

Here is a line "translated" from thinking in G to thinking in D♭. In this particular example, thinking in D♭ results in fewer accidentals, but that should not be your ONLY consideration. Think in terms of LOGICAL chord sequences: G7-5 to C, D♭7-5 to G♭.

Some G7 lines. These fit G7+, G7-5, G7+5-9, etc. "Translate" each from G to D♭.

Extend this chord scale:

to this:

Two more examples. Try to play a chord with the melody, to help your ear, and resolve into an appropriate chord: G to C, D♭ to G♭.

Improvising

One way to develop improvisational skills is to take any common chord pattern and isolate it for study. Each of the following studies shows a chord pattern in the top line. Below it are some improvisations which fit the pattern.

When you've finished these, write out any chord sequence that seems to you a "common" pattern; then improvise.

A7
D7
G7
C7
F
A13
Ami6
D7
G7+9
(-9)
C7
F
Emi
Emi7
A7
Ami
Dmi9
G7
C7(-5-9)
F
G
Emi
Ami
D7
G
Gma7
Emi9
Ami7
Ami9
D13
Gma7(6)

The next study fits the pattern: G to Em to Am to D7 (one bar each). No chord symbols appear because you are to make your own analysis.

Blues

These solos are in straight 8th-notes. By eliminating rhythmic variety, you force the ear into building better melodies. 8th-note studies also tend to avoid the practice of playing memorized licks.

Chord symbols are for your analysis, not necessarily for accompaniment.

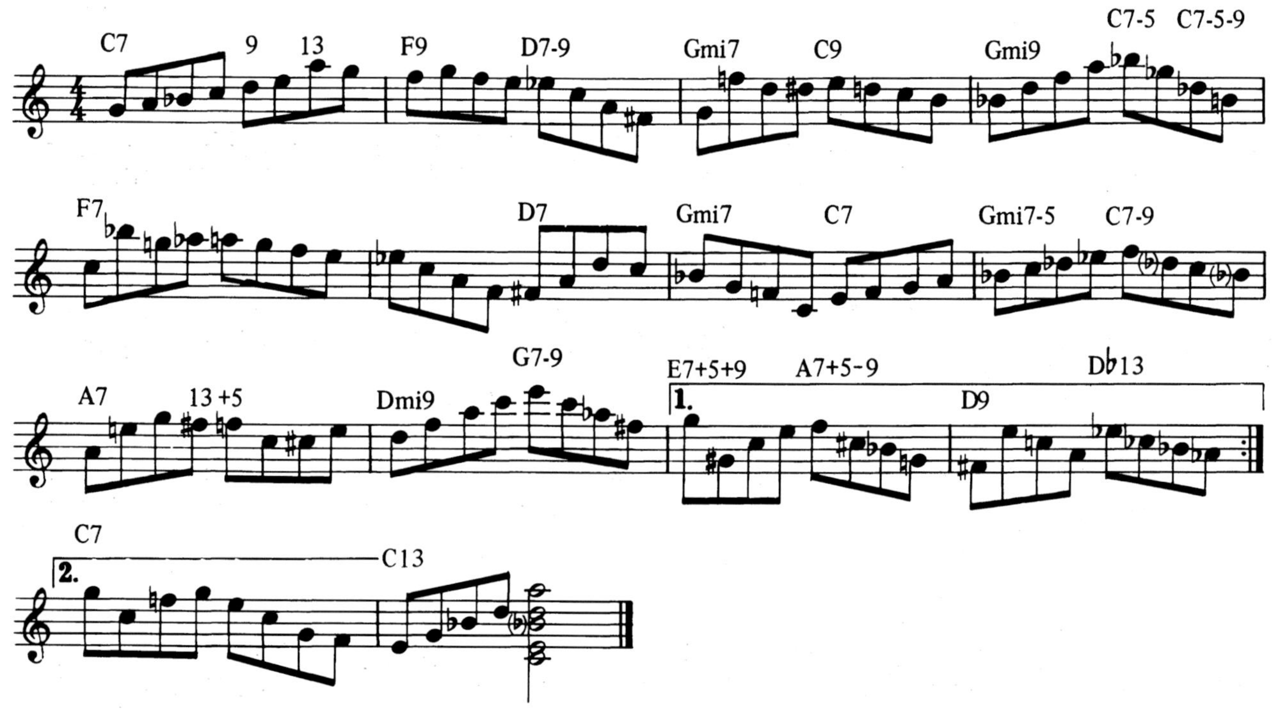

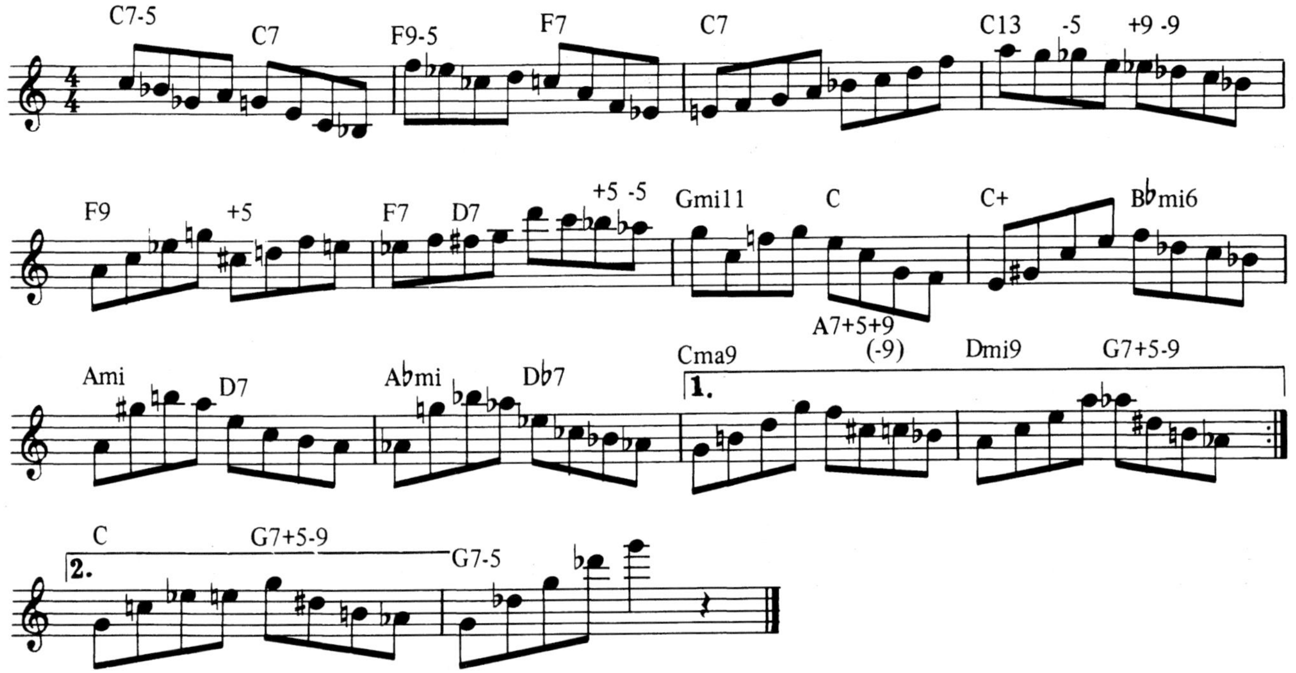

This one is in 16th-notes. It gives you more to play on each chord:

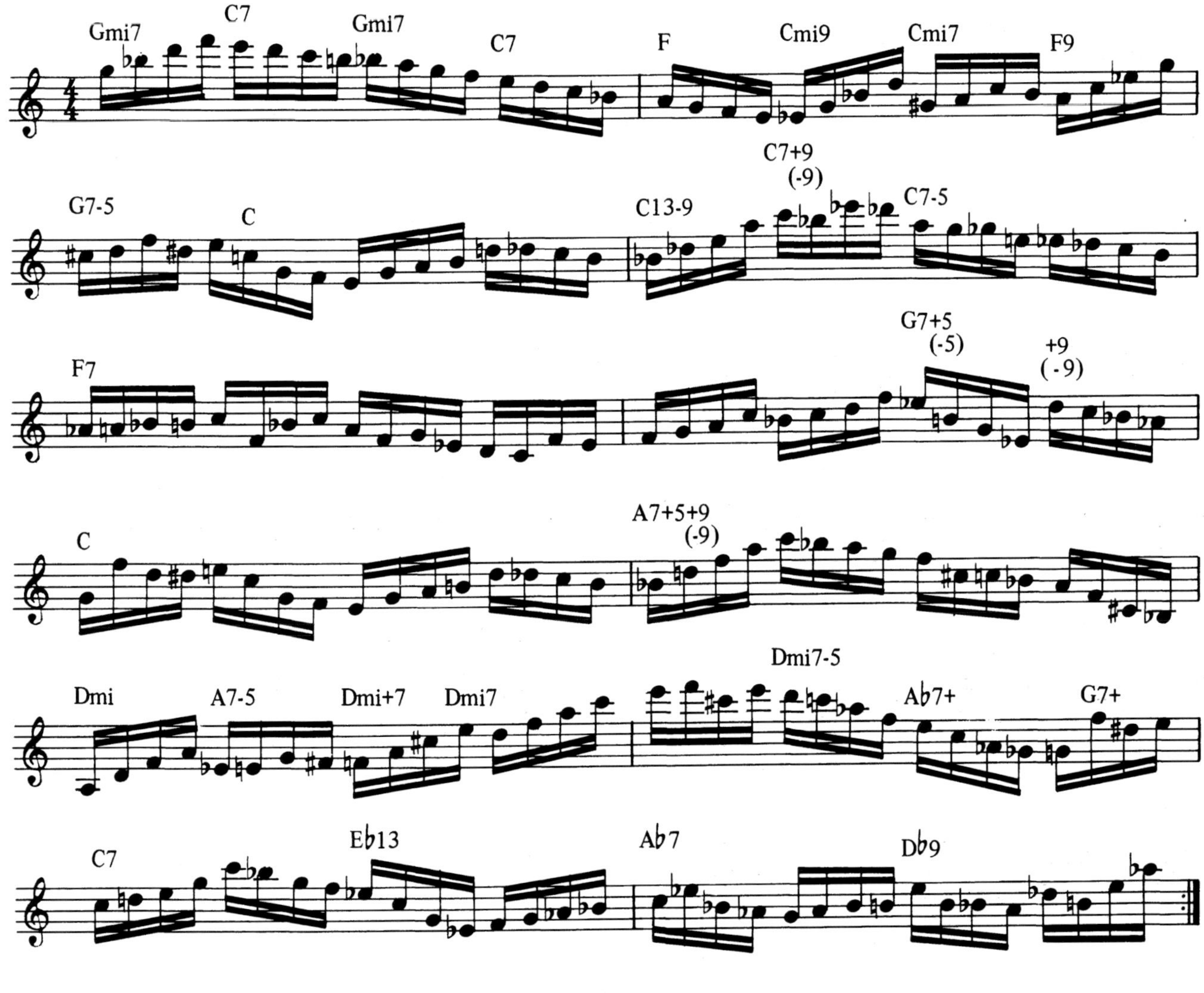

Gmi7 C7 Gmi7 C7 F Cmi9 Cmi7 F9

G7-5 C C13-9 C7+9 (-9) C7-5

F7 G7+5 (-5) +9 (-9)

C A7+5+9 (-9)

Dmi A7-5 Dmi+7 Dmi7 Dmi7-5 A♭7+ G7+

C7 E♭13 A♭7 D♭9

Minor Blues

Chord symbols are for analysis, not accompaniment:

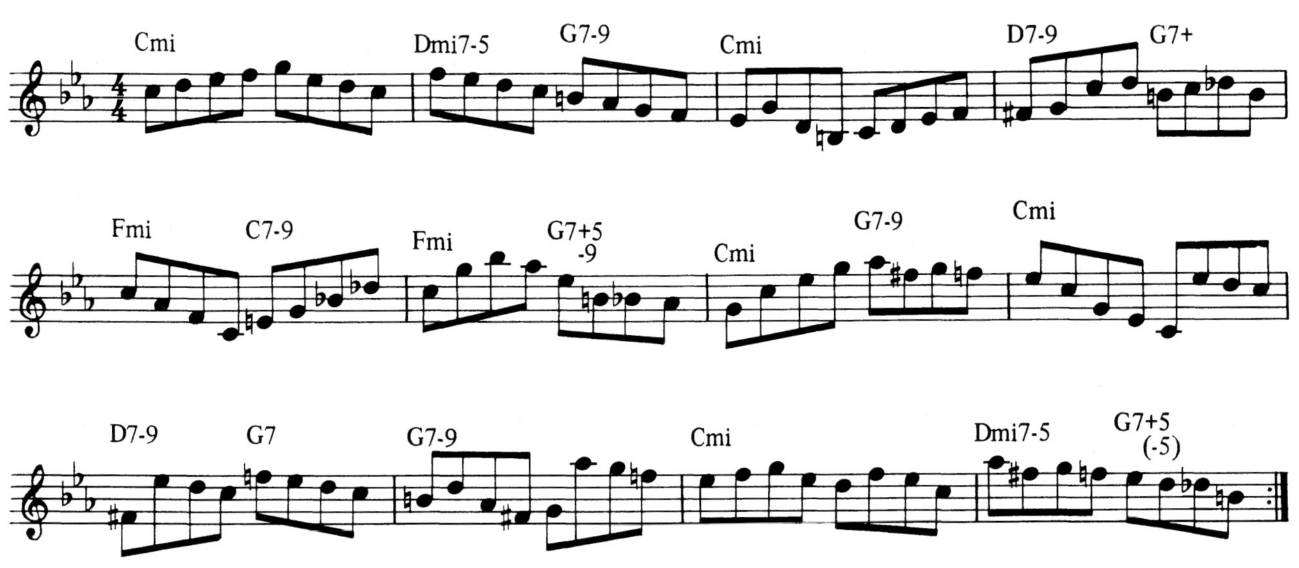
Cmi
Dmi7-5
G7-9
Cmi
D7-9
G7+
Fmi
C7-9
Fmi
G7+5 -9
Cmi
G7-9
Cmi
D7-9
G7
G7-9
Cmi
Dmi7-5
G7+5 (-5)

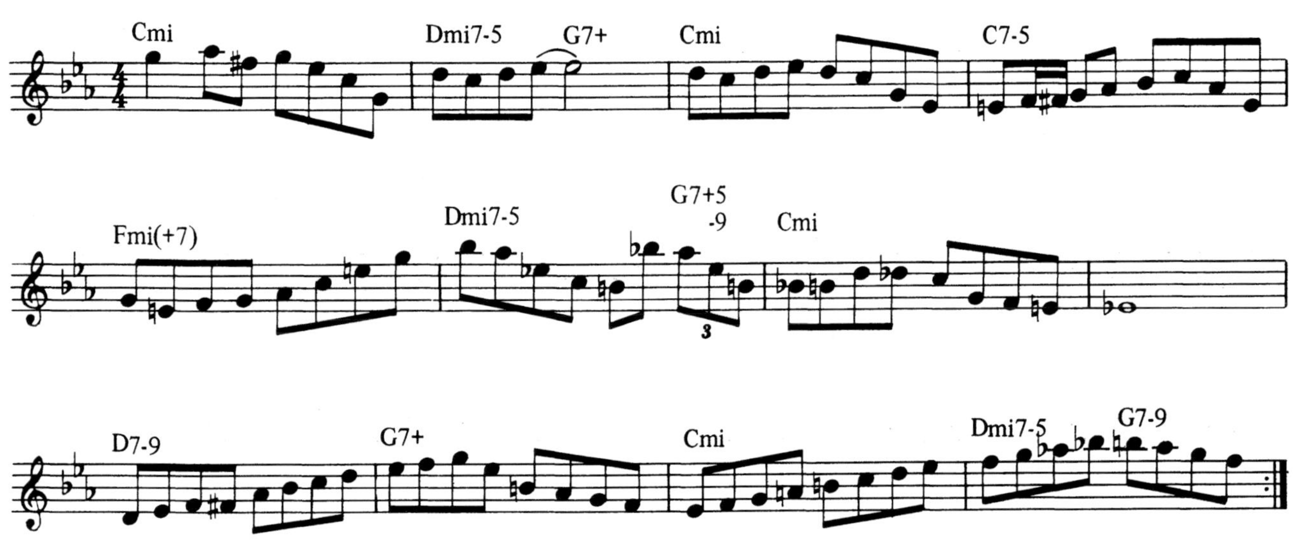
Cmi
Dmi7-5
G7+
Cmi
C7-5
Fmi(+7)
Dmi7-5
G7+5 -9
Cmi
D7-9
G7+
Cmi
Dmi7-5
G7-9

Modern Blues

The chords shown below represent one version of blues changes.

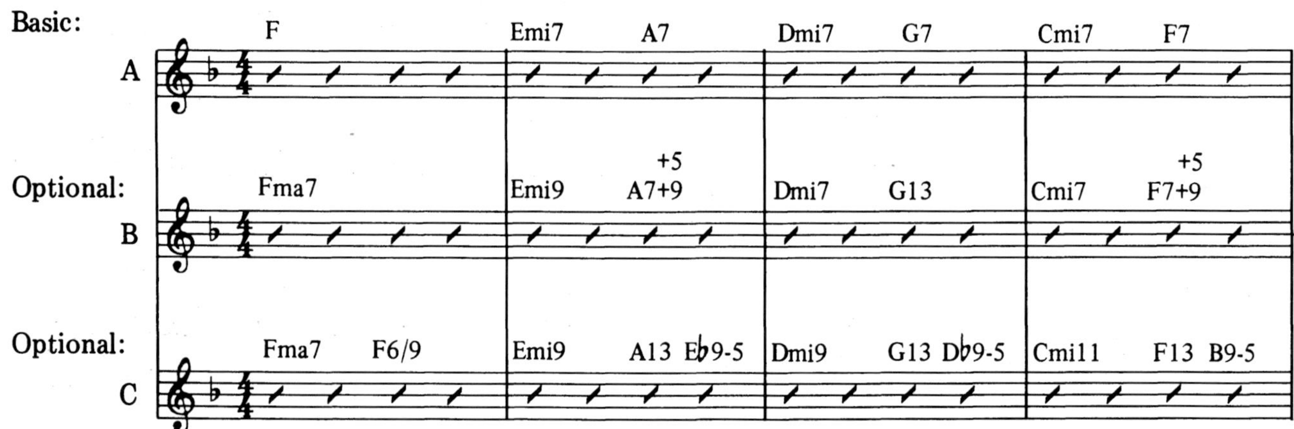

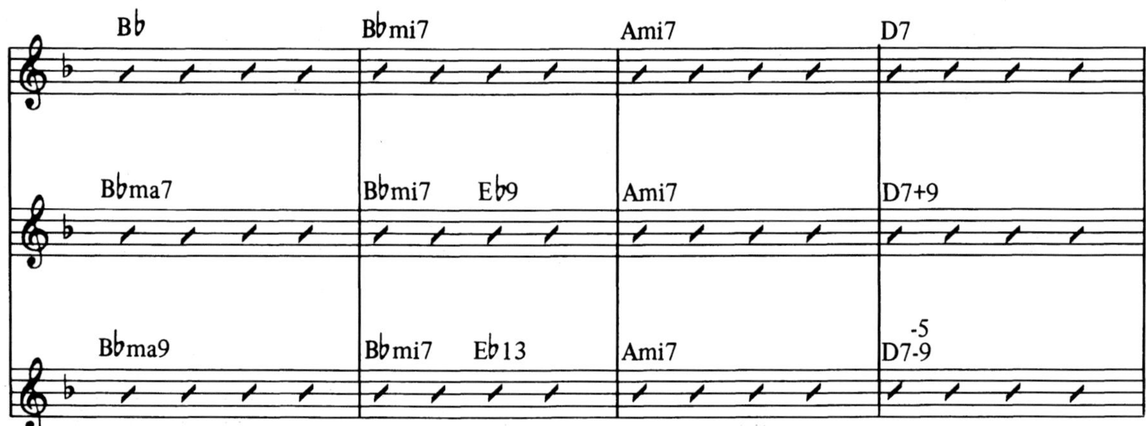

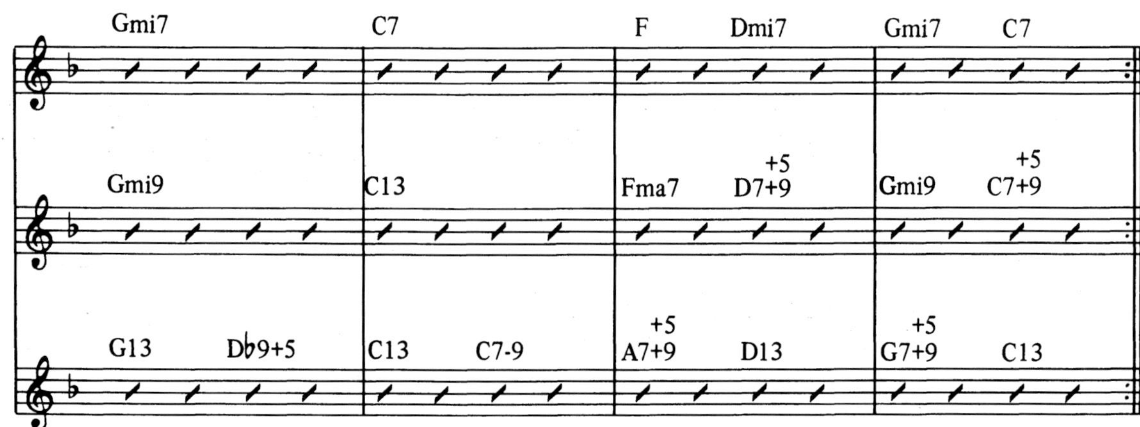

There are many possible variations. The chord symbols in the studies are to help your analysis of the melodic lines, but they'll give an approximation of the proper accompaniment.

These are designed to be played consecutively, so the final measure in each chorus may contain the "pickups" for the following chorus.

Fma7
Emi7
A7-9
Dmi7
G7
Cmi7
F13
B♭ma7
B♭mi7
Ami7
D7
A♭mi7
D♭7
C7
(-9)
Fma7
D7-9
Gmi7
C7
F
Emi7
A7
Dmi9
G7
Cmi7
F13
B♭ma7
B♭6
B♭mi7
Ami9
A♭mi7
Gmi
Gmi7
C+
F(Ami7)
D7+9
(-9)
Gmi7
(G7)
C7+
Fma7
Emi
+5
A7-9
Dmi7
G7
Cmi7
F7+5
B♭ma7
B♭6
B♭mi(+7)
B♭mi7
Ami7
D7
A♭mi7
D♭7
Gmi7
Gmi9
C7(+5)
F6
(Dmi)
Gmi7
C13

F Emi7-5 A7(13) Dmi7 G7(13) Cmi7 F7
B♭ (F7) B♭ B♭mi7 Ami9 D13 A♭mi7(11)
Gmi (+7) (7) C7(-9) F D7+9 (-9) Gmi7 C7
F Emi7 A7 Dmi7 G7 Cmi7 F7+9 (-9)
B♭ Cmi7 C♯° B♭6 B♭mi7(11) (9) E♭7(13)
Ami7 A♭mi7
Gmi7 C7 C13 C7+9 -9 (+5)
F Ami9 +5 D7-9 Gmi9 Gmi7-5 C7-9
F Emi7 A7 Dmi G7
Cmi7 F7-5+9 (-9) B♭ma7 B♭6
B♭ma7 E♭7 Ami7
A♭mi7 A♭mi9 Gmi7 C7-9 F D7-9 Gmi7 C7

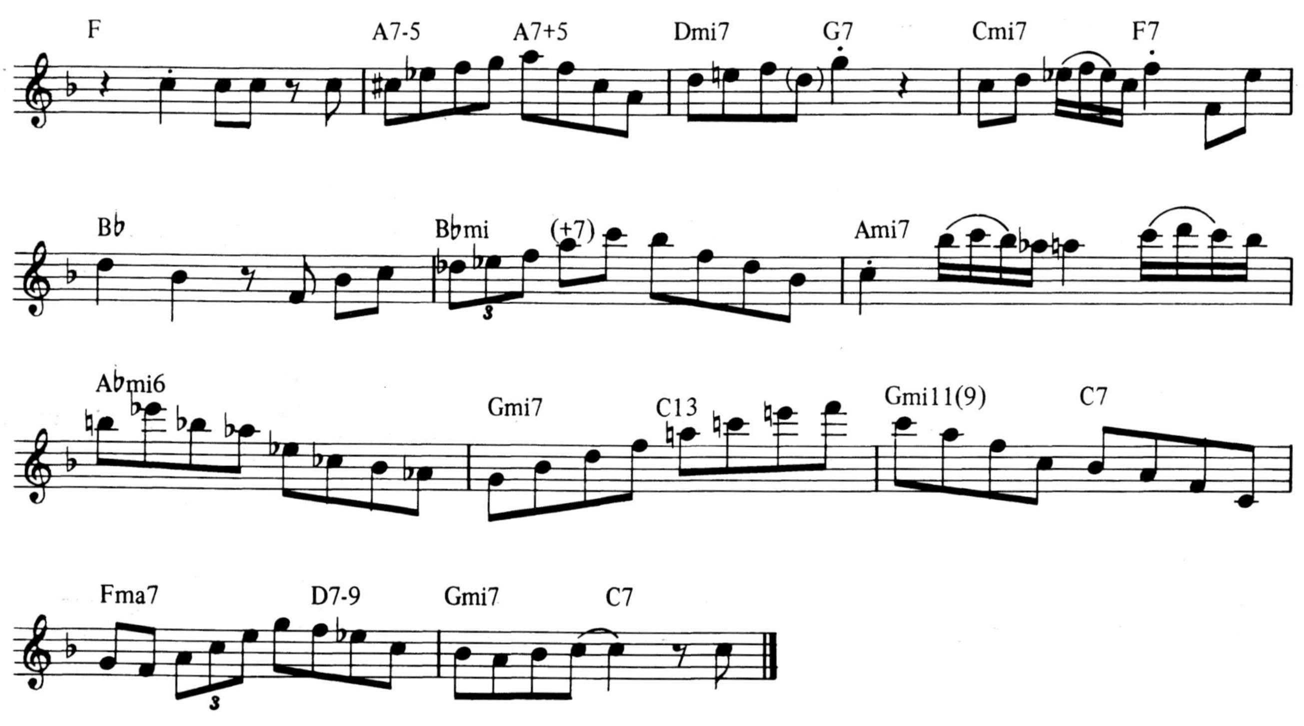
F
A7-5
A7+5
Dmi7
G7
Cmi7
F7
B♭
B♭mi
(+7)
Ami7
A♭mi6
Gmi7
C13
Gmi11(9)
C7
Fma7
D7-9
Gmi7
C7

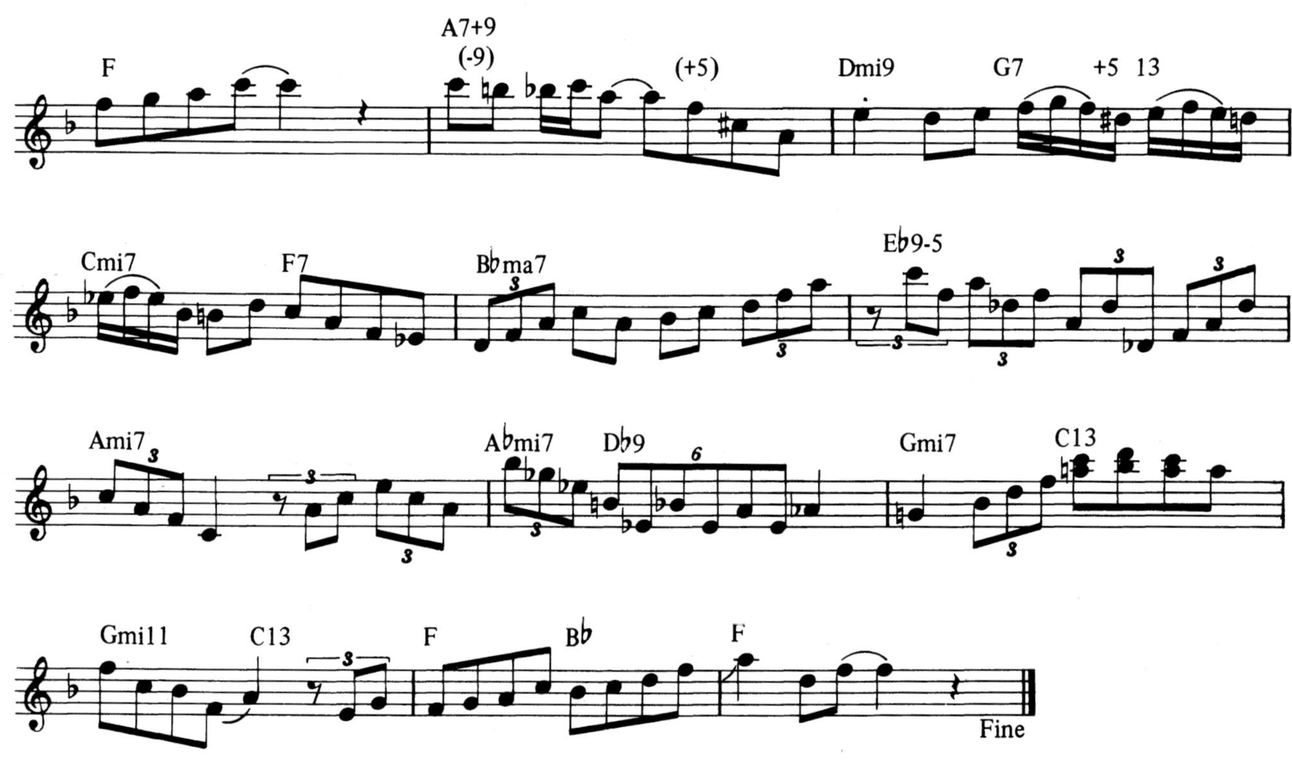
F
A7+9
(-9)
(+5)
Dmi9
G7
+5
13
Cmi7
F7
B♭ma7
E♭9-5
Ami7
A♭mi7
D♭9
Gmi7
C13
Gmi11
C13
F
B♭
F
Fine

Improvise in the blank measures:

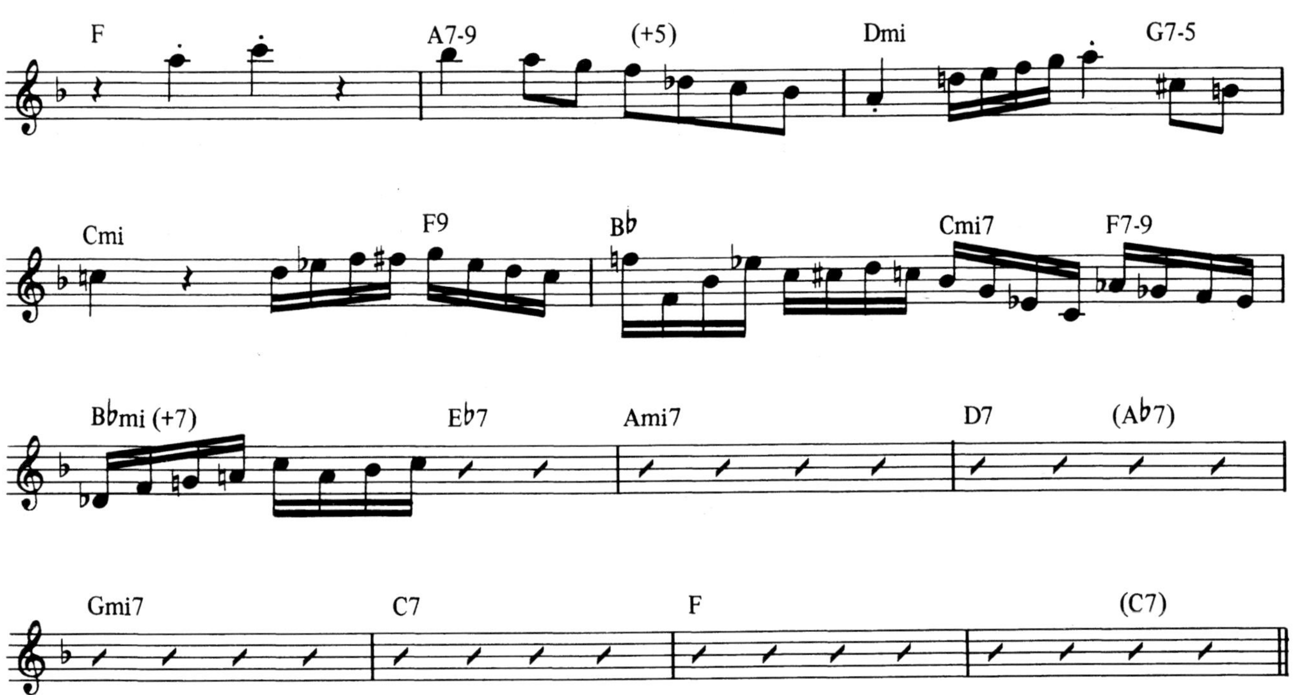

Modern blues are also played against this chord pattern. Use chord embellishment, substitution, etc.

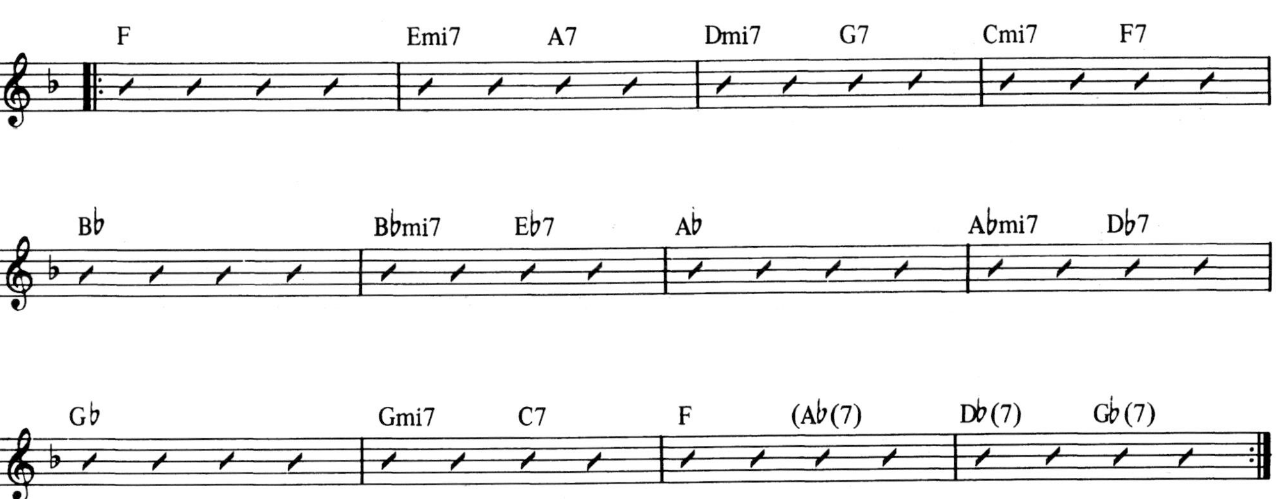

Rhythm Changes

Rhythm changes are normally played at very fast tempos, so the chord patterns vary, depending on the player. The chart shows two BASIC "rhythm" patterns:

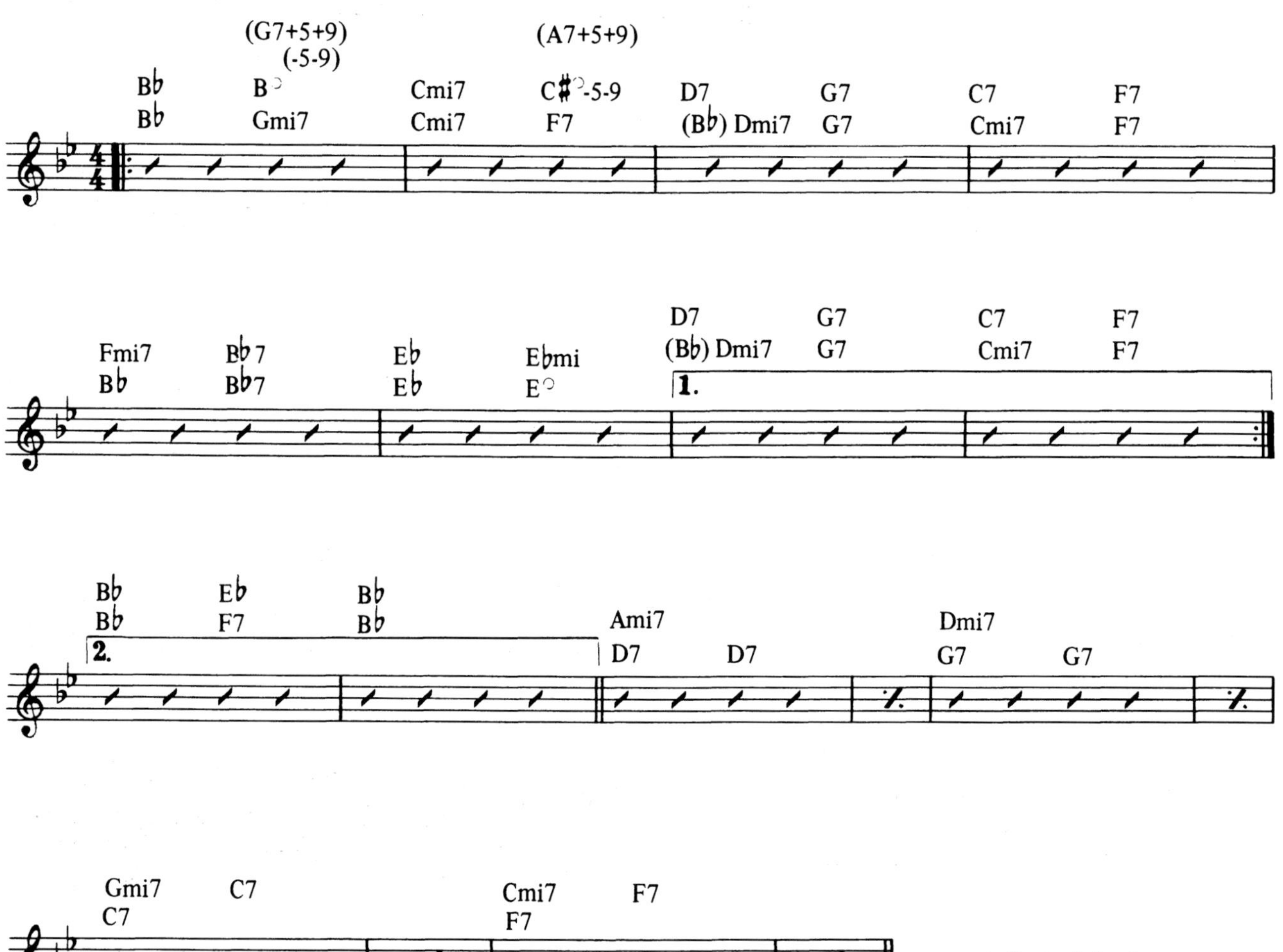

As usual, the chord symbols in each chorus represent the harmonic THINKING in the melody line.

Notice the bridge (starting at bar 17) consists of a single two-bar phrase, repeated through the chords:

B♭
Cmi7
F13
B♭ma7
(Gmi9)
Cmi7
F9
B♭7
E♭ma7
E♭mi7(6)
B♭ma7
Dmi7
G7
Cmi7
F7
B♭
Cmi7
A7
Dmi7
G7+9
Cmi7
F7+
B♭
B♭9(-5)
E♭
Cmi7
F13
B♭(ma7)
D7
(13)
Ami7
D7-9
G7
Dmi7
Dmi9
G7
C7
Gmi7
Gmi9
C7
F7
Cmi7
Cmi9
F7
B♭ma7
Cmi6
F9
D7
G7
Cmi7
F7+5+9
(-9)
B♭ma9(Dmi7)
G7+5+9
(-9)
Cmi7
F7+5
B♭

B♭ma7 Cmi7 F7-9 +5 B♭ (Dmi) G7-9 +5 Gmi7 G♭mi7
Fmi7 B♭7 E♭6 A7 Dmi7 G9 Cmi7 F7
B♭ Dmi7 Cmi7 F13 Dmi7 Gmi9 Cmi7 F13
B♭ B♭9 E♭ E♭mi7 A♭9 B♭
D7+ +9 (-9) Dmi9 G9+5 (-5)
C7 (13) (-5) (+5) (ma7) C7 F13 Cmi7 F9
B♭ (Gmi7) Cmi7 F13 Dmi7 G7 Cmi7 F7
B♭ B♭7 E♭ma7 E♭mi (E°) B♭ma7

The chords in the unmarked measures are just standard "rhythm" changes. The phrase which begins in bar 8 is re-stated during the next few bars. Don't over-analyze this: just play it and LISTEN.

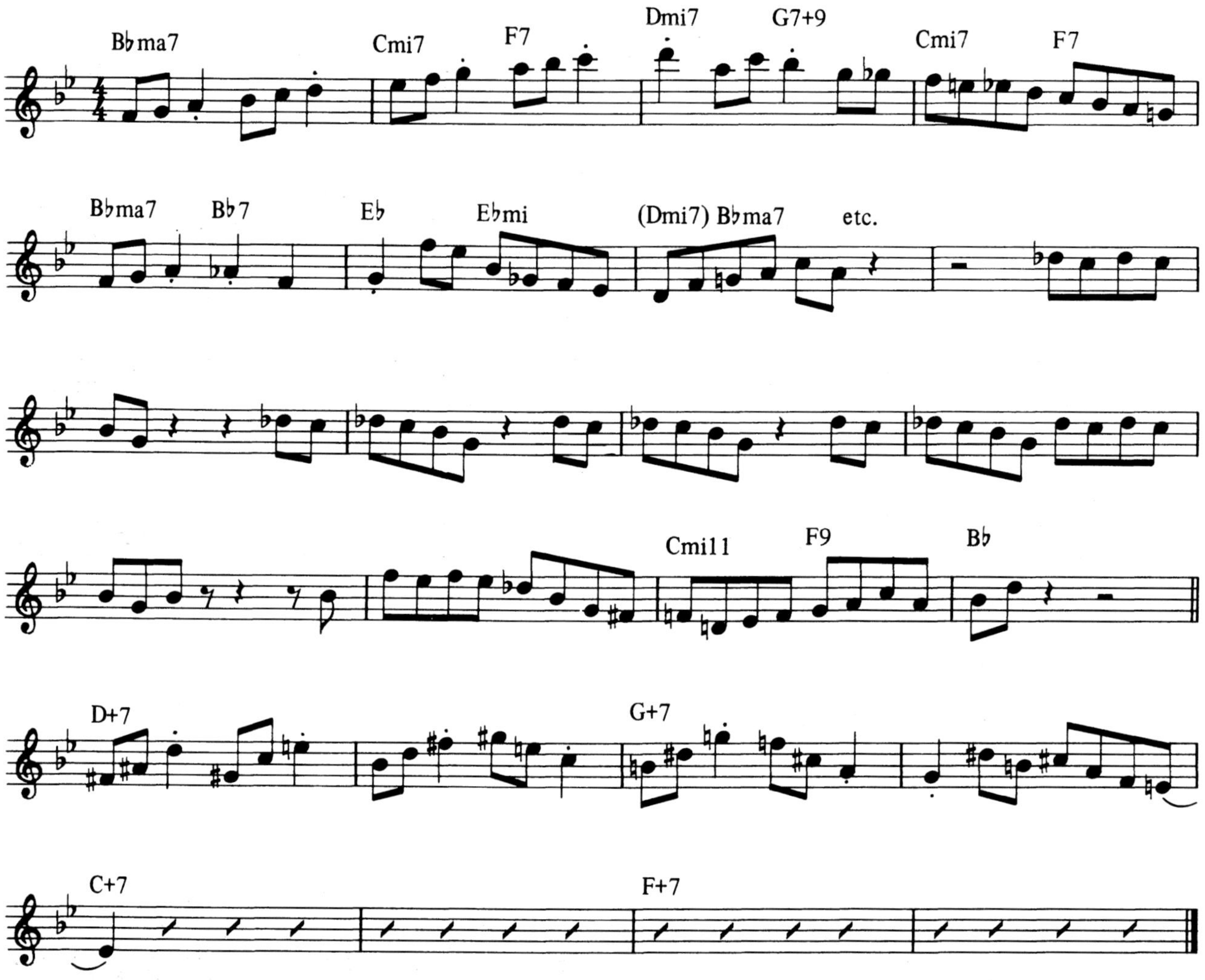
B♭ma7
Cmi7
F7
Dmi7
G7+9
Cmi7
F7
B♭ma7
B♭7
E♭
E♭mi
(Dmi7) B♭ma7
etc.
Cmi11
F9
B♭
D+7
G+7
C+7
F+7

Finish the chorus with something of your own. Below are two examples of two-bar phrases which can be repeated through a line of dominant 7th chords. Try them on the bridge, above.

D7
G7
C7
etc.
D7
G7
etc.

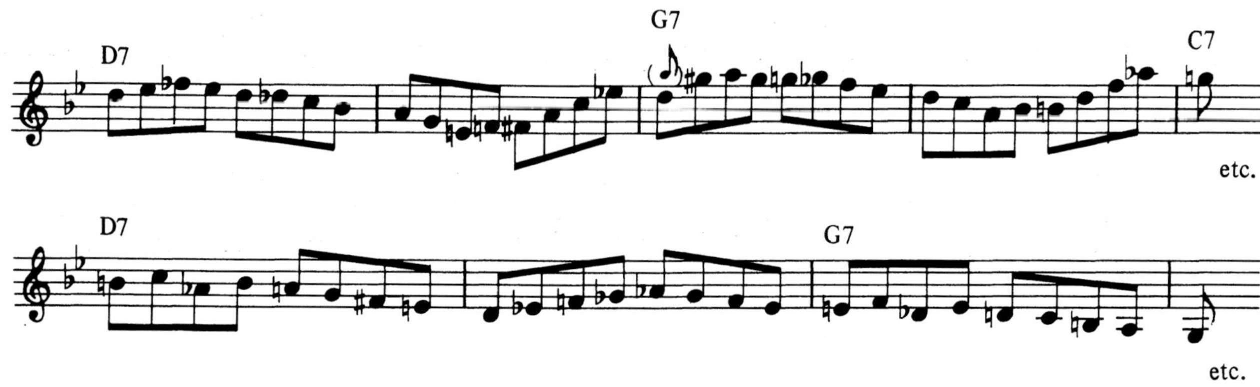

3/4 Blues

This is another set of blues changes, in 3/4 time.

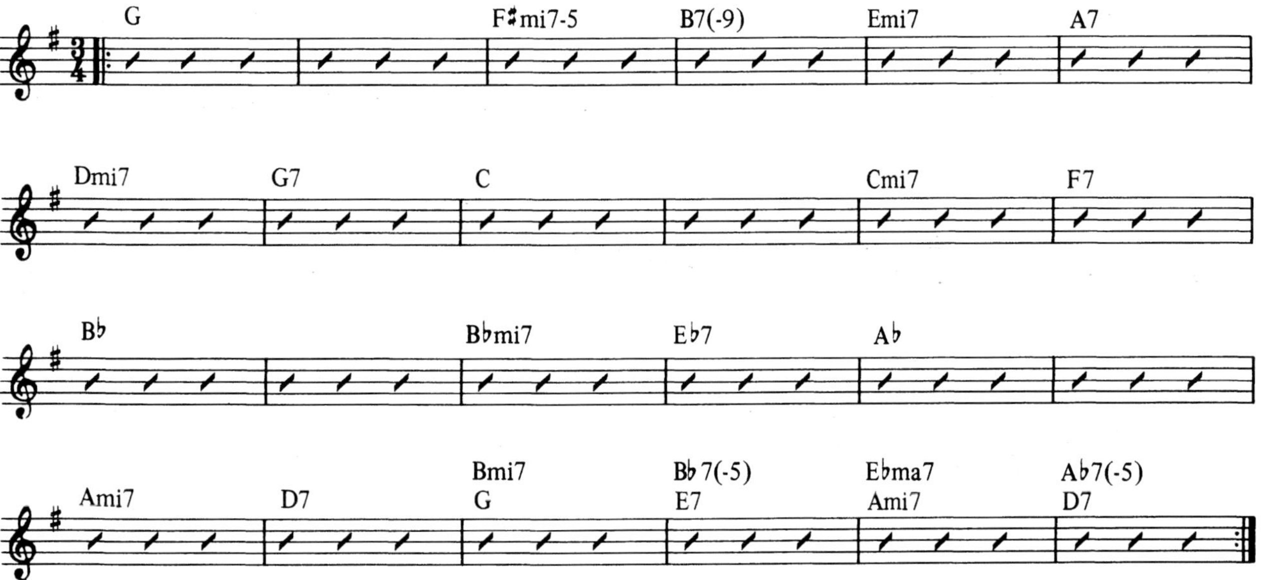

The solos are designed to be played consecutively, so the last bar in each chorus may contain the "pickups" to the ensuing chorus.

INTRO:

B♭ma7
B♭mi7
(+7)
E♭7
A♭ma7
Ami7(6)
D13
Bmi7
E7+5(+9)
(-5)(-9)
E♭mi9
Ami7-5
(D7)

G
F♯mi6/B7
F♯mi7-5
B7-9
Emi
(+7)
Emi7
A7
Dmi7
G7
+9
(-9)
Cma7
Cmi7
(+7)
B♭ma7
B♭mi
(+7)
B♭mi7
E♭7
A♭ma7
Ami7
D13
(-5)
Gma7
Fmi(+7)
B♭9
E♭ma7
D7+5-9

G (♮)
B7-9
Emi7
A9
A7-9
Dmi7
G7
Cma7
Cmi7
F7
B♭
B♭mi7
E♭7(-9)
A♭ma7
Ami9
(+7)
D7-9
Bmi11
E7+9
(-9)
A7-9+5
(-5)
Ami7
D7
G
F♯mi7-5
B7
A7-9
A9
G7-9
Cma7
Cmi7

F7
B♭
B♭mi7
E♭7(-9)
A♭ma7
Ami+7
Ami9
D7
G(Bmi7)
B♭7
E♭ma7
A♭7-5
G
F♯mi7-5
B7
Emi7
A7
Dmi7
G7
Cma7
Cmi7
F13-9
B♭ma7
gliss.
B♭mi7
E♭9-5
A♭ma7
Ami9
D7+5
G(Bmi7)
B♭13
E♭ma7
A♭ma7
D7+9
(-9)

G
F♯mi7-5
B7-9
Emi7
A7
Dmi7
G7+9
(-9)
Cma7
Cmi7
F9
B♭ma7
B♭mi7
E♭9
A♭
Ami7
D13
G(Bmi7)
B♭7
E♭ma7(6)
A♭9
G

Solo as Recorded by Joe Pass on Pacific Jazz PJ-85 album "For Django".

This chart shows some of the basic chordal thinking used in the solo. With chord embellishment and substitution, variations are almost limitless. No chord symbols are indicated throughout the solo, so you must do your own analysis.

A
Bridge
Tacet
B

Bridge
8va
8va
8va
C loco
Bridge

D
Bridge

PART THREE

JOE PASS JAZZ PHRASES

SECTION ONE

(1)
B♭7
Fm7
B♭13 (♭9)
Fm7
B♭7
(2)
B♭
(+5)
(3)
B♭7
Fm11
B♭7
3
3

(4)
B♭

B13
B♭

(5)
B♭

(6)
Fm11
Bm11
E13

Fm11
B♭7

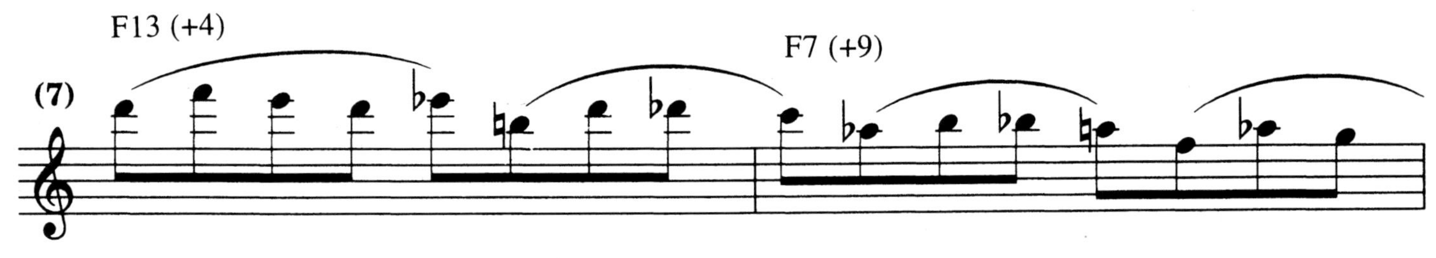
(7)
F13 (+4)
F7 (+9)

F13 (♭9)
F7

(8)
Cm9
F13

F13

(9)
B♭

Cm7
F7 (♭9)
B♭

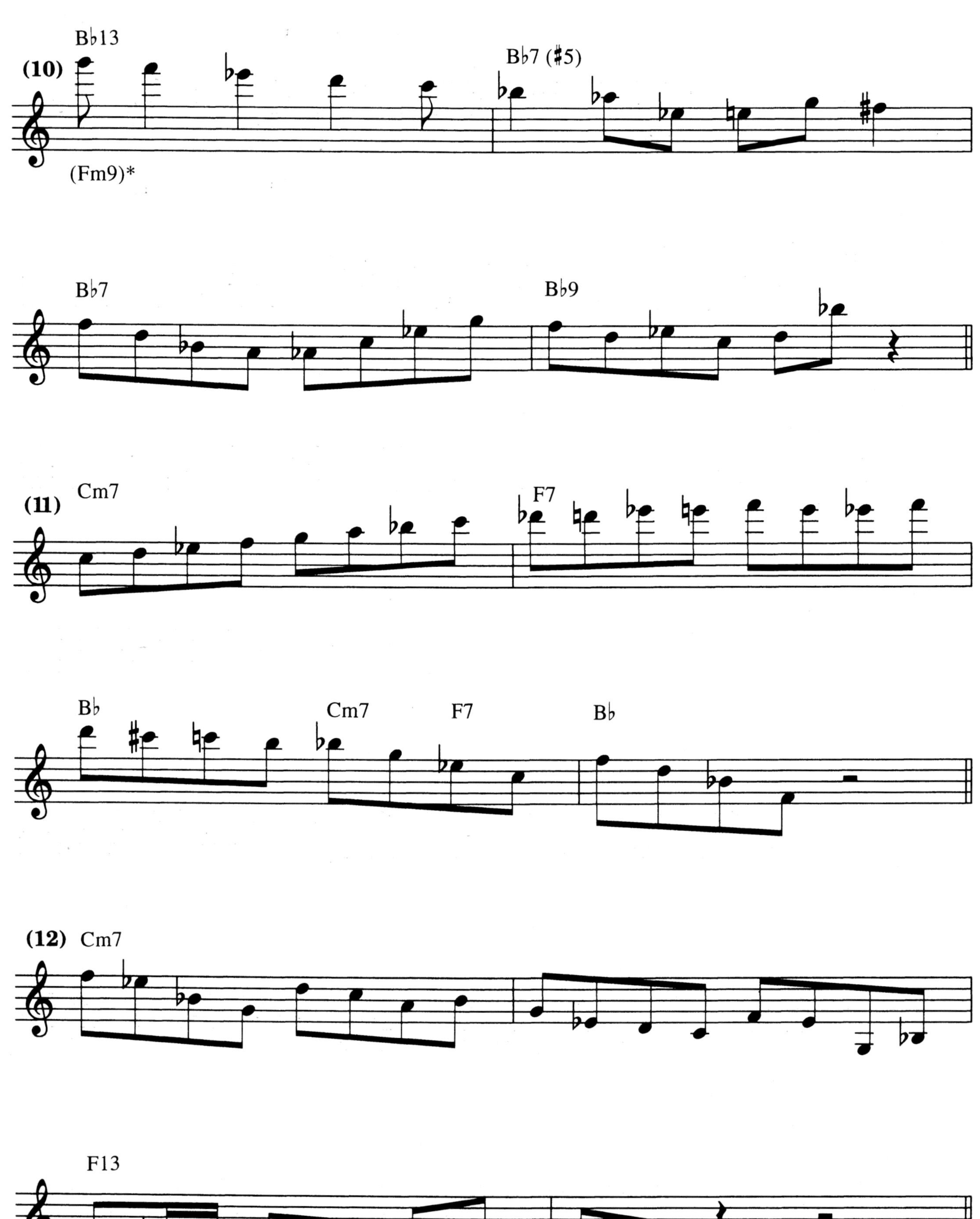

* Chord in parenthesis means: you could probably get along without it, but if you wanted to use a different chord here, you could use the one indicated.

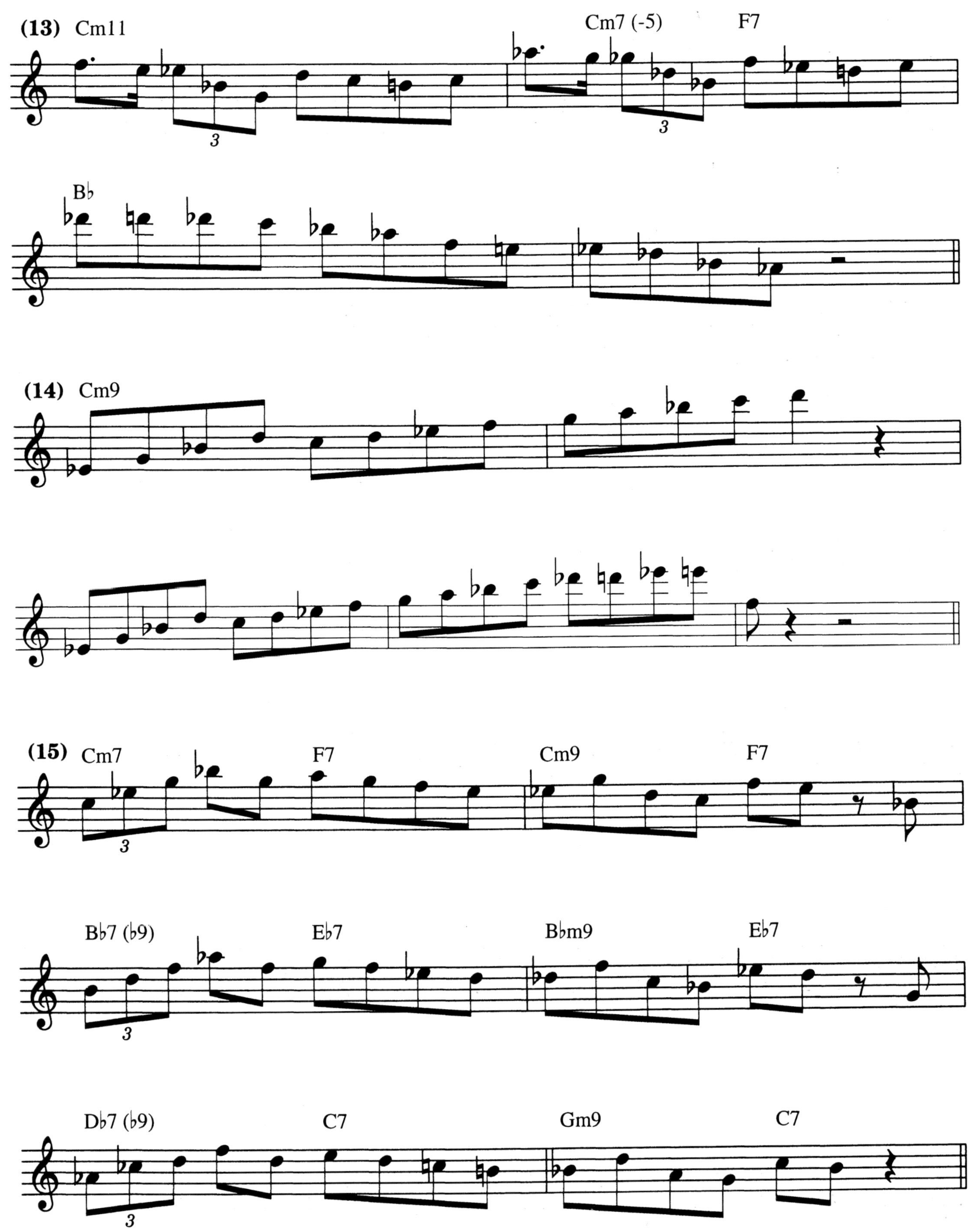
(13) Cm11
Cm7 (-5)
F7
3
3
B♭
(14) Cm9
(15) Cm7
F7
Cm9
F7
3
B♭7 (♭9)
E♭7
B♭m9
E♭7
3
D♭7 (♭9)
C7
Gm9
C7
3

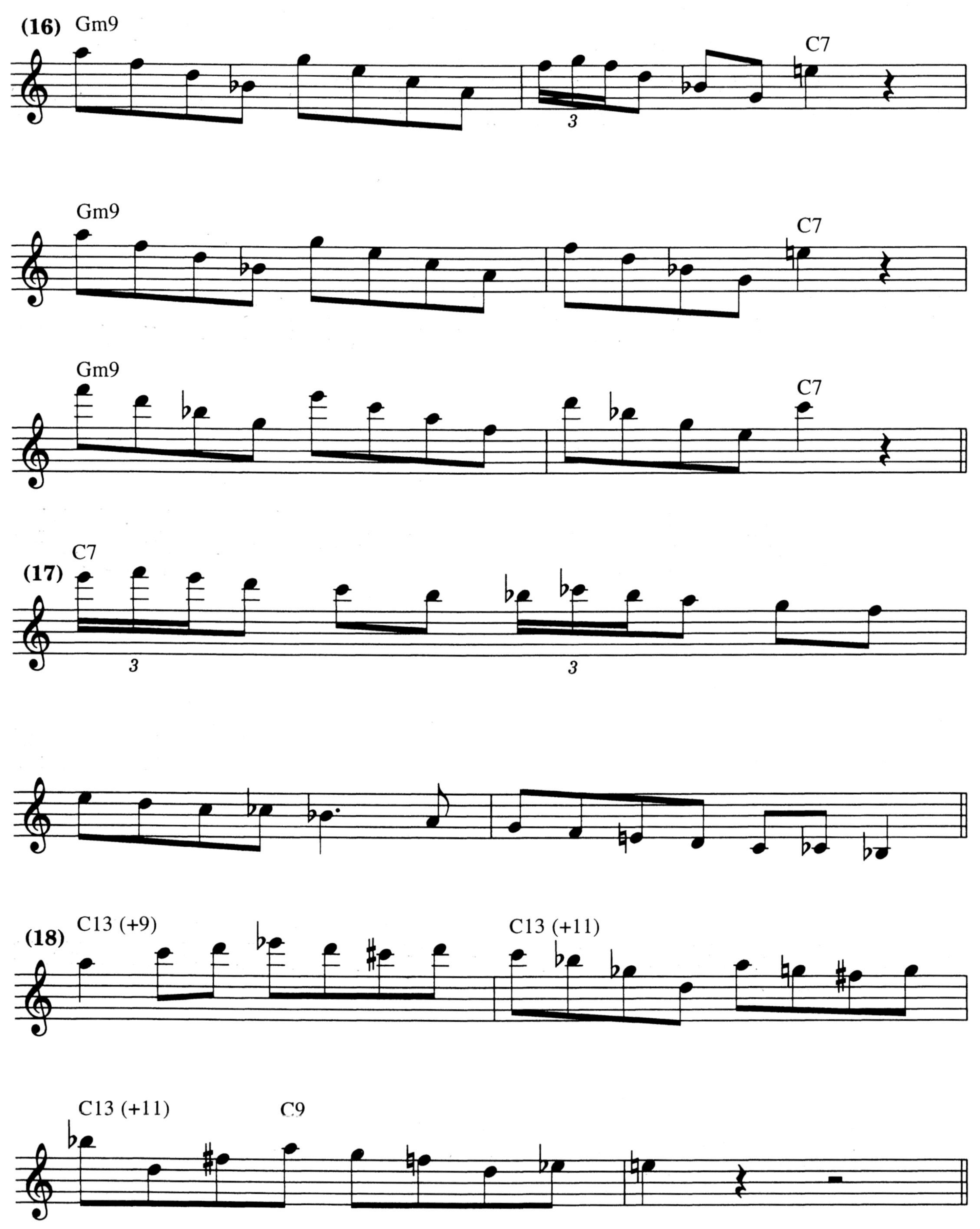
(16) Gm9
C7
3
Gm9
C7
Gm9
C7
C7
(17)
3
3
(18) C13 (+9)
C13 (+11)
C13 (+11)
C9

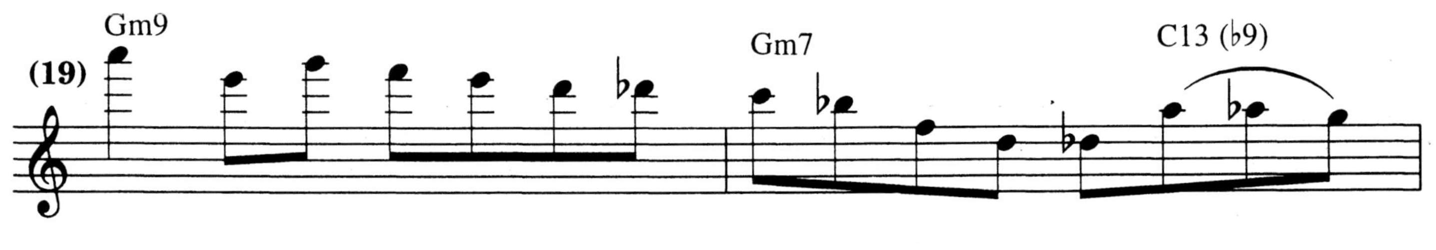
(19)
Gm9
Gm7
C13 (♭9)

Gm7
C13
Gm7
C7

(20)
Gm
Gm △7
Gm7
Gm6
3

Gm △7
Gm7
Gm6

(21)
C7 (♭9)

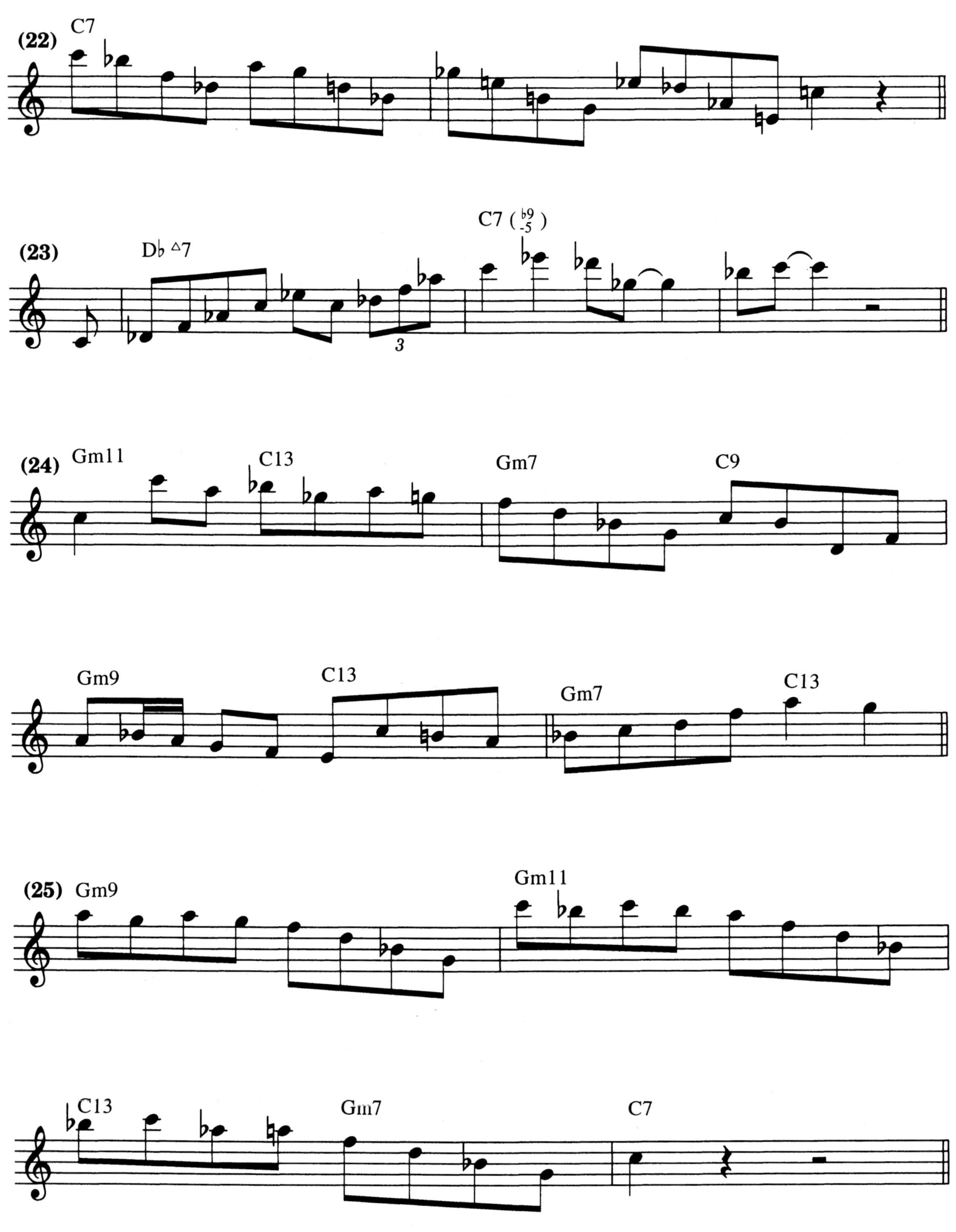
(22)
C7
(23)
Db △7
C7 (b9 -5)
3
(24)
Gm11
C13
Gm7
C9
Gm9
C13
Gm7
C13
(25)
Gm9
Gm11
C13
Gm7
C7

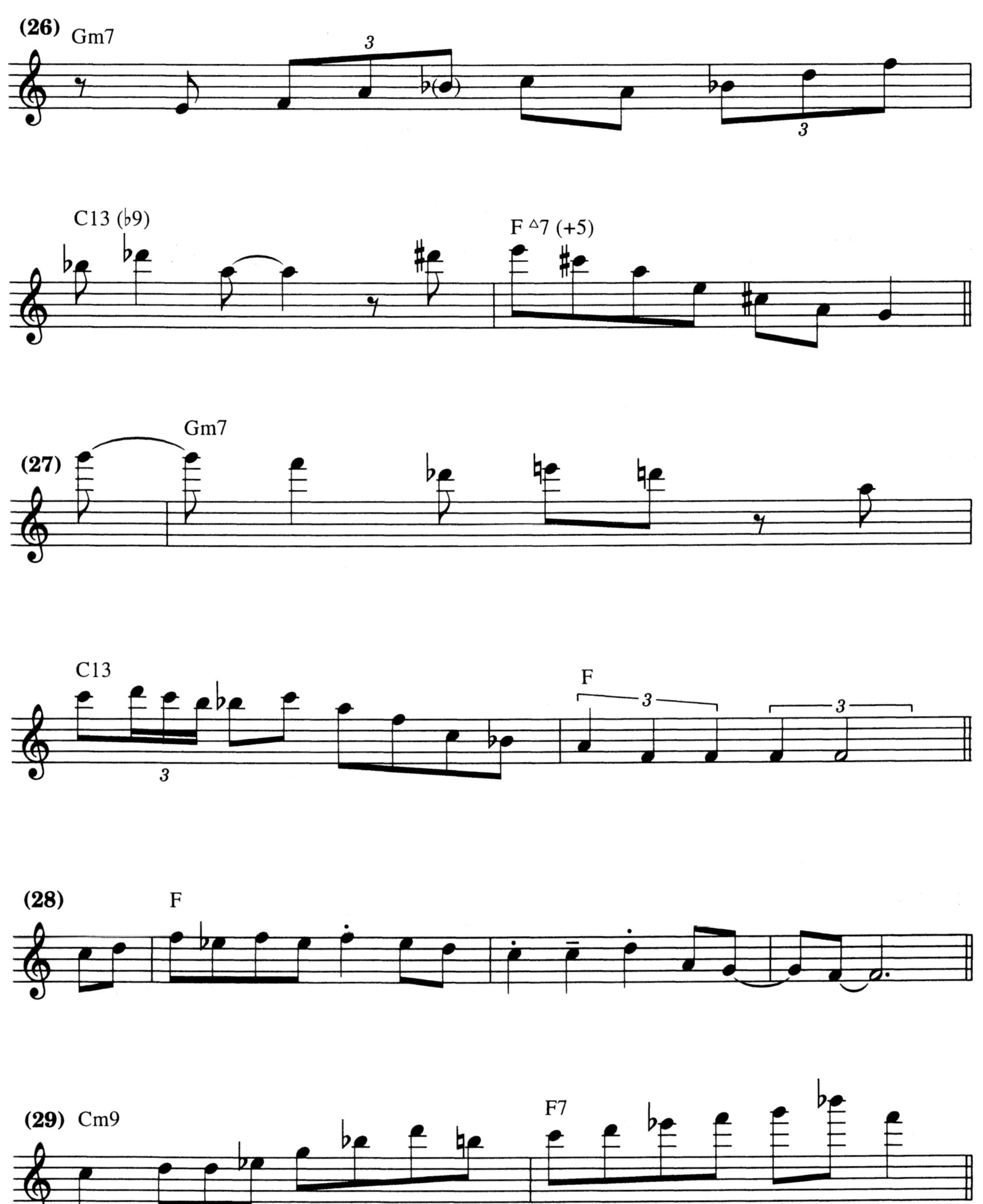
(26) Gm7
C13 (♭9)
F △7 (+5)
(27) Gm7
C13
F
(28) F
(29) Cm9
F7

PART THREE

JOE PASS JAZZ PHRASES

SECTION TWO

"BLUES"

"Blues Sound equals ♭7, ♭3, ♭5."

These three sounds **can** be used in a blues progression, but all three do not **have** to be present to create a sound.

Those passages that have a "Blues Sound" in them will be indicated by name.

(1)
Dm7
G7

Dm7
G7
3

(2)
Dm9
G9

Dm9
G7 (sus4)
G7

(3)
Dm11
3

G9

(4)
Dm9 (-5)
G13 (♭9)
3

Dm7 (-5)
G7

(5)
Dm11

G+7 (♭9)

(6)
Dm11

G7
3
3
3

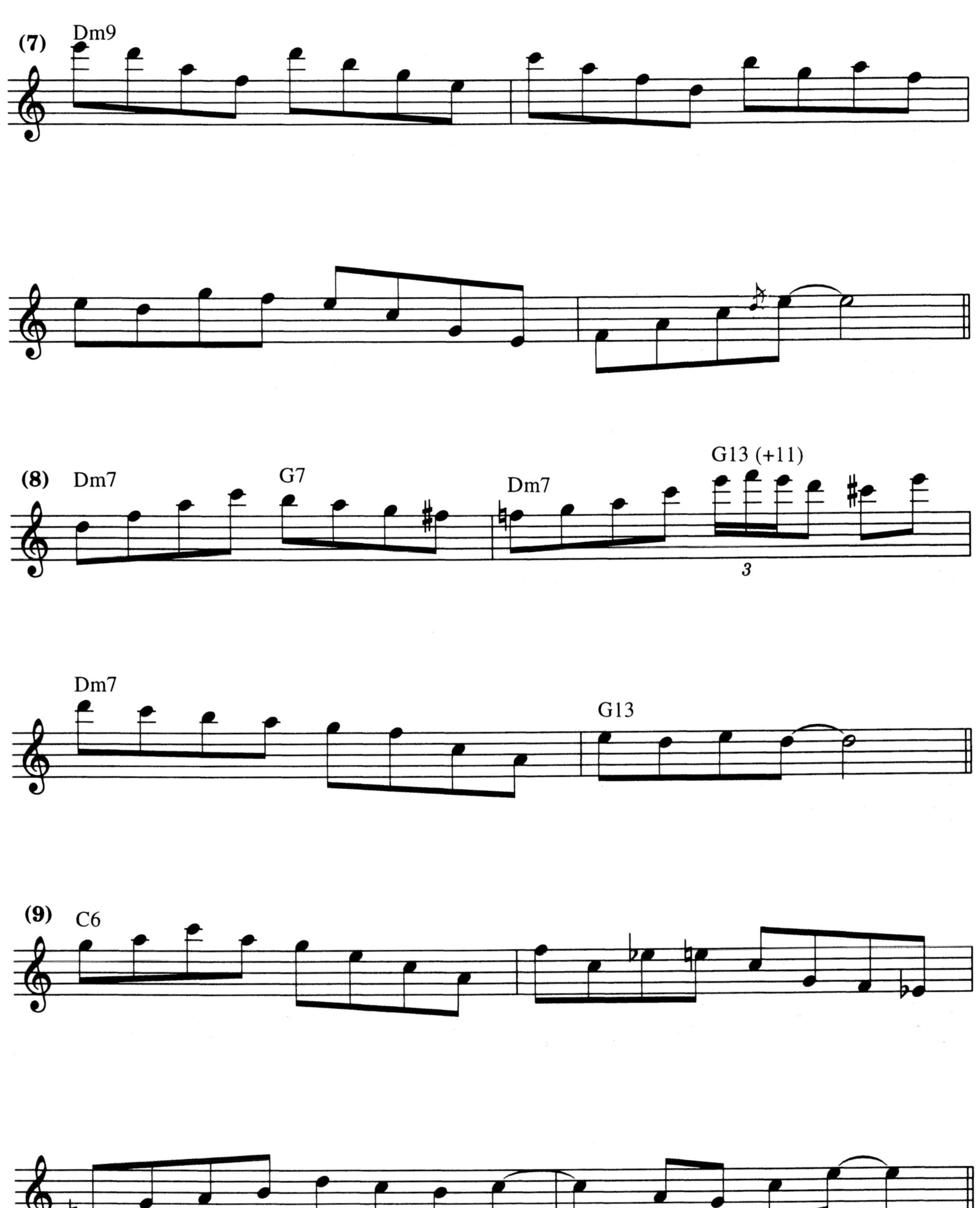
(7)
Dm9
(8)
Dm7
G7
Dm7
G13 (+11)
3
Dm7
G13
(9)
C6

C6
(10)

(11)
C
("Blues sound equals ♭7, ♭3, ♭5")

C6

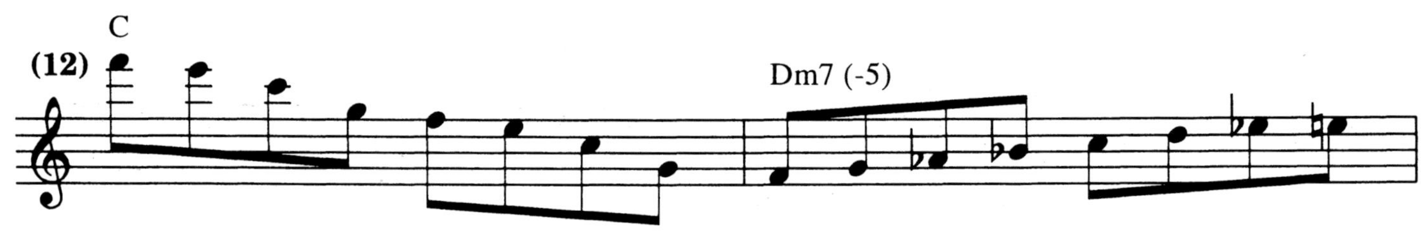
C
(12)
Dm7 (-5)

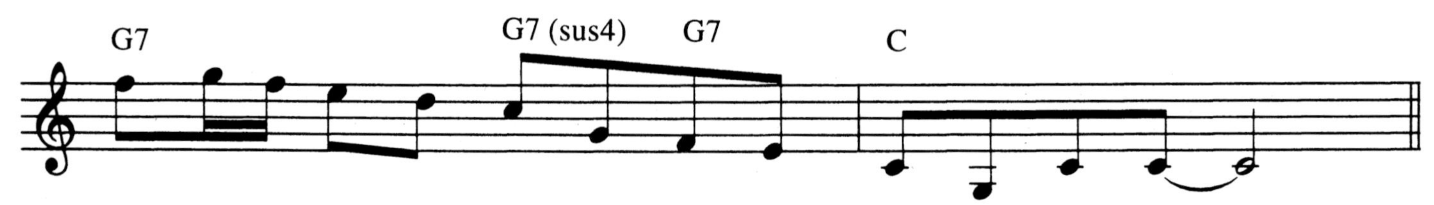
G7
G7 (sus4)
G7
C

(13)
Dm7
3

G+7 (+9)
G13 (♭9)
C6

(14)
C^7
3
3
Dm7
G+9

C6

(15)
C
"Blues sound" (♭7, ♭3, ♭5)

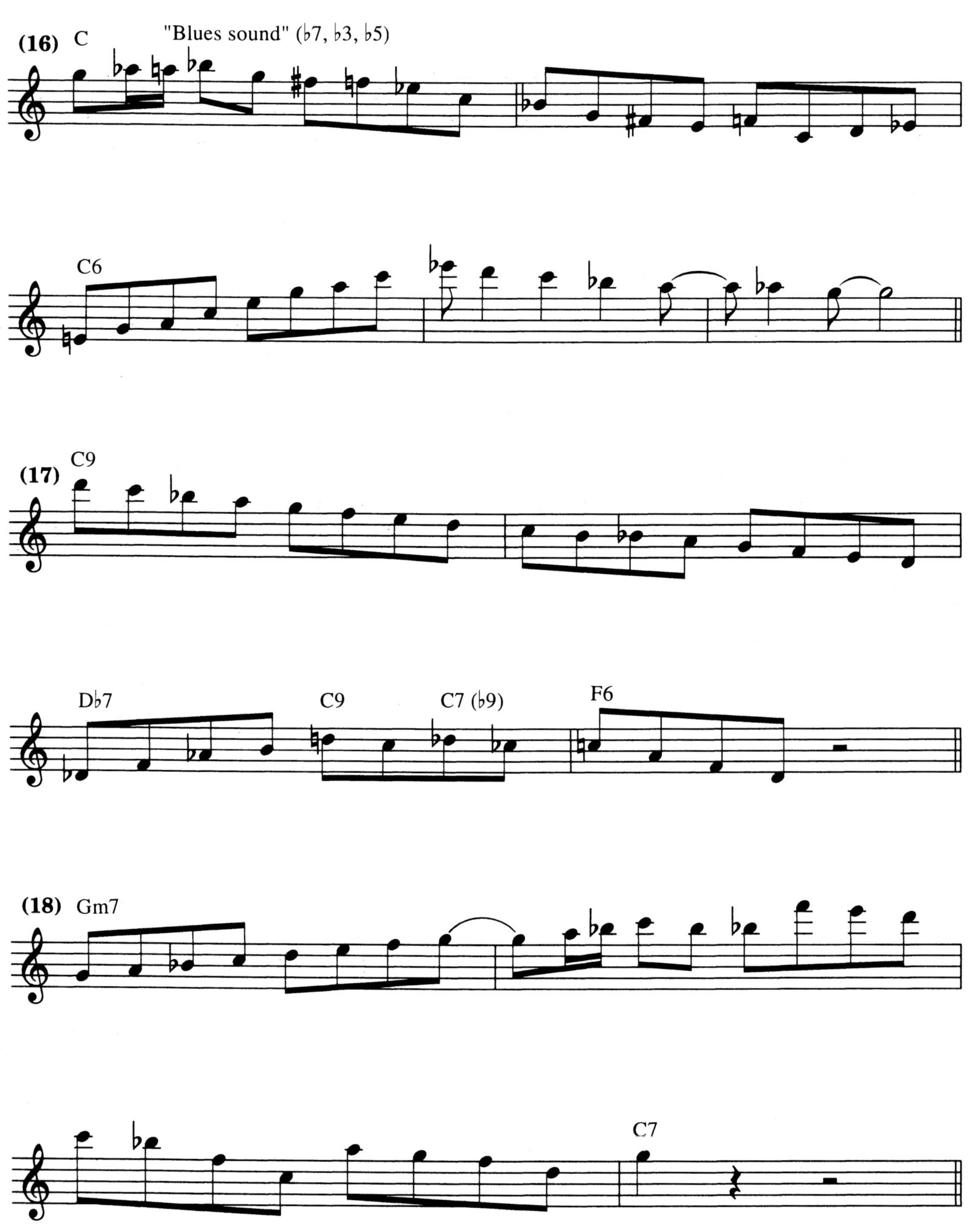
(16)
C
"Blues sound" (♭7, ♭3, ♭5)
C6
(17)
C9
D♭7
C9
C7 (♭9)
F6
(18)
Gm7
C7

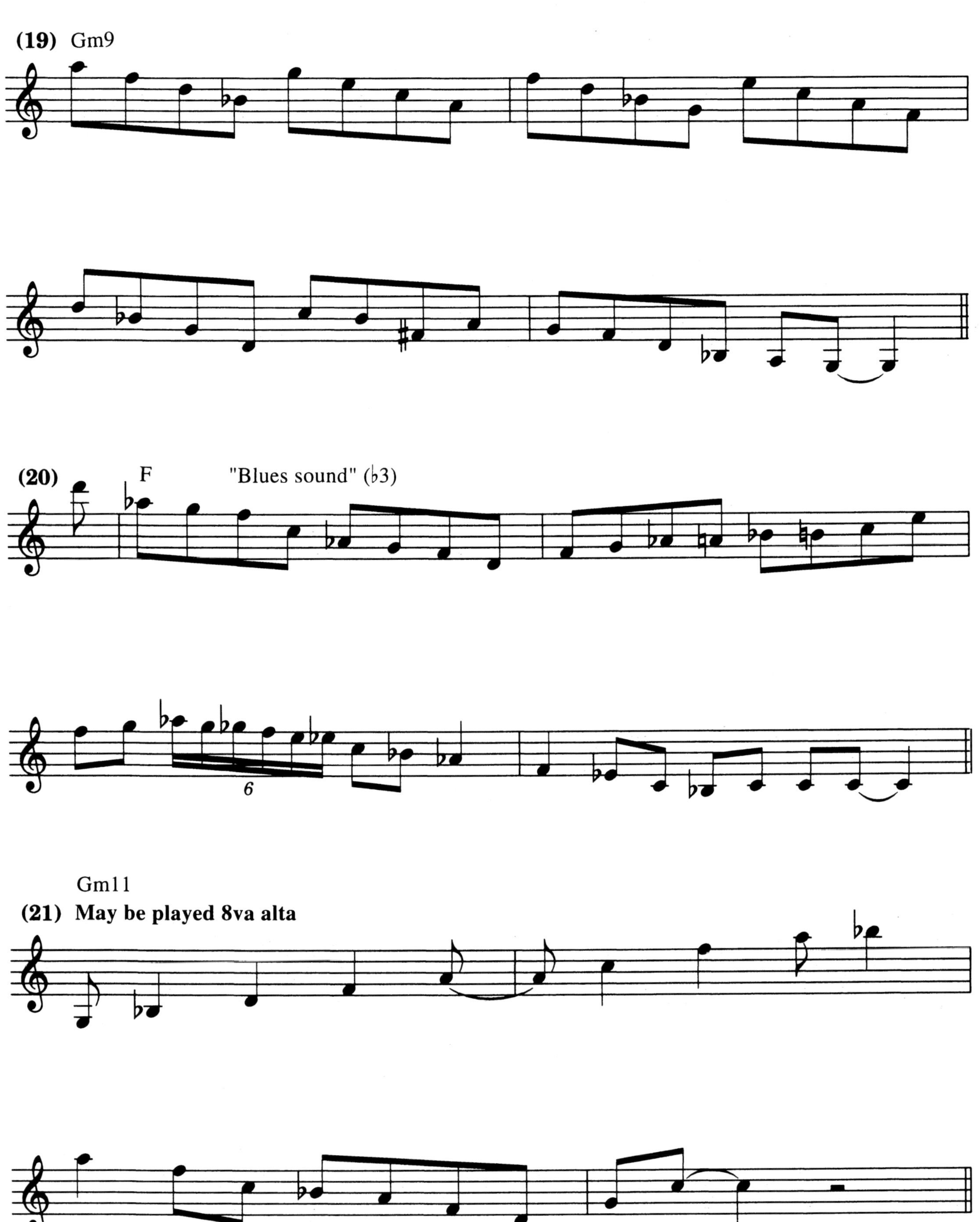
(19) Gm9
(20) F "Blues sound" (♭3)
6
Gm11
(21) May be played 8va alta

(22)
Gm9
(Am7)

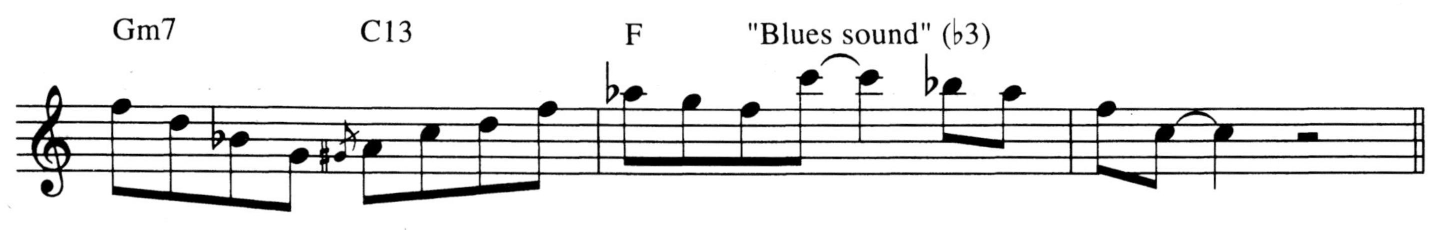
Gm7
C13
F
"Blues sound" (♭3)

(23)
F+7
(+9)

F+7
B13 (+9)
B♭m △7
B♭m6

(24)
F+7 (+9)

B♭m6/9

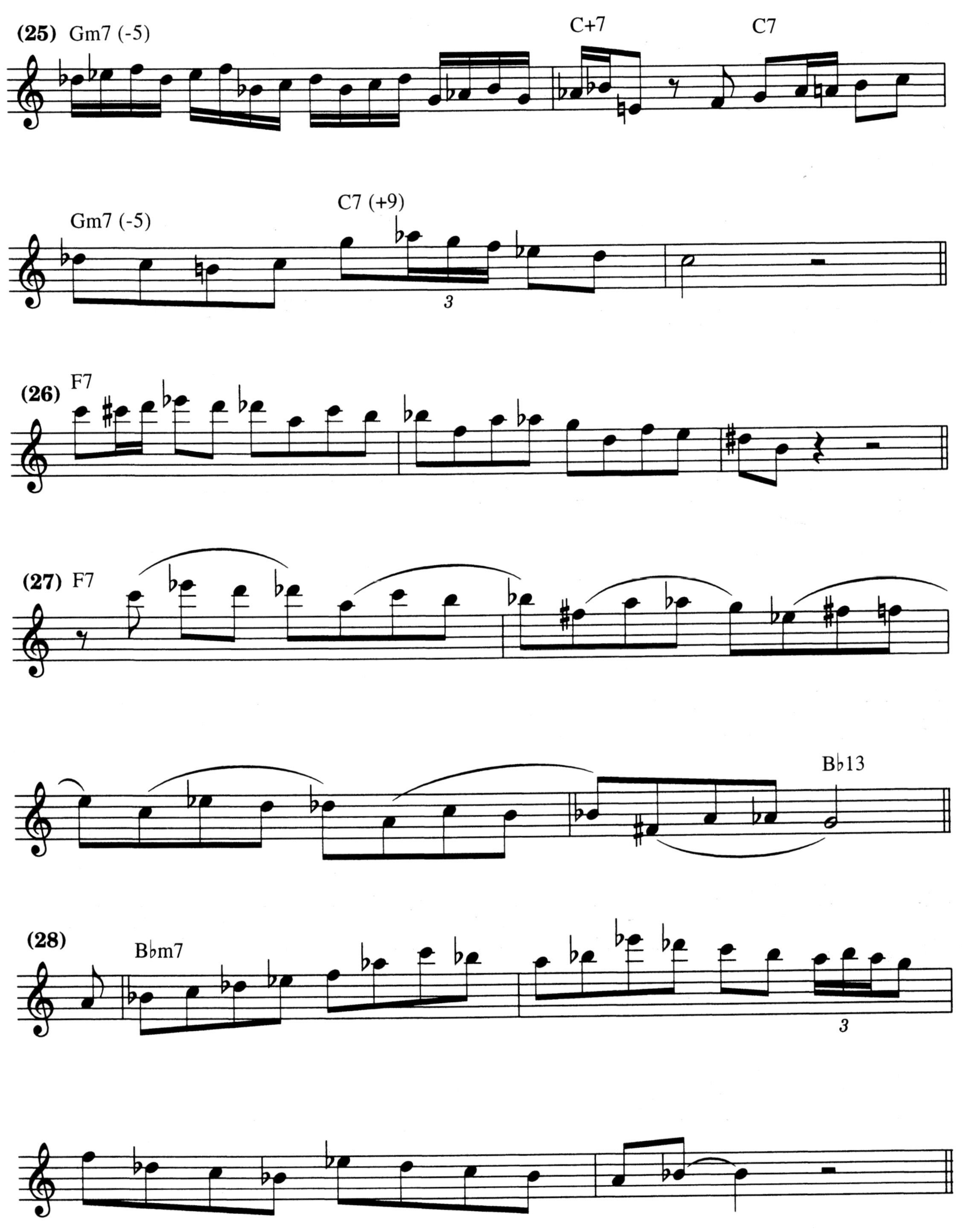

(25)
Gm7 (-5)
C+7
C7
Gm7 (-5)
C7 (+9)
3
(26)
F7
(27)
F7
B♭13
(28)
B♭m7
3

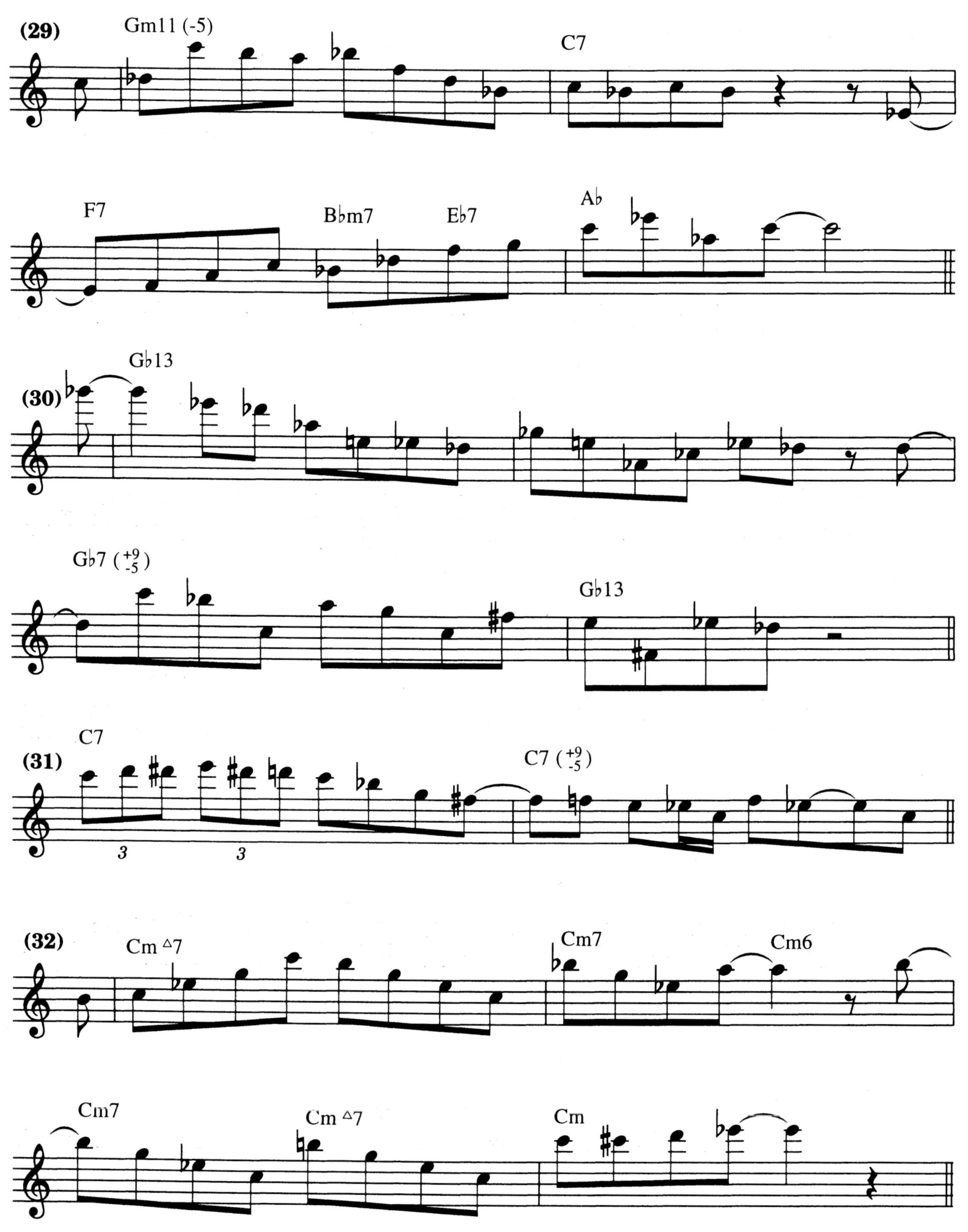
(29)
Gm11 (-5)
C7
F7
B♭m7
E♭7
A♭
(30)
G♭13
G♭7 (+9 -5)
G♭13
(31)
C7
C7 (+9 -5)
3
3
(32)
Cm △7
Cm7
Cm6
Cm7
Cm △7
Cm

(33)
B♭
"Blues sound" (♭3, ♭5)
(34)
B♭
"Blues sound" (♭7, ♭3, ♭5)
B♭
"Blues sound" (♭7, ♭3)
(35)
(F7)
B♭

(36)
B♭
"Blues sound" (♭3)

(E♭)
B♭

(37) B♭ △7
Cm7
C♯ ○7
B♭/D

B♭ △7
Cm7
C♯ ○7
B♭/D

(38)
B♭
B♭ △7

Cm11
F7
B♭6
(F7)
B♭

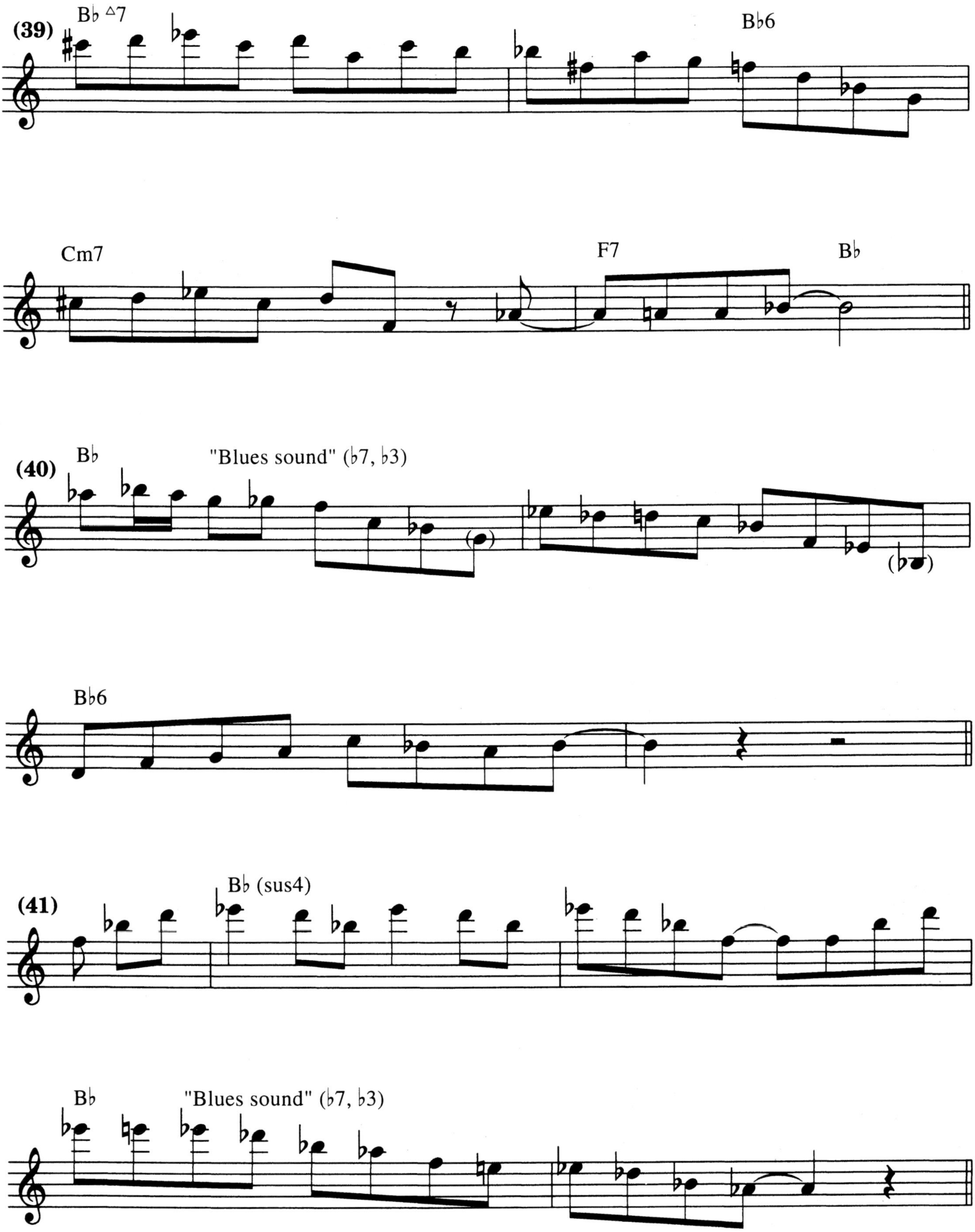
(39)
B♭△7
B♭6
Cm7
F7
B♭
(40)
B♭
"Blues sound" (♭7, ♭3)
B♭6
(41)
B♭ (sus4)
B♭
"Blues sound" (♭7, ♭3)

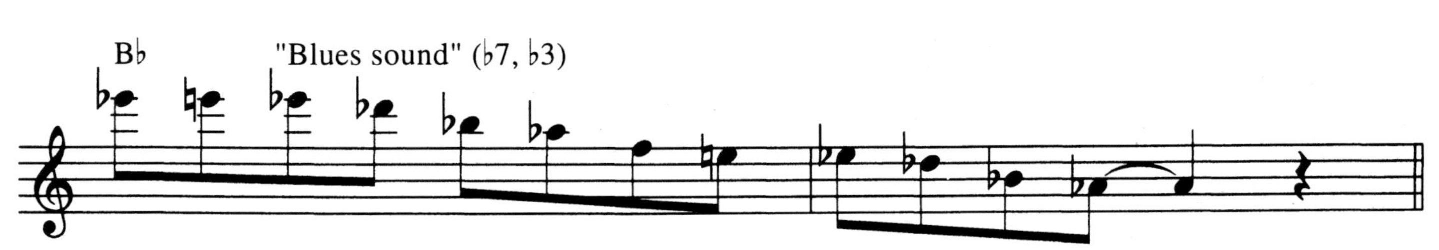

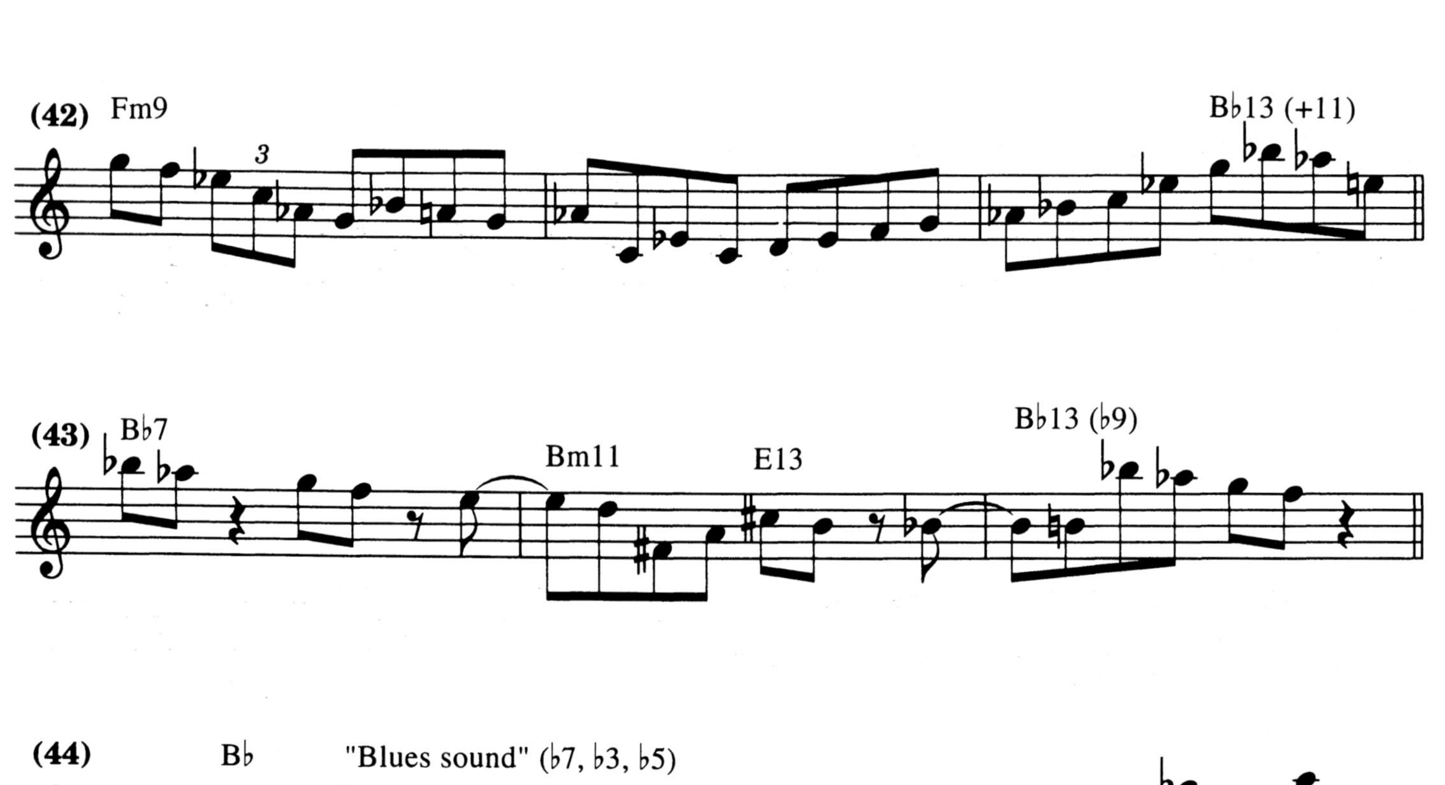
(42)
Fm9
3
B♭13 (+11)
(43)
B♭7
Bm11
E13
B♭13 (♭9)
(44)
B♭
"Blues sound" (♭7, ♭3, ♭5)

B♭7 (-5)

(45)
(B♭7)
B♭
"Blues sound" (♭7, ♭3, ♭5)

(46)
Cm7
F7
Fm7
B♭13

F♯m7
B7
B♭13 (♭9)

B♭+7 (♭9)

All B♭7, or as is indicated

(47) May be played 8va

PART FOUR

TRANSCRIPTIONS

"Bay City Blues"

Joe Pass

A–9
D13
G–9
G–9
C13
(F9)
(B♭9)
(F9)
(C–7)
3
(F9)
(B♭9)
P
P
H
P
3
P
(B♭9)
3
(A–9)
(D7)
(A♭ –7)
(D♭7)
3
(G–9)
(B♭ –9)
P
(E♭9)
H
P
3
(A–7)
(D7)
(G–7)
(C7)
3
(F9)
(B♭13)
P
H
(F9)
H
(F9+5)
3
3
(B♭13)
H
3

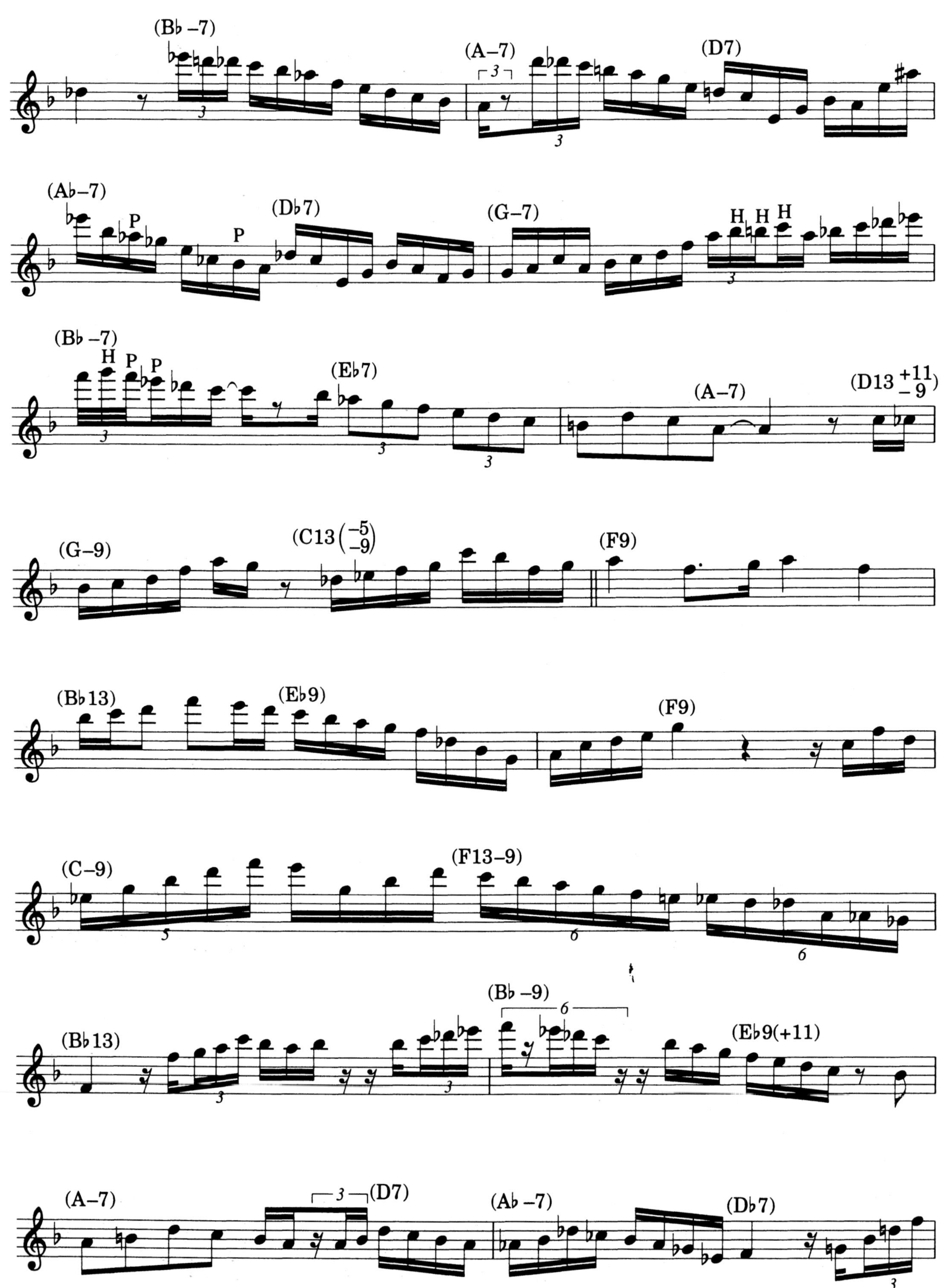
(B♭ –7)
(A–7)
(D7)
(A♭–7)
(D♭7)
(G–7)
(B♭ –7)
(E♭7)
(A–7)
(D13 +11 –9)
(G–9)
(C13 (–5 –9))
(F9)
(B♭13)
(E♭9)
(F9)
(C–9)
(F13–9)
(B♭13)
(B♭ –9)
(E♭9(+11)
(A–7)
(D7)
(A♭ –7)
(D♭7)

(G–7)
(B♭–7)
(E♭7)
(A–9)
(D13(–9 –5))
(G–9)
(C13(–9 –5))
(F9)
(B♭13)
(F9)
(F7alt.)
(B7)
(B♭13)
(B♭13)
(A–9)
(D13)
(A♭–9)
(D♭13)
(G–9)
H
(B♭–9)
(E♭9)
(A–7)
(A♭/D)

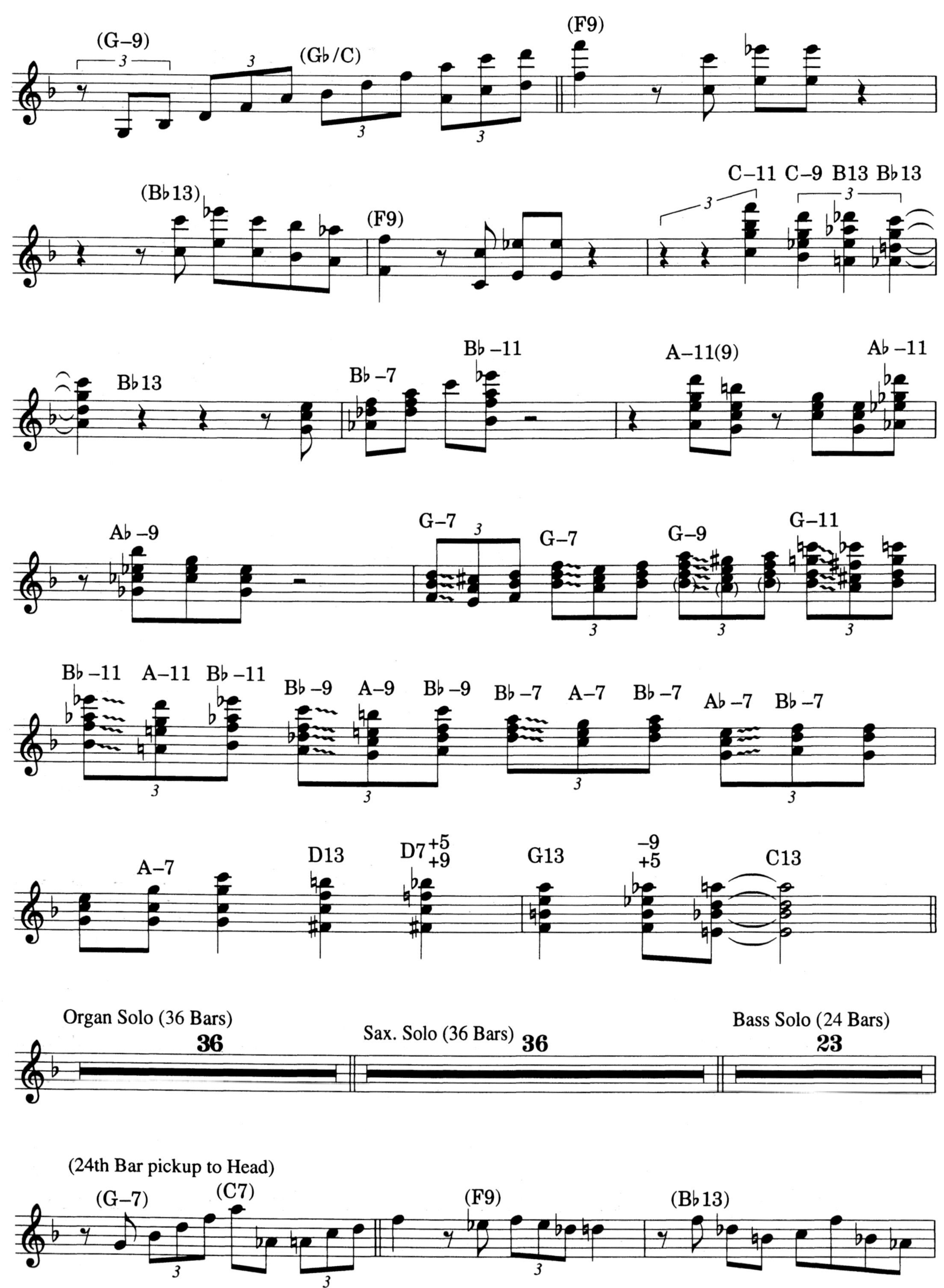
(G–9)
(G♭/C)
(F9)
(B♭13)
(F9)
C–11 C–9 B13 B♭13
B♭13
B♭–7
B♭–11
A–11(9)
A♭–11
A♭–9
G–7
G–7
G–9
G–11
B♭–11 A–11 B♭–11
B♭–9 A–9 B♭–9
B♭–7 A–7 B♭–7
A♭–7 B♭–7
A–7
D13
D7 +5 +9
G13
–9 +5
C13
Organ Solo (36 Bars)
36
Sax. Solo (36 Bars)
36
Bass Solo (24 Bars)
23
(24th Bar pickup to Head)
(G–7)
(C7)
(F9)
(B♭13)

(F9)
B9 B♭9
(B♭13)
B♭ –7
(A–9)
(D9)
(A♭ –7)
(D♭7)
(G–7)
P
(9)
B♭ –11 B–7 B♭ –7
B♭ –9 B♭ –7
A–9
D9
G–9
G–9 C13
F13
(B♭13)
(F9)
(F9)
B13
B♭9
(B♭9)
B♭ –9
B♭ –11 B–7 B♭ –7
A–7
(A♭ –7)
D♭9
G–7
G–9 C7
B♭ –11
B–7 B♭ –7
B♭ –9 E♭9
A–9
D13
G–7
C13
Fine
E7+9

"Foxy Chick and a Cool Cat"

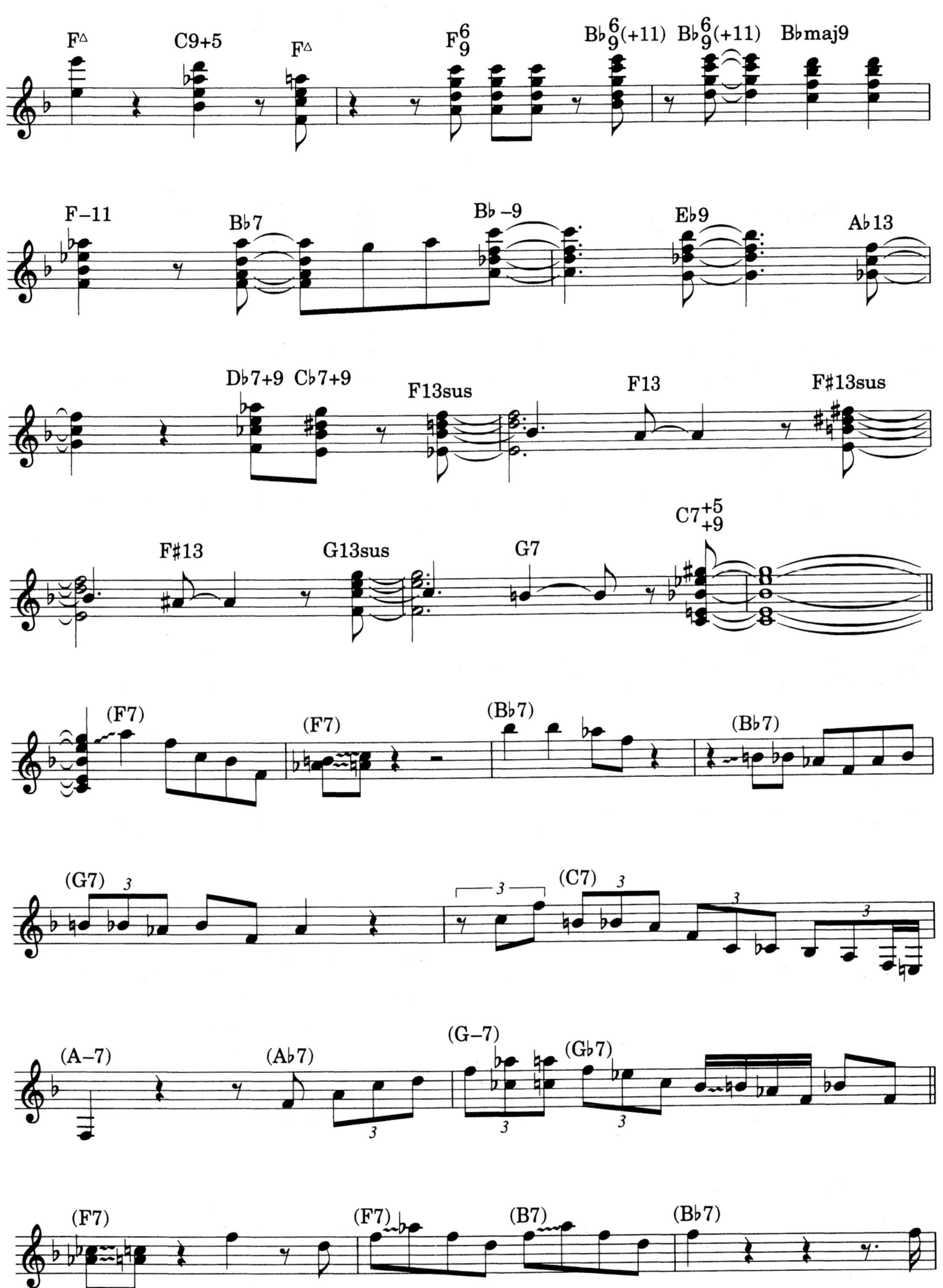

F△
C9+5
F△
F6/9
B♭6/9(+11)
B♭6/9(+11)
B♭maj9
F−11
B♭7
B♭−9
E♭9
A♭13
D♭7+9
C♭7+9
F13sus
F13
F♯13sus
F♯13
G13sus
G7
C7+5+9
(F7)
(F7)
(B♭7)
(B♭7)
(G7)
(C7)
(A−7)
(A♭7)
(G−7)
(G♭7)
(F7)
(F7)
(B7)
(B♭7)

(B♭13)
(G♯–9)
(C♯9(+11))
(G–7(–5))
(C7+5 +9)
(F△9)
(C–7)
(F7)
(B♭–7)
(E♭9)
(E7)
(F△)
(C–7)
(F7)
B♭–7
A–7
B♭–7
B♭–9
E♭13
E♭9
D♭9+5
(A–7)
(D7)
(G–7)
(C7)
(F7)
(F♯7)
(F7)
(B7)
(B♭7)
(B♭7)
(A♭7)
(G7alt.)
(C7alt.)
(F7alt.)
(D7alt.)
(G7alt.)
(C7alt.)
(F△)
(F7)

(B♭7)
B♭7
A7 A♭7 G7
(G7)
(C7)
(F7)
(C7alt.)
(F7)
F7+9
F7+9
(B♭13)
B♭13
(B♭13)
(A♭13)
(G7alt.)
(C7alt.)
(F7)
(C–7)
(F9)
(B♭–7)
(E♭9)
(E7)
(Fmaj)
E7
F7
(B7–5)
B♭–9
(7)
B♭–9

E♭13
D9+5
D9
D♭9+5
G–9
C13+9
(F7)
(F9)
(B♭13)
(+11)
(B♭13(+11)
(G13–9)
(C7alt.)
(F7+9)
(D7+9)
(D♭7+9)
(C7+9)
(F7)
(C–9)
(F7)
(B♭13)
(B♭13)
(G7+11)
(C7alt.)

(F7)
(D7)
(D♭7)
(C7)
(F7+9)
(F7+9)
(B♭13)
(B♭13)
(G7alt.)
(C7alt.)
(F 6 9)
(C7+9)
(C–9)
(F9)
(B♭–9)
(E♭9)
(Fmaj7)
(C–7)
(F7)
B♭–7
F7–9
B♭–7
B–9
E♭13
A–7
D7+9 5
G13
(C7 +9 +5)

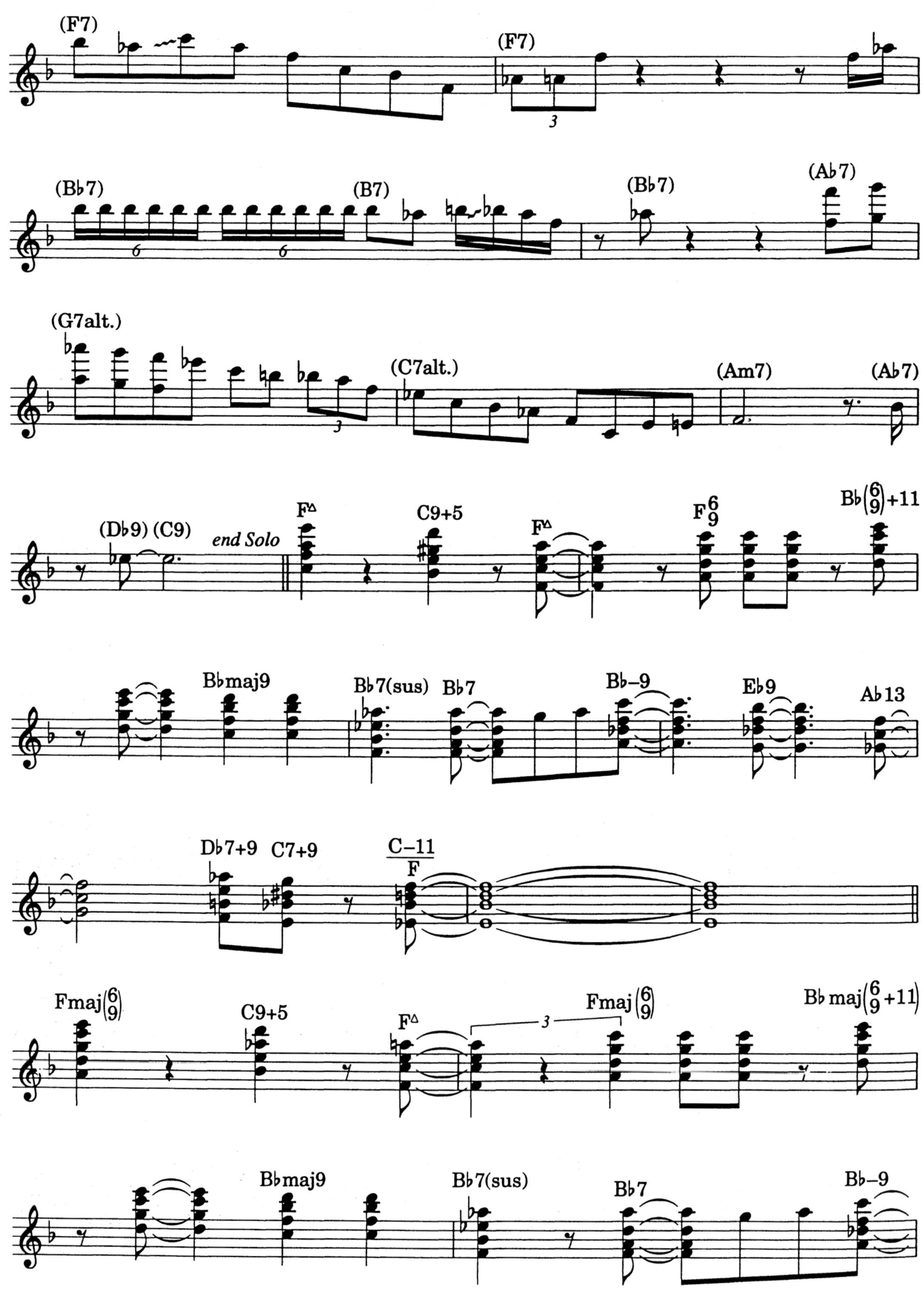
(F7)
(F7)
(B♭7)
(B7)
(B♭7)
(A♭7)
(G7alt.)
(C7alt.)
(Am7)
(A♭7)
(D♭9) (C9)
end Solo
F△
C9+5
F△
F6/9
B♭(6/9)+11
B♭maj9
B♭7(sus)
B♭7
B♭–9
E♭9
A♭13
D♭7+9
C7+9
C–11/F
Fmaj(6/9)
C9+5
F△
Fmaj(6/9)
B♭ maj(6/9+11)
B♭maj9
B♭7(sus)
B♭7
B♭–9

E♭9 A♭13 D♭7+9 C7+9 C–11/F
B♭–9 E♭9 B♭–9 B♭–9 E♭9 B♭–9 E♭9
Fmaj(add6) B♭–9 E♭13 B♭–9
B♭–9 E♭9 D♭9+5 C13+9
F△ C9+5 F△ F6/9 B♭ maj 6/9(+11)
B♭ maj 6/9(+11) B♭maj9 B♭7(sus) B♭7 (13) B♭–9
E♭9 A♭13 D♭7+9 C7+9 C–11/F F13 C♯–11/F♯
F♯13 D–11/G G13 C7+5/+9
Fine

"Time In"

Joe Pass

(G7+)
(C7)
3
(C7/ G♭)
(Fmaj)
(D–7)
(G–7)
(C9)
(Fmaj)
(F♯–7)
(B7)
(B♭7)
(B♭7)
(F7)
(D7)
(G–7)
(C7)
(C–7)
(F7)
(alt.)
(B♭7)
(B♭7)
(B♭7)
(E7/B♭)
(E♭7)
(E♭7)
(B♭7)
(E♭7)
(D–7)
(G7–9)
(C9)

(C–7)
(F7)
(B♭7)
(F–9)
(B♭7+)
(E♭7)
A7(–5)
A♭7
A7
B♭7
E♭7+9
C7+9
B♭–7
E♭7+9
A♭7
(A°)
(E♭7)
(A♭7)
(G–7)
(C–7)
(G♯–7)
(C♯7)
(F^ø)
(E/B♭)
(E♭7)
(B♭–7)
(E♭7–9)
(A♭7)
(E♭13)
(E♭–7)
A♭13
A13
A♭13
A♭7
D♭13
C13
D♭13
D13
D♭7
D♭13
D13
D♭7
G9
A♭9
G9
A♭9
G♭7
G♭9

Gb13 Gb7 F7+9 Bb13 B13 A7 Bb7
Bb –11 Bb –9 (Eb7) (Ab7) (A7) (Ab) Ab13 (–5)
Db6/9 D9+5 Db9
D9 Db9 G7 Gb7 D9+5 Db9
(Db9) Eb –9 E–9 Eb –9 Gb△/ Ab
Gb△/ Ab G△/ A (A13)
(D7) (G7) (G#°) (D7) (Eb9)
(D7+9) Ab13 G7 (G#°)

(D6/9) (F♯–7) (B7) (E–7)
(A13) (Dmaj(add 6/9)) (Cmaj(add 6/9)) (B♭ maj(add 6/9)) (A7alt.)
(D6/9) (A7) E♭9(+5) D9
(A–7) (D7(–9)) (G7) E♭9
D9 (F♯–11) (F–11) (E–11)
(E- 9) (A13) (D7+9) (D7+9)
G7+9 G♭ 7+9 G7+9 C7 F7 B♭7 E♭7 D7 D♭7 D7 D♭7 C7
B7 C7 C♯7 C7 C7

F7
B♭7
A7
D7
(–5)
G7
(E♭maj)
(Emaj)
(Fmaj)
(F♯maj)
(E–7)
(D–9)
(C–9)
(B♭ –9)
(A–9)
(C–9)
(C♯ –9)
(D–9)
(D–7)
(G7–9)
(G7alt.)
(G7alt.)
(C7)
(C7)
(G–9)
(C7 -9 +5)
3
(F9)
(F♯ -7 -5)
(B7alt.)

(Cmaj 6/9) (F9) B♭9 A7 (D–7)
(G7) (Cmaj 6/9) (A7+5) (D7 +5 +9) (G7 +5 –9)
(Cmaj) (B♭maj)
(A♭maj)
(G11) (G7)
C7 (F7) (F♯°) (C7)
C7+9 (F7) (F♯°)
(C7) (F7) (E–7) (A7) (D–9) (11)

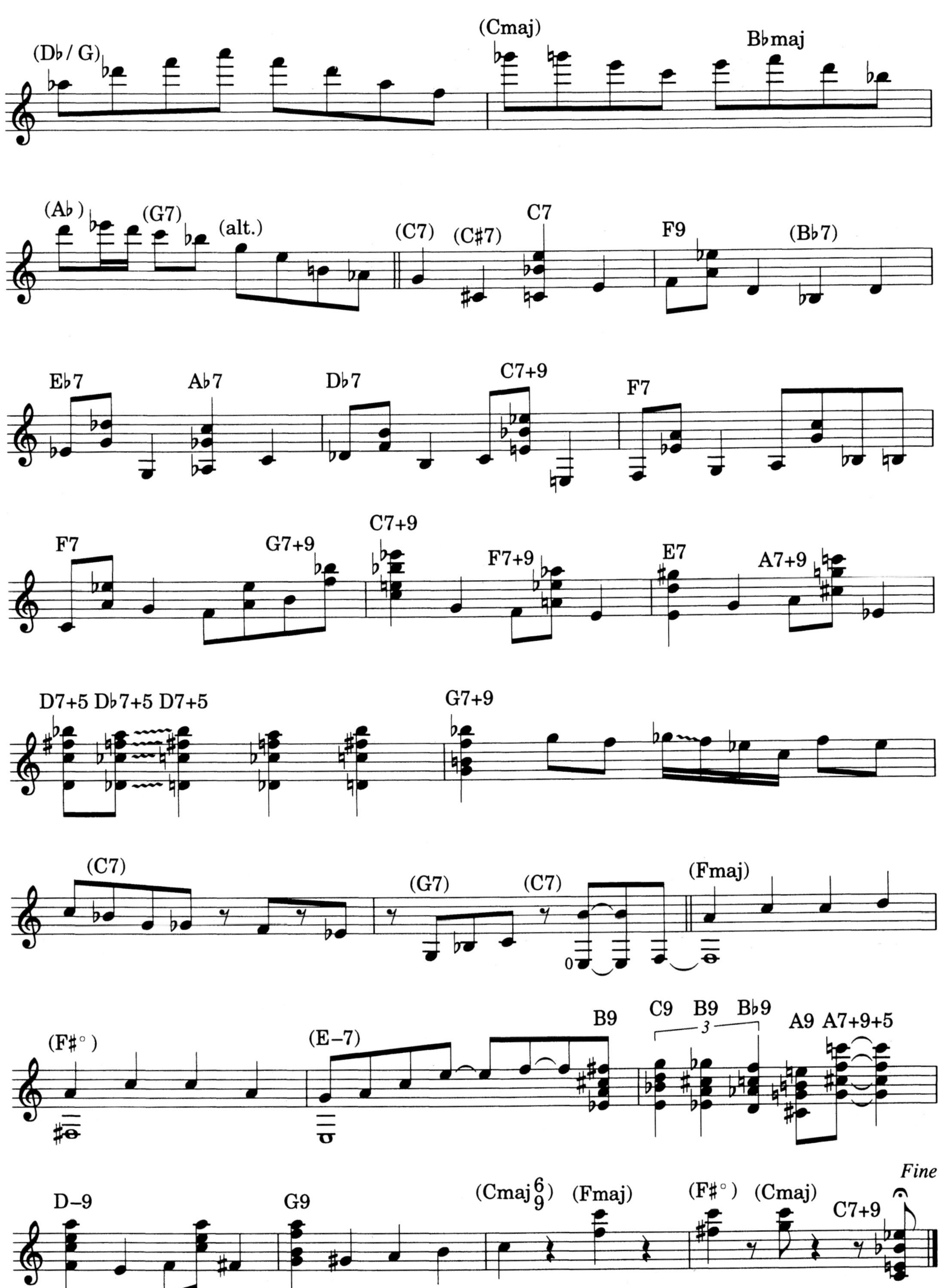

(D♭/G)
(Cmaj)
B♭maj
(A♭)
(G7)
(alt.)
(C7)
(C♯7)
C7
F9
(B♭7)
E♭7
A♭7
D♭7
C7+9
F7
F7
G7+9
C7+9
F7+9
E7
A7+9
D7+5 D♭7+5 D7+5
G7+9
(C7)
(G7)
(C7)
0
(Fmaj)
(F♯°)
(E–7)
B9
C9
B9
B♭9
3
A9
A7+9+5
D–9
G9
(Cmaj 6/9)
(Fmaj)
(F♯°)
(Cmaj)
C7+9
Fine

Blues In G

♩ = 170
a tempo
(GM) F7 F♯7 G7
(G7) (A♭7) (G♭7)(G7)
(C7) B♭7 B7 C7
(C7)
H P P
(C♯°)
(GM) (B7) E7
(B♭7)+11
A7
D7+9
A♭7
G7
F♯7 F7 E7
(B♭7)
A7
D7+9
(A♭7)
(G13) F7 F♯7 G7
(G13)
H P P
(D♭7+9/G)
(C7) B♭7 B7 C7
(F7)
(F♯7)
(G7)
E7+9
B♭13
A9
(open/pos.)
D7+9
A♭7
G7
Cmaj
(C♯○)
(GM)
A♭7
G7
(F7)
F♯7
(G♯7)
A7
B♭7
B7
B♭7
B7
E7
C♯-7
C11
B-7
(F7)
E7
E7/B♭

(A9) (A13) (A13) (A13/E) (C/D)
(A-7) (D7) FM F♯M G7+9 (G♯7+9) (G7+9) D♭7
C7 F7 B♭7 E♭7 A♭7 D♭7 C7 C♯○ (GM) (F7) E7 B♭7(+11)
A9 D7+9 G7+9 F♯7(+9) F7(+9) E7 (E7/B♭) A9 D7+9 A♭7
G7 (A♭7) (G7) D♭9 C9 (D♭9)
(C9) (C♯○) (G7+9) (B7) E7+9 B♭7+11 A9 D7
G7+9 (B7) E7+9 B♭7 A9 D7+9 A♭7 G7 (D7+9)
(G13) (D♭7+9) (C9) (D♭9) (C9) (C♯○)

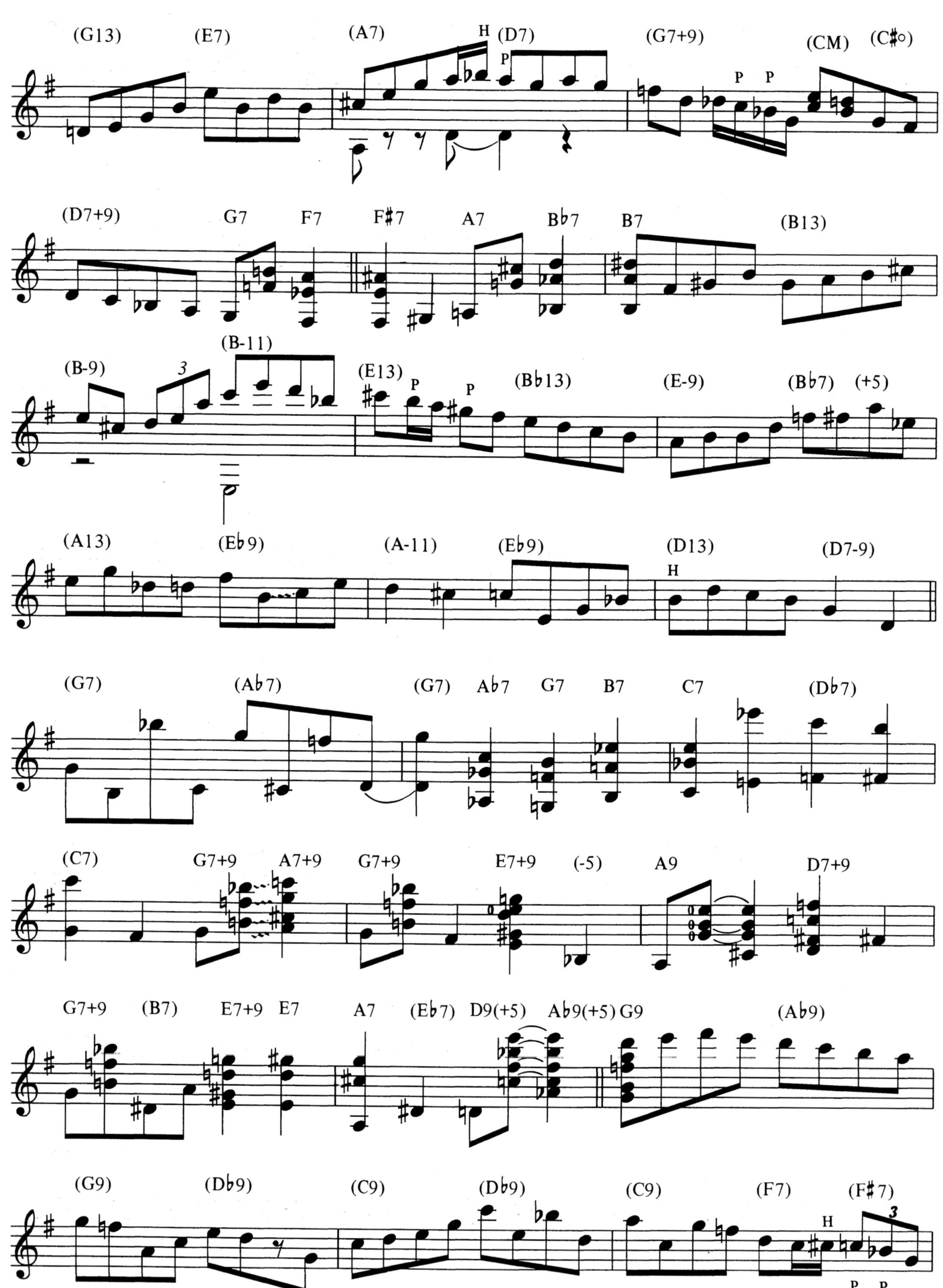
(G13) (E7) (A7) H (D7) P (G7+9) P P (CM) (C♯○)
(D7+9) G7 F7 F♯7 A7 B♭7 B7 (B13)
(B-9) 3 (B-11) (E13) P P (B♭13) (E-9) (B♭7) (+5)
(A13) (E♭9) (A-11) (E♭9) (D13) H (D7-9)
(G7) (A♭7) (G7) A♭7 G7 B7 C7 (D♭7)
(C7) G7+9 A7+9 G7+9 E7+9 (-5) A9 D7+9
G7+9 (B7) E7+9 E7 A7 (E♭7) D9(+5) A♭9(+5) G9 (A♭9)
(G9) (D♭9) (C9) (D♭9) (C9) (F7) (F♯7) H 3 P P

(G7) (E7+9) A7 D7 G7+9 E♭7+9 E7+9 (B♭13-9)
A9 D7+9 A♭7 G7 H (D9) (D-9) (D♭9) (+5) P
(G-9) (G-11) (G-9) (C9) H 6 (F9) (E7+9)
(E♭maj9) (D7+9) (GM7) (C9+11) (GM9) (G♭M9) (GM9)
(F♯ø) +9 (B7+5) 6 E9 C♯-7 C11 B-7
(F7) +5 E7+9 (B♭7) A7 (A7-5) (A7/E♭)
(C/D) H 3 P (D13) (D13(-9) (G7+9) (G13)
(G7) D♭7 C7 (D♭9) H P (C9) (F7) (F♯7)

Blues
B7 E7 (-9) B♭7(+11) A9 D7+9 (A♭7) G7 (F♯7) (F7) E7 E7/B♭
A9 D7+9 A♭7 G13 (G♭13) G13 G13 (G♭13) G13
(open/pos.)
C9 B9 C9 C9 B9 C9 G7+9 (B7) (open) E7+9 B♭7
A9 D7+9 (♮9) G7+9 (F7) E7(-9)(+5) (A9) A9 (E♭7) D7(-9) A♭9
ant.
G9 (A♭9) (G13) (D♭7+9) (C9)
(C9) (D7+9)(-9) (B-9) (B♭-9) (A-9) (D13)
(GM9) (C13) (B-7/G) (F♯-7) (C9)
(B9) (B13) (B13/F) E7+9 F7+9 E7+9 (E7) E7+9 E9 (B♭7)

A7+5 H (Bb-7) (Eb9) (C/D) -5 (D7-9)
(Ab7/D) (G13) (Ab13) H (D-9) H H P P P (Db7+9)
(C9) H (Db9) P (C#o) (D Bass Pedal)
(G7) (Bb7) A7 Ab7
G7 Bb7 B7 C7 Db7 D7 Db7 C7 F7 Bb7 Eb7
Ab7 Db7 C7 A– (GM) (F7) E7 E7-5 A9 D7+9 (Ab7)
G13 F#9 F13 (E9) Eb9 D13 Ab7(+9) (DBL. 3rd) G13 (Ab13)
(G13) Ab7 G7 B9 C9 (G-7) (G-9) H P (C13)

(D Bass Pedal) (D Bass Pedal) (G7) (CM) (C♯○)
(G7) (F♯-7) (B13) (F/B)
(D/E) (E13) (B♭7) (A7) (E9)
H—H—H
(A7) (E♭9) (A-7) (B♭-7) (D9) (A♭13)
H P
6 (G9) 6 (G9) +5 (D♭7+9) (C9) (D♭9)
H H H
(C9) (C9+11) 6 (G9) (B♭○) (A-7) +5 (D7+9)
H H H H
G7 A♭7 B♭7 (D7) E♭7 D♭7 D7+9 A♭7 G7 A♭7 G7 A♭7
G7 A♭7 G7 C7 (B7) (C9) (F7) (F♯7)

(B-7) (E9) (A7) E♭7 D7 (A♭7) G7+9 E7 E7+9 B♭13-9
A9 D7+9 A♭7 G7 H (G♭7) (G7) H P (D♭7+9)
C9 H H H B9 (C9) (C♯°) H P (GM) (F♯7) (F7) (E7)
(A-7) (D13) (G13) (D7+9) P (G7) B♭7
B7 (C7+5) (B13) H (F9) P P (D/E) P
(E7+9) P P (E7-9) (A7) H H H (B♭7) (A7)(-5) (A7)
(A-11) (E♭9) P (D9) P (A♭7) (GM) (CM) C♯°
(GM) A♭7 G7 B7 (C7) (B7) (C7) D♭7 C7 A♭9(+5)

G9 F7 E7+9 -9 B♭13 A9 C♯7+9 D7+9 A♭7 G7 B7 E7+9 B♭7
A9 D7+9(-5) (G7) (D7+9) (G7) P P (G7/D♭)
(C9) (D♭9) (C9) P P (F7) (F♯7) (G7) (F7) (E7) (B♭7)
(A-7)(+5) +5 (D7+9)(-9) (GM+5) (A♭M+5) (AM+5) H H (B♭M+5) H
(G9) (A♭9) H P (G9) (D♭9) (C9) (D♭9)
(C9) (C♯o) P (G7+9) (E7+9) (A13) P (D7+9)
add (GM7)(9 6) +5 (D7+9) 6 (G9) C7 B7 B13 C13
B13 B♭13 B13 F9 E9 (E9+11) (E7+9) P (E7-9) P

(E-9) (F-9) (B♭13) (E-9) (A13/E♭) (C/D) (D♭/E♭)
(C/D) (D7-9) (G7+9) (A♭13) (G13) (D♭7+9)
(C9) (B9) (C9) (C♯o) (G7+9) (E♭7+9) (E7+9) (B♭13)
(A13) (E♭7+9) (D7+9) (A♭13)(GM7 add 6/9) (E7 +5/+9) (E♭9+5) (D13)
(G13) (G7) (G7-5) (D♭7-9) (C9) (C♯9)
(D9) (F9) (B-7) (B-9) (B♭-9) (E♭13)
(A♭9 6) (C/D) (D13)(-9) (G9 6) E-7 E♭-7
D-7 A♭7 G7 C9 (B9) (C9) (C♯o)

(G7+9) E♭7+9 E7+9 B♭7 A9 D7+9 A♭7 G7
(G7) F♯7 (F♯-7) B13 C13 B13 F9
accel.
E9 (F9+5) (E9) (E7+9) (E-9) H H (E-11) P P P
(E-9) P P (A13) (A-9) (B♭-9) (A-9) +5 (D7+9)
(G7+9) (G7+9) (D♭7) (C7)
(C♯o) (G7+9) (E♭7+9) (E7+9) (B♭13) P (A13) (E♭7+9) (D7+9) (A♭13)
(G13) D7 C7 C♯7 F♯7+9 G7+9 F♯7(+9) G7(+9) F♯7 (+9) G7+9
G7(+9) G♭7(+9) G7(+9) D♭7 C13 B13 C13

C♯○
C○
C♯○
G♭7(+9)
G7(+9)
E7+9(-5)
E9(add+5)
A7(-5 -9)
E♭13
D7(-9 +5)
G♭7(+9)
G7(+9)
D♯7(+9)
E7(+9)
B♭13
A9
D7+9
(G7+9)
H H
3
(G7+9)
D♭7
D♭9
C9
H
3
(C9)
(C♯○)
P P
(G7+9)
(E7+9)
H P P
(A13)
D7(+5 +9)
(G6 9)
(A♭6 9)
(G6 9)
B7/F
(-5 E7-9)
F13
B-9/E
B-11
B-9
F9
E9
F9
E7+9
B♭7
A9
(A13)
H
3
(E-9)
(E♭7+9)
P P P
(C/D)
(+5 D7+9)
P P
(A♭13)

(G13) (A♭13) (G13) (D♭7+9) (C9) (D♭9)
3 3 3
(C9) (C♯○) G7 C7 B7 B♭7 A7 (+5) D9
3
G7 G♭7 G9 -9 D7+5 (A♭13) P (G13) (A♭13) P
(G13) (D♭9) (C9) (C♯○)
(C♯○) (A-7) P (D9) (GM9) (A-7)
(B♭M) (A♭M) (G13) (A♭13) (G13) (D♭9)
C9 G-11 G-7 G-9 C9 (F7) P P (F♯7) (G7) (F7) E7(-5)
3
A9 D7(+9) G♭7(+9) G7(+9) (D7+9) (GM7) (add9)

B7 (B♭7) B7 C7 B7 B♭7 B7 (D♯7) E7 C♯-7 C11
B-7 (F7) E7 (-5) A9 E-7 E7+9
(A-7) D13 E♭13 A♭9 G9 (A♭9+5)
(G9) P D♭9 C9 (B9) (C9) (C♯○)
(G7+9) E♭7 E7(+9) (B♭13) A9 D7(+9) A♭7
G7 G7 D♭9 C9 H H H (D♭9)
(C9) B9 C9 H H (B9) H (C9) (C♯○) G♭9
G9 (A♭9) (G9) (C7) F7 E7 (E7+9) P

(E7+9) (B♭13) (A13(-9)) (E♭9) (D9)
(E♭9) (D9) (C♯7) (D7) (E♭7) (D7)
(C♯7) (D7) H (G7) H (D♭9) C9 C♯○
GM7 C♯○ C9 GM9/B (F7) (E7) (+5) (-5)
A7 (E♭7) D7 G7 C♯7 C7 B7 B♭7 A7 A♭7
G7 D♭9 C9 (B9) (C9) C♯○ (D7) A♭9+5 G♭9 G9
F7+9 E7+9 B♭7 (A-7) (B-7) (CM) (C♯○) (C/D) (D13-9)
G6 9 (CM) (C♯○) GM G6 9 G13
Fine

Dante's Inferno

(G7) (D♭7) C7 (Fmaj) (F♯○) (G7) (D♭7)
C7 (F7) (C7) D♭7
D♭9 C9 (F7) (F7) (B○)
(C7) (B7) (B♭7) (A7) (D7+9)
+9
(G7+5) (CMaj) (A7) (D9) (G13) H P
Solo
(C7) (F7) P (C7)
(G-7) (C9) (F7) (F7) H P P (F♯○)
(C7) (B7) (B♭7) P (A7) (D7+9) H P

+9
(G7+5)
P
(C7)
(A7)
(D9)
(G13)
(C7)
(F7)
(C7)
H P
(G-7)
(C9)
(F7)
P
(F7)
(F♯○)
(C7)
H
(F9)
(E-7)
(B♭9)
(A7)
(E♭7)
(D9)
(A♭7)
(G13)
(C7)
(B♭7)
(A7)
(E♭9)
(D9)
(A♭7)
(G7)
(D♭9)
(C9)
(F7)
(G-7)
(D♭9)
(C9)
(G♭7)
P
(F7)
(F7)
P
P
(F♯○)
(C7)
(F9)
(E-7)
P P
(B♭7)
(A7)
(E♭9)
(D-7)
(A♭7)

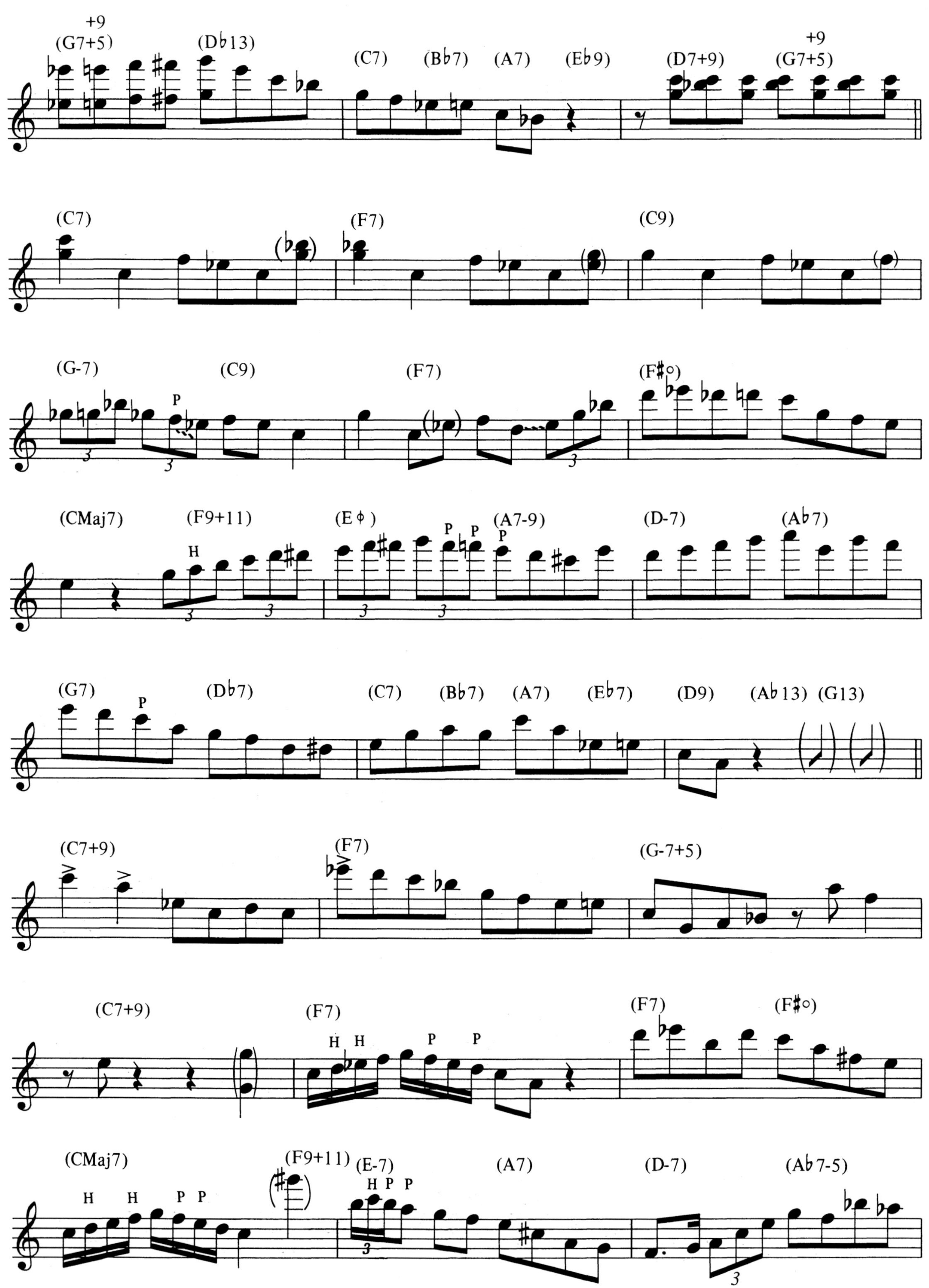
(G7+5) +9
(Db13)
(C7)
(Bb7)
(A7)
(Eb9)
(D7+9)
(G7+5) +9
(C7)
(F7)
(C9)
(G-7)
(C9)
(F7)
(F#○)
(CMaj7)
(F9+11)
(E ϕ)
(A7-9)
(D-7)
(Ab7)
(G7)
(Db7)
(C7)
(Bb7)
(A7)
(Eb7)
(D9)
(Ab13)
(G13)
(C7+9)
(F7)
(G-7+5)
(C7+9)
(F7)
(F7)
(F#○)
(CMaj7)
(F9+11)
(E-7)
(A7)
(D-7)
(Ab7-5)

+9
(G7+5)
-9
(G7+5)
(E-7)
H
(A7)
(D-7)
(D♭9)
(C7)
(G♭7)
F9
C13
(C7)
(G-7)
(G♭7)
(F7)
H
(F7)
(F♯○)
C△+11
H P
(F9+11)
(E-7) (B♭7)
(A7)
(E♭9)
D9(+11)
(G13-9)
(E⦰)
(A13-9)
P
(D⦰)
-9
(G7 13)
C7+9
(F7)
P
C7+9(11)
(G-7(+5)
(G♭13)
(F7)
H
P
H P
H
(F7)
H
(F♯○)
H
(C7)
(F9)
(E-7)
(E♭-7)
(D-7)
H P P

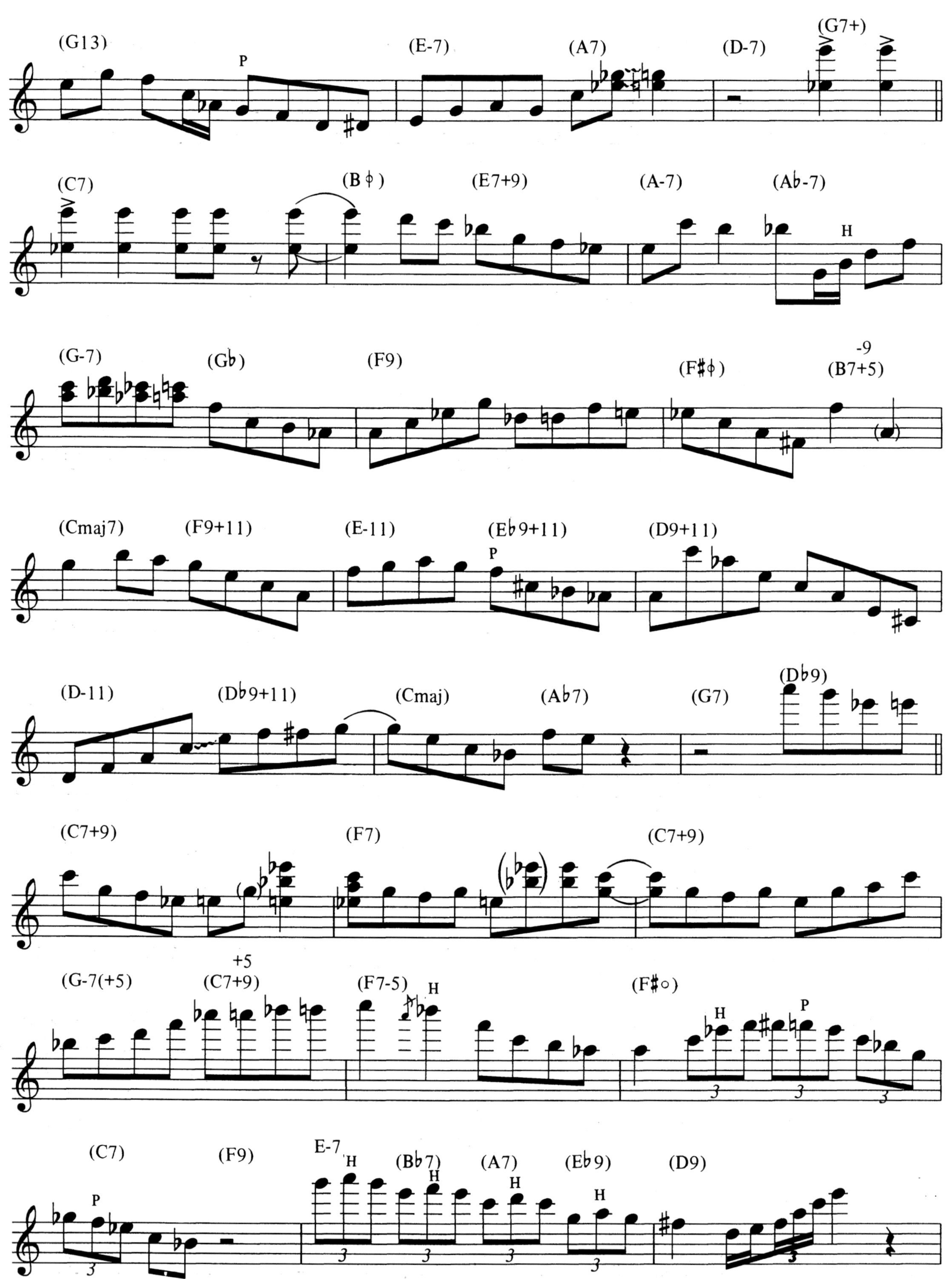
(G13)
P
(E-7)
(A7)
(D-7)
(G7+)
(C7)
(Bø)
(E7+9)
(A-7)
(A♭-7)
H
(G-7)
(G♭)
(F9)
(F♯ø)
-9
(B7+5)
(Cmaj7)
(F9+11)
(E-11)
(E♭9+11)
P
(D9+11)
(D-11)
(D♭9+11)
(Cmaj)
(A♭7)
(G7)
(D♭9)
(C7+9)
(F7)
(C7+9)
(G-7(+5))
+5
(C7+9)
(F7-5)
H
(F♯○)
H
P
(C7)
P
(F9)
E-7
H
(B♭7)
H
(A7)
H
(E♭9)
H
(D9)

(D-9) P (G13) H P (Eϕ) (E♭9) (D9) (D♭9)
(C9) (F13) H P P (C7)
(G-7) (G♭7) (F9) (C-7) (F9)
(Eϕ) (A13-9) (D7+9) H P
+9 (G7+5) H (E-7) (A7) (D-7) +9 G7+5 C13
C13 +5 G7+9 C13 G♭13 F9 E9 F9 +5 G7+9 C13 C13 +5 G7+9 C13 +5 G7+9
(C7-5) (C7) C7(+9) F9 F9 F13-9 C° C♭° C° C♭° C° B7+9
C7+9 C13 C7 B♭7 A7 A7+5 D-9 D-9

(G13-9)
H
6
(C9)
C9 (anticipated)
C9
Cb9 C9 Cb9 C9 Cb9
Cb9 C9
(G-7)
H
(C13)
(F9)
(F#ø)
(B7)
(C7)
(Bb7)(+11)
(E - 7)
(Eb9(+5)
(D-7)
(Ab7)
(G7)
(Db9)
(C7)
(A7)
P
(D-7)
(G7)
(Cb7+9) C7+9
F9
F9
Cb9
C9
+9
(C7+5)(C7)
C13
C13
(Gb13)
(F7)
(F#○)
(Cmaj)
(F9)
(Eø)
(A7)
(D-7)
(Ab7)

(G7)
(D♭9)
(C9)
+9
(A7+5)
(D-7)
+9
(G7+5)
P
(C7+9)
P
(F7)
P
(C7+9)
[simile/attack]
P
P
(C7)
(G♭7)
P
(F7)
P
(F♯○)
(C7)
(F9)
(E-7)
A13(+9)
(D7+9)
P
P
(D♭7+9)
(C7+9)
+9
(G7+5)
(C7)
F9
(F♯○)
(C7)
(G-7)
(G♭7)
(F7)
(F♯○)
(C13)
(F13)
(E-7)
(A7)
(D9)
(A♭7)

(G7) (D♭9) (Cmaj) (A7) (E♭9) (D9) (A♭7) (G7) (D♭9)
(C7) (F-7) (B♭7) P (C7) (G-7)
(G-7) H (C7+5) (C-9) (F9) (F♯○)
(C7-5) P (C7) (C7) (B♭7) (A7) A7(+5) D-9 D-9
(G7) (Cmaj) (B♭7) (A7) (E♭9) (D-7) (A♭7) (G7) (D♭9)
(C7+9) (F7) (C7+9)
(G-7(+5) (C7) (F7(+9) (F7) (F♯○)
6
(C9) (F9) (E-7) (E♭-7) (D-7) (A♭13)

(G13) (D♭13) (C13) (A13) (A♭13) (G13) P
(C7) (F7) (G-9) H 3 3 3
(C13-9) (F7) (F7) (F♯○)
(C△) H P P (F9+11) (E-7) (E♭9) P (D-11) 3
(G7+5) 6 (C9) (B♭7) (A♭7) (G7)
(C7) (F7) (C7) D♭13 C13
(C7) (G♭7) (F7) (F7) (F♯○)
(C7) B♭13 A13 (A13-9) (D7+9)

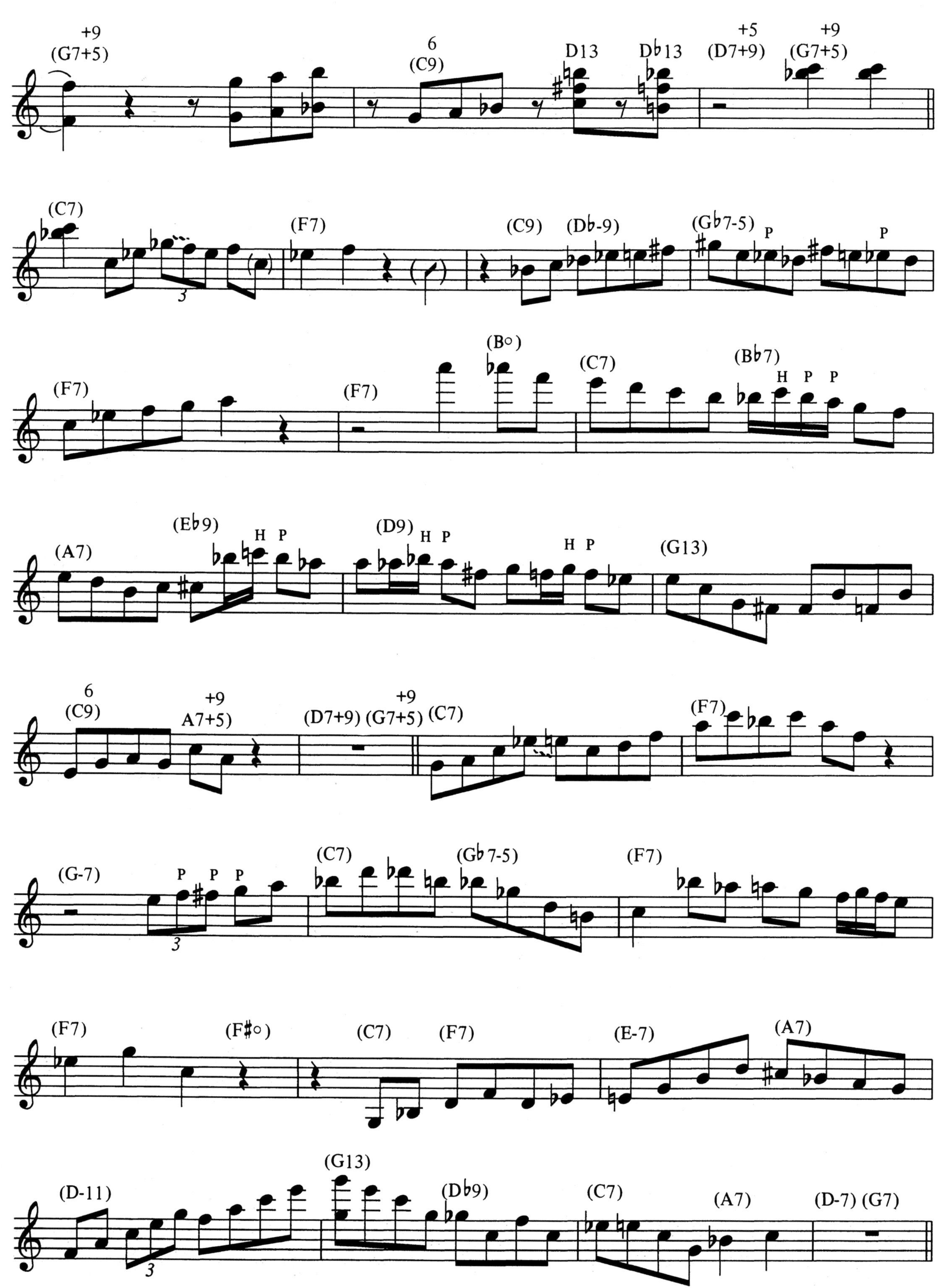
+9
(G7+5)
6
(C9)
D13
D♭13
+5
(D7+9)
+9
(G7+5)
(C7)
(F7)
(C9)
(D♭-9)
(G♭7-5)
P
P
(F7)
(F7)
(B○)
(C7)
(B♭7)
H P P
(A7)
(E♭9)
H P
(D9)
H P
H P
(G13)
6
(C9)
+9
A7+5)
(D7+9)
+9
(G7+5)
(C7)
(F7)
(G-7)
P P P
(C7)
(G♭7-5)
(F7)
(F7)
(F♯○)
(C7)
(F7)
(E-7)
(A7)
(D-11)
(G13)
(D♭9)
(C7)
(A7)
(D-7) (G7)

(C13)
P
(F13)
P
(G-9)
P
(C9)
(G♭7)
(F7)
(F7)
(F♯○)
(E-9)
(A13-9)
(D9)
(G13-9)
-9
(+5)
6
(C9)
(E♭9)
(D7)
(D♭9)
(C7)
(F7)
(G-7)
(C7)
(G♭7)
(F7)
(F7) F○
F♯○
(C7)
(F7)
(E-7)
(B♭7)
(A7-5)
(E♭9)
(D9)
(A♭13)
(G13)
(D♭9)
6
(C9)
(Fmaj)
(E♭9)
(D9)
(D9)
(F/G)
(C7)
(F7)
F♯○

(C7)
(D♭9) (C9)
(F7)
(F7) F♯○
(C7)
(F9)
(E-7) B♭7) (A7)
(E♭9)
(D7+9)
+9
(G7+5)
6
(C9)
(A7)
(A♭7)
(G7)
(C7)
F7
F9
(C7)
C7+9
(F7)
(F7) F♯○
(C7)
(F9)
B♭7
(E-7) A7
(D9)
(G13)
Rubato
6
(C9)
(Fmaj) (F♯○)
(Cmaj/G)
C-7
H P P
P P
3
3
Fine

Grēte

P
P
3
f
3
G-9
F♯-9
F-9
E-11
E♭7+9

P
P
P
3
8va
8va
8va
8va
3
G-11
(G-7)
C13(+5)
F♯-11 F-11 F♯-11
B13 (+5)
B7
3
F-11 F♯-7
F-7 (11)
E-11 E-11
F-7
E-7
(A13) A7+5
A7

D7(+9)
EM
E♭M
D7+9
EM
E♭M
D7+9
G7
DM6
DM6
G7
A♭○
P
P
P
P
H
H
P

C7 B♭7 B7 B♭7 A7
D7+9 G7 A7 A7 A♭7 A7 A♭7 A7
fz
C7 B7 A♭7 A7
C7 B7 B♭7 A7
C7 B7 E7
B7 B♭7 A7
A7 A♭7 F♯7 G7 F♯7 G7

H H
B7
E7
A7
D7+9
D♯○
E - 7
F-7
F♯7
C7
B7
E-7
A7
D7+9
G7
G♯○

3
H
C7
B7
B♭7
A7
D7+9
F9
E9
A7(+5 -9)
G11
G11
G13
D♭9
DM6 9
B7(-9 +5)
B7+5
B♭7+5
A7+5
F9
E9
E♭9
B7+5
B♭7
A♭7
A7
A♭○
A♭-7
G-7
F♯-7
F-7
3

E-7
3
Tempo primo (Piano)
rit.
Rubato Freely
6
Fine

PART FIVE

JOE PASS & HERB ELLIS

JAZZ DUETS

INTRODUCTION

When one thinks of jazz guitar at its best, the names Joe Pass and Herb Ellis come instantly to mind. While each is known for his outstanding solo work, they both have the unique ability to blend with and complement other jazz musicians when playing in ensemble. It is with great pleasure that we at Mel Bay Publications present this outstanding collection of jazz guitar duets by two of the world's finest guitarists.

William Bay

Bonnie

Arr. by JOE PASS
and HERB ELLIS

3
3
3
3
3
3

3

Jazz Waltz

By JOE PASS
and HERB ELLIS

A7
Dm7
G7
Cm7
F7
B♭
Cm7
C♯o
Dm7
E♭o
Eo
3
3
B♭
A♭7
G7
Cm7
F7
Dm7
G7
Cm7
F7
C
B♭
F7
F7

3
3
3
3
3

3
3

Some Of These Days

Arr. by JOE PASS
and HERB ELLIS

G7
C
C7
F
F7
B♭
A7
D7
Gm7
Gm
A7♭9
B7
E7
F7
B♭7
E♭7
D7
G7
C7

G Blues

By JOE PASS
and HERB ELLIS

Hot Stuff

By JOE PASS
and HERB ELLIS

D7
G7
E7
3
A7
D7
G7
G^O
G
G^O
A7
D7
G7
E7
A7

D7
G7
E7
A7
D7
G7

3

Ballad

By JOE PASS
and HERB ELLIS

Bbmaj7
Bb7+9
Bbm6
Eb7+9 +5
Emaj7
Fmaj7
ritard ad lib
F7
Bbmaj7
faster
Abmaj7
ritard ad lib
faster
Bbmaj7
Abmaj7
Bbmaj7
Abmaj7
Gmaj7
Gmaj7